CIVIL RIGHTS IN WARTIME

To those Sikhs, including my parents, who came to the West in pursuit of a better life for themselves and their children

DSS

To those courageous Sikhs who put their ideals before themselves

NSG

Civil Rights in Wartime
The Post-9/11 Sikh Experience

DAWINDER S. SIDHU
Georgetown University Law Center, USA

NEHA SINGH GOHIL
Sikh Coalition

ASHGATE

Published by
Ashgate Publishing Limited
Wey Court East
Union Road
Farnham
Surrey, GU9 7PT
England

Ashgate Publishing Company
Suite 420
101 Cherry Street
Burlington
VT 05401-4405
U.S.A

www.ashgate.com

British Library Cataloguing in Publication Data
Sidhu, Dawinder S.
Civil rights in wartime : the post-9/11 Sikh experience.
1. Sikh diaspora. 2. Sikhs--United States--Social conditions--21st century. 3. Sikhs--United States--Public opinion. 4. Public opinion--United States. 5. Sikhs--Violence against--United States. 6. Sikhs--Civil rights--United States. 7. Terrorism--Religious aspects.
I. Title II. Gohil, Neha Singh.
305.6'946'073-dc22

Library of Congress Cataloging-in-Publication Data
Sidhu, Dawinder S.
Civil rights in wartime : the post-9/11 Sikh experience / by Dawinder S. Sidhu and Neha Singh Gohil.
p. cm.
Includes index.
ISBN 978-0-7546-7553-2 (hardback) -- ISBN 978-0-7546-9925-5 (ebook) 1. Sikhs--Civil rights--United States. 2. Discrimination--Law and legislation--United States. 3. Minorities--Legal status, laws, etc.--United States. 4. War on Terrorism, 2001---Law and legislation--United States. 5. September 11 Terrorist Attacks, 2001. 6. Terrorism--United States--Prevention. I. Gohil, Neha Singh. II. Title.

KF4755.S59 2009
342.7308'73--dc22

2009031264

ISBN 9780754675532 (hbk)
ISBN 9780754699255 (ebk)

Mixed Sources
Product group from well-managed forests and other controlled sources
www.fsc.org Cert no. SGS-COC-2482
© 1996 Forest Stewardship Council
FSC

Printed and bound in Great Britain by
TJ International Ltd, Padstow, Cornwall

Contents

Contributions

Partap Singh Ajrawat
Manpreet Anand
Harmeet Kaur Dhillon
Rajdeep Singh Jolly
Valarie Kaur
Gurinder Singh Mann
Saburo Masada
Amandeep Sidhu
Gurharpal Singh
I.J. Singh
Khushwant Singh
Prabhjot Singh
Darshan Singh Tatla
Eric W. Treene

Our history has shown us that insecurity threatens liberty. Yet, if our liberties are curtailed, we lose the values that we are struggling to defend.

9/11 Commission

Sometimes law lags behind justice – and it is up to us to bridge that distance.

Barack Obama

Foreword

Amy Chua

After the fall of the Berlin Wall, a triumphal consensus emerged, not only in the U.S., but to a considerable extent all around the world. Communism and authoritarianism had failed, therefore markets and free elections were the answer. Conveniently spread by globalization, free market democracy would transform the world into a community of productive, peace-loving nations, and individuals into civic-minded citizens and consumers. In the process, ethnic hatred, religious zealotry, and other "backward" aspects of underdevelopment would be swept away.

Unfortunately, if you look at the last two decades, something very different has taken place. Since 1989, we have seen escalating discrimination, religious extremism, nationalism, xenophobia, confiscations, expulsions, and repeated episodes of ethnic persecution and violence.

For Muslims in the former Yugoslavia, persecution arrived in 1992, when thousands were raped, tortured, and killed in the name of Serbian nationalism. In Rwanda in 1994, 800,000 Tutsis were killed by the Hutus over a period of three months. For white Zimbabweans, persecution came when their homes were taken from them by President Robert Mugabe's Zanu-PF government. And for my own family, it came with the murder of my aunt in the Philippines – just one instance among many hundreds of the kidnapping or killing of wealthy ethnic Chinese, almost invariably by ethnic Filipinos. What happened in each of these communities can happen anywhere. Time and time again, we have seen situations where the anger of a majority community combined with the rise of an identifiable minority community produces explosive results.

This type of hatred – directed by a majority against a minority – is fueled by any number of factors. Where a minority controls the markets and the nation is impoverished, resentment can be especially rife. Pair market domination with an ancient rivalry, as in the case of the Hutus and the Tutsis, or a colonial history, as in the case of the whites in Zimbabwe, and the outcome is almost predictable.

This book is about a variant of the same phenomenon, playing out within America's borders. The experiences the authors describe arise out of hate triggered by a need for revenge after the tragic events of September 11, 2001. The images flashed across 24-hour news channels in the days and months following the attacks represented to many Americans the very face of the enemy. The anger being felt towards that enemy manifested itself within our own borders, against fellow Americans.

When Balbir Singh Sodhi was killed just days after the al Qaeda attacks in New York and Washington, DC, it marked the beginning of a new phase of ethnic violence in the United States. What followed was Sikhs and Muslims being removed from their jobs, attacked on our streets, and excluded by our own government. Sikh children mistreated in schools because of their religion are at the forefront of this battle. Some, such as those whose stories are told in this book, have decided to fight back.

This text breaks new ground. Dawinder S. Sidhu and Neha Singh Gohil have chronicled the beginnings of America's newest civil rights movement. This book is necessary, not only to tell the stories of how it began, but more important, to show how our existing laws have failed our newest citizens. The new forefront of the civil rights movement comes at a complex intersection of race, religion and nationality, a point the authors highlight in this work.

The United States is unique in that we are a nation bound together not by race or religion, but by our ideals. After 9/11, Muslim Americans and those perceived to be Muslim or Arab became targets. Following the horrific attack on the World Trade Center, many Americans saw those who practised Islam – a faith that few Americans knew much about prior to the attacks – as disloyal and hostile to their country. At the same time, the identity of Muslim Americans became tangled up in their appearance, often misleadingly. Based on television reports, those who wore turbans and had long, flowing beards – including Sikhs, who are *not* Muslim – became associated with either the Taliban or al Qaeda. This appearance became a proxy for the hatred that has followed.

The values of the Sikh faith – equality, public service, and hard work – are closely aligned with those of America. But the plight of visible minorities like turban-wearing Sikhs or hijab-wearing Muslim women is that they stand out, and can easily be identified as "alien." What is unique about the Sikh turban, closely bound up with Sikh identity, is that it has always been intended to do precisely that. Wearing a Sikh turban has never been easy in any part of the world.

Sidhu and Gohil take on the assumption that conformity in appearance is a prerequisite for American values. They remind us that Americans have never looked exactly alike. The differences began with the Native Americans that inhabited the land far before the nation's founding fathers landed here from Europe. Since then, Germans, Polish, Italians, Jews, and more recently Asians, Africans, and Latinos, have flocked to this country. And each new wave of immigrants – whether identifiable by their appearance or their accents – has had to fight anew for their rights among the majority.

Another visible minority, identified by their race and their last names, was the scapegoat decades ago. In the middle of the last century, thousands of Japanese Americans were removed from their homes and taken to internment camps because of Japan's actions in World War II. At that time, the Supreme Court sanctioned this implicit blaming of the "other" with its landmark decision in *Korematsu v. United States*. Today, although the outcome of that case is largely considered misguided, it has never been explicitly overturned.

Even as we have elected our first black president, another community continues to be targeted for the way they look. Their children have the same ideals, see the same dreams, but are being asked to give up their traditions in exchange for acceptance as Americans. Like the Sikh faith, America is very young. The Sikh American experience can teach us a great deal, not only about how far we have come as a nation, but also how far we still have to go in order to live up to our democratic ideals.

Preface

On September 11, 2001, we, like many Americans, were in an unparalleled state of grief, confusion and fear. And, like others on that fateful Tuesday, we exchanged numerous calls and emails with loved ones and friends, asking if everyone was "OK" and recollecting how, and under what circumstances, we learned of the morning's tragedies.

As Sikhs, we also received dozens of messages of a different sort. We were inundated with calls, emails, and text messages from members of our community, informing us that turbaned Sikhs were being targeted, verbally abused, and harassed around the country. We were on edge not only because of the specter of another terrorist attack, but also because of a more personal and immediate concern: that our people – and, by extension, our fathers, mothers, brothers, and sisters – had become targets for aggressive and potentially violent behavior. We were unnerved by the threat to our physical safety posed by terrorists from afar and by Americans all around us.

Then, on September 15, 2001, the Sikh community's worst fears were realized: a Sikh in Mesa, Arizona was shot to death because, in the county prosecutor's words, he was wearing a turban and had a long beard. The man who killed the Sikh claimed he was "a patriot."

Quickly, the post-9/11 backlash became a confirmed and all too dangerous reality. In the subsequent weeks and months, the number of hate crimes against Sikhs climbed to the hundreds; an online database, hastily created the day after the 9/11 attacks, chronicled the growing acts of hate against Sikhs across the country. The incidents assumed many forms (from stabbings and assaults to verbal abuse and vandalism), took place in various settings (for example, the schoolyard, grocery stores, streets, and the workplace), and affected children, adults, and the elderly from coast to coast and Main Streets in between.

To help stem the tide, Sikhs mobilized to condemn violence against Muslims and groups perceived to be Muslim, and to spread awareness of Sikhs and Sikhism. Sikh advocacy organizations were formed to bring the voice of the Sikh community to the table. They undertook the responsibility of protecting the rights of Sikhs, educating America's leaders and its people about Sikhs and the backlash, and developing relationships with law enforcement agencies, among other things. It was the beginning of the Sikh civil rights movement.

At the same time, another prong of the Sikh response was missing: there was a conspicuous absence of academic literature that would aid judges, lawyers, scholars, and commentators in understanding, first, the nature and effect of the backlash on Sikhs, and, second, the significance of this particular story in the larger context of America's struggle to safeguard the rights of visible minority groups in times of war or national emergency.

In those early days after 9/11, the nation's focus was understandably fixed on other issues – within, on how and when terrorists of the same group were going to strike again, and without, on finding and eliminating the perpetrators of the 9/11 attacks. To the extent that the national gaze had turned to the backlash, it was even then directed at Muslims in the United States – since those responsible for killing over 3,000 Americans on 9/11 invoked Islam as the moral and religious reasoning for their terrorist behavior. Sikhs, therefore, were fighting an uphill battle. Not only did we have to divert the people's attention from the external threat, but also bring it to bear on a group that wasn't Muslim, and that hardly anyone seemed to know anything about. The point had to be made, nonetheless, that a group of Americans were being killed and otherwise targeted, that the safety of these people and American ideals (which were hanging precariously in the liberty and security balance) were at stake.

Even with improbable chances of success, in short order Sikh organizations arrived in the halls of Congress, courtrooms, corporate offices, classrooms, and other locations, informing people of the escalating mistreatment of Sikhs. Despite their tireless efforts and the appeals for tolerance from leading government officials, however, Sikhs continue to be subject to noxious behavior even today – years after the towers fell and the backlash began. It has become evident that the American public is still unfamiliar with the Sikh identity – despite the fact that Sikhism is the fifth largest religion in the world – and, in particular, is still conflating the Sikh turban with terrorists – despite the fact that 99 percent of turbaned individuals in the United States are Sikhs. It has been a sobering fact to absorb, namely that Sikhs still have to explain who they are and that they exist as a distinct faith, even before describing that they have been subject to bias and hate violence. In short, Sikhism and the severity, complexity, and ongoing nature of discrimination against Sikhs still have not been sufficiently conveyed to government entities, the legal community, and the general public.

In recognition of this, we drew upon our Sikh heritage and legal backgrounds to prepare a law review article that surveyed challenges to turbaned Sikhs in the wake of the 9/11 terrorist attacks. Our goals were: (1) to provide an overview of the Sikh faith and the importance of the Sikh turban, the item of clothing that superficially and visually links Sikhs to Osama bin Laden and al Qaeda, (2) highlight prominent incidents in which Sikhs have been subject to discriminatory conduct after 9/11 (for example, harassment, detention by law enforcement, racial violence, denial of entry into public places, employment discrimination, and airport profiling), and (3) examine the call in Western societies after 9/11 for visible minority groups like turbaned Sikhs to abandon their articles of faith in order to adopt a more homogeneous national and secular appearance. It was a single effort, to be sure, but it was something. We hoped that the article would serve to educate and explain a situation that we were intimately aware of, but which was largely obscured from the public's consciousness.

In 2008, the article was published in a leading university journal that focuses on the intersection of law and religion. To our knowledge, it is the first and only legal article dedicated to the post-9/11 civil rights of turbaned Sikhs in America. The reaction to the article was overwhelming, and overwhelmingly positive. We were pleased in a sense – we had described the peaks of the issues affecting our community where the landscape in academic journals was otherwise barren.

We realized, however, that much more needed to be done on the academic front – the valleys and other peaks on the horizon also required description. The law review article was limited in focus to legal issues, and in its audience to legal practitioners. We supplied an article to one subset of the American populace, but to diminish ignorance regarding Sikhs and the backlash, information of a different sort needed to be disseminated and offered more widely. In contrast to an article that was circumscribed in its scope and rather dense and technical in its language, we wanted to create something that would be more accessible in tone and more contextual in substance. As we wrote, more incidents were coming to light, and debates about assimilation were evolving and touching other areas of the globe. This book represents our attempt to do just that – to offer a more comprehensive and comprehensible academic text on the post-9/11 experience of turbaned Sikhs in America.

The text that follows reflects our unique background as individuals who have helped lead the Sikh community's attempts to respond to the post-9/11 backlash for over eight years. For example, we have both worked for or closely with each of the leading Sikh advocacy organizations. There are a finite number of individuals who may be able to directly speak to the Sikh identity and ordeal after 9/11. We are two individuals from that limited set of people who may be able to write this book in a meaningful and expansive fashion – from the inside.

As extensive as our work in the post-9/11 Sikh civil rights world may be, there undoubtedly are other individuals who have been intimately involved in or implicated by the post-9/11 backlash. There are, for example, other Sikh civil rights leaders, Sikhs who responded to the discrimination in non-traditional ways, Sikh victims, and so on. We readily recognize that their perspectives, informed by their unique roles in the post-9/11 experience, would invaluably enrich this book. Indeed, we view this book as an opportunity for these individuals to discuss, often for the first time, their reactions to and impressions of the post-9/11 backlash against turbaned Sikhs. Accordingly, we have asked these individuals who have been the forefront of the Sikh experience in one form or another to contribute to these pages. These first-hand narrative accounts will provide the reader with additional views "from the trenches."

Their narratives also serve another purpose – they are a departure from the factual information and analysis, and instead express the Sikh experience in a deeper, personal way. In short, these contributions add a more human element to the book. They can be found interspersed in various parts of the book that correspond with the contributor's area of expertise, interest, or involvement.

* * *

Before embarking any further, it would be appropriate to thank a number of individuals whose assistance, guidance, and encouragement were instrumental to the preparation of this text. We are the beneficiaries of the generosity of these individuals, and hope that this text properly reflects and honors the time and energy that they have invested in our vision. We pay tribute to these individuals not only to express our personal gratitude, but to remind the reader that – despite the appearance of two names on the cover – this book is the product of a collective and collaborative effort.

We acknowledge the contributors who have taken time of out their busy schedules to pen insightful, and often very personal and emotive, accounts of their experiences after 9/11. Their contributions have immeasurably enhanced both the quality and the depth of this book. We hope that this text does justice to those contributions.

We wish to thank Eric Levy and the staff at Ashgate Publishing for their work on the manuscript, and for believing in the book's ability to make a meaningful contribution to the existing understanding of how religion and law intersect. Eric has been an invaluable resource, and has put up with a constant and seemingly endless flow of questions from us regarding the preparation of this book. His assistance and professionalism throughout the publication process are greatly appreciated. We thank Morgan Hargrave, our intern, who worked independently and efficiently to help prepare and update sections of the book. The staff of the *Rutgers Journal of Law and Religion* also provided useful revisions on the underlying law review article.

Dawinder Sidhu extends his deepest gratitude to his intellectual mentors, whose example, instruction, and wisdom have shaped and continue to inform his professional life and his worldview, jurisprudential and otherwise: Bhai Gurdarshan Singh Ji, the Honorable David G. Campbell, Jacques Toliver, David F. Black, Jeffrey Rosen, Arthur Wilmarth, Jr., and Catherine Ross. He also wishes to acknowledge, with great respect and humility, those individuals who have profoundly influenced his thinking even in the absence of a personal relationship: the Gurus and the Founding Fathers. Finally, he wishes to thank above all his parents, Dr. Jaswinder S. Sidhu and Satwinder K. Sidhu, for their love, instilling in him the importance of living an honest life, and for allowing him to be part of the American dream. They are his heart and soul, and in his view, model Sikhs.

Neha Singh Gohil is forever indebted to the Gurus for showing us the way, and to her parents, Mokshinder Singh Vahali and Renu Vahali, for always encouraging her to stand behind her beliefs. She is awed by the sincere commitment and steady guidance of Amardeep Singh and each of her colleagues at the Sikh Coalition in their efforts to defend the Sikh way of life. She expresses her gratitude to her GTMO team – Scott Sullivan, Douglas Cox, and Sarah Havens – who accompanied her on her first foray into the world of civil rights. She would also like to thank Amy Chua for her mentorship in crafting the initial draft of the paper that formed the foundation for this book, and the Discrimination and National Security Initiative for developing it. Finally, none of this would have been possible without the unflinching support of her best friend and partner, Amit.

The aforementioned acknowledgements indicate that we have benefited greatly from the work, kindness, and influence of many individuals. In light of this, and in consideration of the contributors whose writings are included herein, this book should be viewed as a collaborative effort. Indeed, we intentionally seek to convey the impression that this is a work not just of two isolated writers, but of a community and others. That said, we remain responsible for the ultimate product, and therefore express regret for any errors.

Moreover, we note that while this book contains information on the Sikh religion, we ourselves are no theologians. The historical events in a faith's development and the meaning of its beliefs may be subject to many different interpretations, and those interpretations may be very closely held. This book, however, reflects our understanding of the faith based on the established resources we consulted. To the extent that our presentation of Sikh history and doctrine conflicts with another's view on those subjects, we note that we attempted, in good faith, to present an account of Sikh history and beliefs that we believed to be accurate and supported by credible authority. There was no interest or intent to promote or denigrate any one school of thought with respect to Sikhism.

That said, we resisted the temptation to enter the thicket of selecting between differing interpretations and concepts of past events, and to avoid reinventing the wheel with respect to the major Sikh historical and doctrinal developments. The reader will notice that the discussion of Sikh history and beliefs contains materials written by some of the most revered Sikh scholars in the world. In including this material, we have deferred to the writings of these scholars in those areas that are most critical to the faith – its founding by Guru Nanak, the establishment of the Khalsa brotherhood by Guru Gobind Singh, the formulation of the Sikh holy scriptures, and three twentieth-century events that have helped define the modern-day Sikh. Prudence dictates that this is the proper course of action with respect to sensitive areas within a religion's formation and ongoing existence.

This aspect of the book does not, however, immunize us from our own responsibility to offer a faithful account of the Sikh religion. A Sikh, upon reciting or explaining a hymn, traditionally utters the saying, "Bhul chuk maaf," which roughly translates into "Forgive me for my errors." It is a humbling reminder to us that human intelligence is limited in its comprehension; it is also an apology for anything that fell short of complete apprehension. It is only proper that, in writing a text on the faith, we seek the same forgiveness at the outset of our discussion.

With these preliminary thoughts in mind, we proceed with the book. It represents our modest attempt to shed light on the problems faced by turbaned Sikhs after 9/11. At a minimum, we hope it will be informative and interesting to the reader as a matter of religion, law, pluralism, diversity, and national security. Our overarching hope, however, is that this book can help eliminate the ignorance about Sikhs that permits one man to commit an act of hate against his fellow, albeit distinguishable, man.

Dawinder S. Sidhu,
Georgetown University Law Center, USA
Neha Singh Gohil,
Sikh Coalition
(Affiliations listed for identification purposes only)

Introduction

The Sikhs are members of the Sikh faith, which was founded in fifteenth-century South Asia and is doctrinally distinct from the other religions prevalent in the Indian subcontinent, especially Islam and Hinduism. An independent and sovereign faith, Sikhism has over 20,000,000 adherents worldwide, making it the fifth largest religion in the world, behind only Christianity, Islam, Hinduism, and Buddhism. Indeed, there are roughly 9,000,000 more Sikhs than there are followers of Judaism.

Sikhs are unique, not only because they have a separate and identifiable belief system, but also because of their appearance. Members of the Sikh faith are required to keep their hair unshorn. Therefore, Sikh men traditionally wear turbans to cover their unshorn hair. The turban carries deep religious significance for Sikhs because it is an instrument that is inextricably intertwined with the unshorn hair that Sikhs must keep. The turban and beard render Sikhs an easily noticeable people.

In the late 1800s, Sikhs migrated from the Punjab area of South Asia to other parts of the world, most notably Britain, Canada, and the United States. Sikhs cultivated land on the U.S. west coast, land that was similar to the farmlands of Punjab. They were also laborers for public projects, and brought professional skills with them.

Their arrival in these areas triggered situations in which natives had to make sense of these turbaned immigrants. The transition, as you can imagine, and as was relatively common for other foreign-looking migrants, was not particularly smooth. Above the stares and odd looks, Sikhs were struggling to prove they were industrious workers, loyal to their new countries, and decent people, in the same way that Mahatma Gandhi spoke of the brown-skinned Indians' attempts in South Africa to prove to the locals that they rightfully belonged and were upstanding members of their adopted homeland.

These difficulties were largely common for general immigrant communities. But they would pale in comparison to the situation Sikh Americans faced after the terrorist attacks of September 11, 2001, on the Twin Towers, the Pentagon, and in Pennsylvania. As Justice John Paul Stevens wrote in the landmark *Hamdan v. Rumsfeld* case: "Americans will never forget the devastation wrought by these acts."[1] The acts were carried out by a network of terrorists based in Afghanistan – al Qaeda. The head of al Qaeda, Osama bin Laden, issued recordings of speeches in which he took responsibility for the atrocities, praised the hijackers for their

1 *Hamdan v. Rumsfeld*, 548 U.S. 557, 568 (2006).

actions, and railed against the United States. Bin Laden and the al Qaeda leadership, including bin Laden's principal deputy, Ayman al-Zawahiri, wore turbans and had long beards.

Bin Laden's video messages were played prominently and frequently on the news, were readily available and viewed on the Internet, and were on the front pages of newspapers and magazines throughout the beleaguered and fearful nation. Bin Laden's image, complete with his white turban and flowing beard, had been seared into the American consciousness, which was still reeling with grief and anger. The visual connection between a turbaned bin Laden and a dark-skinned, turbaned male had been forged. Worse, it was continually reinforced by replays of the attacks, reports on the tragedies, explanations of how the attackers carried out their mission, speculation about future attacks or the existence of other sleeper cells in America, the American leaders' and public preparation for war, and bin Laden's continuous rhetorical attacks against the American infidels.

In contemporary post-9/11 America, the perceived similarity between bin Laden and turbaned Sikhs made Sikhs, already one of the most visible minority groups in the United States, a superficial and accessible proxy for the elusive bin Laden and his distant al Qaeda regime. Americans – bombarded by reminders of the attacks, still contending with the horror and nature of the attack as well as the attendant emotions, on the path to war and under the threat of future terrorism – needed look only to turbaned individuals in America for a trigger for that unresolved emotion, and as a recipient for the rage that had been stewing and festering.

As a result, in the wake of the 9/11 attacks, turbaned Sikhs in America were victims of significant violence and discrimination. As one law professor noted: "Sikh men, who are religiously mandated to wear turbans, have been conflated with Osama Bin Laden," and "suffered significant violence" as a consequence.[2] In particular, Sikhs with turbans in the United States were murdered, stabbed, assaulted, verbally harassed, discriminated against in the workplace, and refused service in places of public accommodation, among other things. Although post-9/11 rage may have been intended for Muslims, it is perhaps unsurprising that Sikhs – with the visual cues of the turban and beard – bore "the disproportionate brunt of hate violence in the aftermath of September 11."[3]

The attacks of that fateful Tuesday morning also provoked another set of reactions in the United States and elsewhere. A sense of nationalism and protectionism set in, wherein natives reconsidered who were proper inhabitants on their society and what the new terms of residency or occupancy in that society would be. The questions were insular and directed inward – Who are we? Who are

2 Leti Volpp, "The Citizen and the Terrorist," 49 *UCLA L. Rev.* 1575, 1590 (2002).

3 Muneer I. Ahmad, "A Rage Shared by Law: Post-September 11 Racial Violence as Crimes of Passion," 92 *Cal. L. Rev.* 1259, 1330 n. 174 (October 2004): "Many Sikh men, who wear turbans and long beards, were targeted in post-September 11 hate violence because they were mistaken to be Muslim. As a result, Sikhs have borne the disproportionate brunt of hate violence in the aftermath of September 11."

they? Do we want them here? If so, should we let "others" be themselves and still be part of "us," and if so, how?

September 11 therefore changed the ballgame with respect to general acceptance of the gradual assimilation that was rather amiably taking place between minority communities in Western societies. The reinvigorated immigration and assimilation conversation was focused particularly (and rather predictably, in light of 9/11) on Muslims. Sikhs, with their superficial resemblance to the extremists who invoked Islam to justify the 9/11 attacks, were clumsily implicated by the second-guessing taking place in town squares and city halls throughout the West.

While in the last century or so Sikhs had been becoming intricately woven into the fabric of Western societies, 9/11 questioned whether individuals with such a peculiar and religious-based identity should be part of those societies – in short, Sikhs were not only being treated differently on account of their appearance; their identity marked them as different, and therefore a suspect element in the West.

* * *

The purpose of this book is to examine how the Sikh turban has transformed from a sacred piece of attire for Sikhs to a target for discriminatory conduct and an object of marginalization after 9/11. In order to appreciate this transformation and understand the Sikh experience during the latter stage, it is first necessary to ask, "Who are Sikhs?" Part I will examine this threshold question. It will begin by providing an overview of the Sikh faith, including its central beliefs, founding, and other historical developments that help explain who the Sikhs are today. It will also address why the turban came to be an integral part of the Sikh identity, and why it is considered important by members of the faith.

Amardeep Singh, a leading Sikh civil rights attorney, has observed that defending Sikhs in the courts "is unlike litigation in any other community you can think of because what we're doing … is beyond arguing the law; we're giving a little mini-history and religion lesson" on the Sikhs.[4] "How can you apply the law against a group you don't understand?" he added.[5] Part I aims to promote that understanding.

Following the background of who Sikhs are, the book will shift to a discussion of turbaned Sikhs in the post-9/11 world. Part II will summarize prominent incidents in several areas in which Sikhs who wear turbans have been subject to discriminatory conduct after 9/11: harassment, detention by law enforcement, racial violence, denial of entry into public places, employment discrimination, and airport profiling. Part II attempts to convey the breadth, scope, and ongoing nature of the backlash against turbaned Sikhs. Indeed, these cases demonstrate that discriminatory incidents have taken place every year since 2001, beginning with

4 See the video *DASTAAR: Defending Sikh Identity*, available at <http://www.alsolikelife.blip.tv/file/17779>, statement of Amardeep Singh, Executive Director, Sikh Coalition.

5 Ibid.

the moments after the Twin Towers were hit, and that they have also taken place in diverse areas of the nation – some small towns, some major cities.

Not only have Sikhs been targeted, but the wearing of the Sikh turban itself has been called into question. While Part II addresses direct discrimination, Part III will discuss a broader challenge to conspicuous articles of faith, especially the Sikh turban, as an acceptable feature in Western societies. In particular, it will review the calls in Western societies after 9/11 for visible minority groups, including turbaned Sikhs, to abandon their articles of faith in order to adopt a more homogeneous, national, and secular appearance. As evidence of the long-standing Sikh contribution to Western societies, this part will describe the celebrated participation of turbaned Sikhs in the military and security forces of the very Western nations that are now attempting to restrict the wearing of turbans.

If a Sikh's civil rights have been infringed in a manner outlined in Part II, or if a Sikh's identity has been compromised by state policy in the ways described in Part III, what legal recourse is available to him or her? Parts II and III discuss these respective questions where appropriate, and in particular, examine the legal apparatus before 9/11, how it has been applied to post-9/11 circumstances, and how it has been modified.

The analysis of available legal remedies suggests that the present legal system is inadequate to protect Sikhs from discrimination. Accordingly, Part IV looks into non-legal approaches that Sikhs have used to mitigate the backlash and eradicate the ignorance that permits acts of hate and bias against Sikhs. These preventative measures, including outreach programs and training efforts, explore the relationship between the Sikh community and their American neighbors, and between the community and the federal government and law enforcement authorities. Part IV will also comment on the human consequences of such mistreatment, where Sikhs have wrestled with the efficacy of maintaining their religious identity in the face of persistent threats.

Finally, we will offer some concluding thoughts that we hope will crystallize the preceding discussion.

* * *

If it is the case that the Sikh experience has been a difficult and at times oppressive one after the terrorist attacks of 9/11, and if it is true that Sikhs have been targeted on the basis of their appearance following the horrific attacks by the ignorant, highly emotional, or self-proclaimed patriotic, the question remains why this is an important area of inquiry. In other words: why should we care?

First, Sikh Americans *are* Americans. This was established for the first time by a Congressional resolution in the aftermath of the 9/11 attacks. Following the murder of Balbir Singh Sodhi, the then Arizona Attorney General and later Secretary of the U.S. Department of Homeland Security Janet Napolitano remarked: "We are all Americans." This is so even if some of those Americans happen to wear turbans or look a certain way. If a subset of Americans is being treated differently due to their appearance, where such mistreatment includes not only harassment and assault, but death, it seems the subject matter becomes important because it explores a marginalized part of America that has not been brought to the light of day. Indeed, the American consciousness has been fixated on the overseas response to the terrorist attacks, including campaigns in Iraq and Afghanistan, but the parallel and internal conflict in the United States – the impact of the post-9/11 environment on Muslims and those perceived to be Muslim – is relatively unknown.

This book also serves as a standard by which we may view the American commitment towards religious freedom. The book indicates how far – or how far short – we have come in fulfilling the ideal of a land where individuals can freely practice their religion without fear of discrimination, let alone death. Indeed, the Framers of this magnificent land escaped Britain for this very reason, to form a nation where the citizens of the political community would enjoy the freedom of religion and a reprieve from religious persecution. As the Supreme Court noted: "the place of religion in our society is an exalted one, achieved through a long tradition of reliance on the … inviolable citadel of the individual heart and mind."[6] Although recent historic moments may provide encouragement to those who think we, as Americans, are reaching the goal of religious tolerance, the experience of Sikhs after 9/11 shows that the goal still eludes us.

This book also examines the ongoing American struggle to create a society that is not only religiously diverse, but also equal. The American theory of pluralism is based on the notion of both civil and political rights for all citizens, irrespective of economic class, race, religion, or gender.[7] America has struggled to preserve this lofty notion of equality. Slavery and segregation exist as the most blatant examples of this difficulty. Beyond such distant examples is the distinct possibility that the moral imperative of equality in America is situation-specific. Some argue, for instance, that equality does not filter down in practice to the inner cities of the United States, where there are a disproportionate number of low-income and minority citizens. Most relevant to this book is the plausible contention that equality in America does not apply in certain circumstances, namely when America is involved in a military conflict. American wartime behavior is an established instance in which equality is quite vulnerable. An examination of the Sikh American experience during another wartime period, the post-9/11 era, should also indicate that we have not maintained a truly equal society irrespective of circumstance. In other words, the nation did not remain faithful to the American ideal of equality in the aftermath of the terrorist attacks.

Make no mistake, we do not intend to suggest that the backlash against turbaned Sikhs is a closed case – the mistreatment of Sikhs persists. With the emotional residue from 9/11 still present and terrorism-related military campaigns still taking place,

6 See *Abington School District v. Schempp*, 374 U.S. 203, 226 (1963).

7 See *Plessy v. Ferguson*, 163 U.S. 537, 559 (1896) (Harlan, J dissenting): "[I]n the eye of the law, there is in this country no superior, dominant, ruling class of citizens. There is no caste here. Our constitution is color-blind, and neither knows nor tolerates classes among citizens. In respect of civil rights, all citizens are equal before the law."

Sikhs continue to encounter discrimination and social marginalization. Because turbaned Sikhs still confront difficulties in America, and because discrimination against turbaned Sikhs may intensify if future attacks occur, the factual predicate justifying a substantive inquiry into the Sikh experience after 9/11 undoubtedly exists. In other words, looking into this subject may not only serve as another lesson in the ongoing American struggle to safeguard equality in times of crisis for tomorrow, but also prevent further mistreatment of Sikhs today.

Justice Sandra Day O'Connor noted emphatically: "It is during our most challenging and uncertain moments that … we must preserve our commitment at home to the principles for which we fight abroad."[8] The post-9/11 Sikh experience demonstrates that our commitment to the principles of religious diversity, pluralism, and equality is wanting. The extent to which the nation has failed to uphold those ideals is regrettably clear in these pages.

Moreover, Sikhs are part of the global community – they can be found in every corner of the world, from India to Canada, and Australia to France. Despite the fact that Sikhs represent such a large segment of the world's religious population, with over 20,000,000 adherents, Sikhs have encountered discrimination in various countries. Their post-9/11 difficulties are not limited to the United States, but instead extend to many Western societies. Although particular incidents may seem like isolated events, when pieced together they suggest a global crisis of civil rights for turbaned Sikhs.

Altogether, this book presents a story about certain religious followers, and how their lives in various parts of the world changed after 9/11. It is a story about a group of Americans, and about American conduct towards them. It is a story about religion and a religious article of faith. It is a story about civil rights and security. It is about American ideals when America itself is in danger. It is a story about pluralism and hate. It is a story about violence and ignorance. It is also a story about a community and a government's response to this hate, violence, and ignorance. It is a story, ultimately, about humans. This story has been silenced, and when touched upon, has been largely dulled. It needs to be told.

8 "Excerpts from Monday's Supreme Court Rulings," *Knight Ridder Newspapers*, June 28, 2004, available at <http://www.realcities.com/mld/krwashington/9033877.htm>.

Part I

Sikhism and the Sikh Turban

The Sikh religion is one of the world's youngest and most progressive faiths. Of the major world religions, Sikhism is probably the least understood. Part I aims to correct that ignorance by providing basic information on the faith's creation and development, its central historical figures, fundamental religious beliefs, its entry into the West, and its articles of faith, especially the Sikh turban.

First, a note on why this background is necessary: before Sikhs are able to meaningfully press their rights and live free of undignified treatment based on their religion, they must first sufficiently explain who they are. If they meet this challenge, others may fully appreciate the significance of the harassment Sikhs have received, and may recognize a turbaned individual as a Sikh, and not a person to be associated with terrorist extremists and thereafter targeted.

In light of the educational purpose of this part, we have included materials written by some of the most respected and learned Sikh scholars. Specifically, Sikh historian and journalist Khushwant Singh takes us through two of the most important players in Sikh history – Guru Nanak (who founded the faith and laid down its essential philosophical principles), and Guru Gobind Singh (who created a brotherhood of followers known as the Khalsa, and in doing so, established the Sikh identity to be observed then and for ever).

This part also features a segment by Gurinder Singh Mann, a leading Sikh academic, on the contents of a Sikh holy text that operates as the living guru of the Sikhs following the death of Guru Gobind Singh. In addition, Gurharpal Singh and Darshan Singh Tatla share their understanding of how Sikhs made their way from the lands of Punjab to various parts of the Western world.

Patwant Singh, another celebrated Sikh historian and scholar, leads us through three of the most critical events in Sikh history in the modern age – the 1919 massacre of Sikhs in Amritsar, India, the political indifference towards Sikhs at India's independence from Britain in 1947, and the killing of Sikhs following the death of India's Prime Minister, Indira Gandhi, in 1984 – a time of considerable mistrust and instability between the Sikh community and the Indian government. These historical situations have undoubtedly shaped the Sikh people as they are today.

Finally, Prabhjot Singh offers his thoughts on the significance of the turban to Sikhs. Some may remark that if the turban has caused Sikhs so much trouble, why not simply take it off? This last narrative should indicate to the reader why this course of action is not acceptable to a Sikh.

We begin by bringing you to the ancestral home of the Sikh faith: Punjab.

Chapter 1
Punjab: The Sikh Homeland

Sikhism was born in an area rife with sacred rites and spiritual leaders. It all began just over 500 years ago in Punjab, a region now split between northwest India and eastern Pakistan. "Punjab" means the "Land of the Five Rivers" – the Beas, Chenab, Jhelum, Ravi, and Sutlej – and its soil is some of the most fertile on the continent. The Sikhs originated in this rural, agrarian corner of the globe.

Punjab is rich in history. One of the earliest civilizations known to man, the Indus Valley, was found in Punjab. From the third to second millennium BC, Punjab was home to the Indo-Aryan civilization. Although the height of the Aryans had passed, Aryan settlers still lived in Punjab from the second to first millennium BC.

Punjab is the birthplace of Indian civilization. During the Vedic period, over a thousand years BC, the Rig Veda and the Upanishads, two seminal and sacred Hindu texts, were written in Punjab. The Bhagavad Gita, a fundamental Hindu scripture and a revered religious composition dated to approximately 500 BC and 200 BC, is said to have been recited in Punjab by Lord Krishna. The Bhagavad Gita is part of the Mahabharata, one of the two major epics in Hinduism. The battles depicted in the Mahabharata took place in Punjab. Around 300 BC, the Ramayana, the other epic story that is central to the Hindu teachings, was also authored in Punjab. Following the Epic Period, Buddhist elements entered Punjab.

With its prosperous lands and strategic location, near the famous Khyber Pass to the west to the Himalayan Mountains and Kashmir to the north, Punjab has been home to many rulers, invaders, and transient opportunists. Five centuries prior to Christ's birth, the Persians reigned over Punjab. In the third century BC, Alexander the Great invaded Punjab, including the region in his vast dominion. Alexander gave way to the Mauryans. The Greeks, under King Menander and others, ruled the land one century later. The Kushan Empire, led by the great Kanishka, then took control of Punjab until the third century AD. The nomadic Huns assumed control of Punjab around the fifth century AD.

From the sixth century AD to twelfth century AD, Arab, Muslim, and Turk rulers governed Punjab. This succession culminated in the rule of the Mughals – Muslims of Turkish, Iranian, and Mongol descent. Their territory was expansive, stretching from present-day Kashmir in the north to present-day Bangladesh in the south. But although the Mughals had wise rulers in their past and had cultivated knowledge and diversity of thought, the Mughal Empire was in a peculiar state in this period. It was not a time of religious harmony, but rather significant inter-faith tension between the ruling Muslims and the majority Hindus. It was into this fray that Sikhism was born.

Chapter 2
Founding and Early Development of Sikhism

The development of Sikhism can be neatly divided into two parts. The first is a rather pacifist period in which the faith was founded by Guru Nanak and continued onwards through the life of the fifth steward of the faith, Guru Arjun. The second is a period of righteousness in which the faith is actively defended and religious intolerance challenged. This second stanza starts with the sixth Sikh leader, Guru Hargobind, and culminates with the tenth master, Guru Gobind Singh, who formed the Sikh brotherhood, the Khalsa.

We turn to the writings of Khushwant Singh, a noted Sikh historian, to describe in detail the two central figures in these two periods – Guru Nanak during the first time frame, and Guru Gobind Singh during the second. In between, we will fill in the necessary gaps. Our discussion starts with the man who founded the Sikh faith: Guru Nanak.

* * *

Khushwant Singh[1]

> Nanak was born on April 15, 1469. His father, Mehta Kalian Das Bedi, was an accountant in the village of Talwandi Rai Bhoe, now named Nankana Sahib, about forty miles from Lahore [in present-day Pakistan]. It is likely that Nanak, like his elder sister, Nanaki, was born in the home of his mother, Tripta, and like her, named after his maternal home, Nanake.
>
> Nanak was a precocious child; at the age of five he started asking questions about the purpose of life. At even seven he was sent to a pandit to learn the alphabet and numerals, and two years later to a Muslim mullah to learn Persian and Arabic. He took little interest in his studies and began to spend his time discoursing with holy men or in solitude, "without confiding the secrets of his heart in any one."
>
> At the age of 12 he was married to Sulakhni, the daughter of Mool Chand Chona of Batala. Even the marriage did not turn his mind towards mundane matters.

---

1 From Khushwant Singh, *The Illustrated History of the Sikhs* (New Delhi: OUP India) reproduced by permission of Oxford University Press India, New Delhi.

Nanak was 19 when his wife came to live with him. For some time she succeeded in turning his attention to herself and two sons were born to them, Sri Chand in AD 1494 and Lakhmi Das three years later. They also probably had a daughter or daughters who died in infancy. Then Nanak's mind went back to spiritual problems and he again sought the company of wandering hermits for guidance. His father tried his best to get him to tend his cattle or to set up as a tradesman, but it was of no avail. His sister brought him over to her home in Sultanpur [about 30 miles from Delhi], and through her husband's influence got him a job as an accountant with the Nawab Daulat Khan Lodhi, a distant kinsman of the reigning Sultan of Delhi. Although Nanak took over the post with some reluctance, he discharged his duties diligently and won the affection of his employer.

[A] Muslim minstrel, Mardana, joined Nanak and the two began to organize the [singing] of hymns in the town. ... "Every night they sang hymns .... They fed everyone who came .... An hour and a quarter before sunrise [Nanak] would go to the river to bathe, by daylight he would be in the durbar doing his work."

During one of these early morning ablutions by the river, Nanak had his first mystic experience. [It is described] as a communion with God, who gave him a cup of *amrit* (nectar) to drink and charged him with the mission in the following words:

> Nanak, I am with thee. Through thee my name will be magnified. Whosoever follows thee, him I will save. Go into the world to pray and teach mankind how to pray. Be not sullied by the ways of the world. Let your life be one of praise of the Word (*nām*), charity (*dān*), ablution (*iśān*), service (*sevā*), and prayer (*simran*). Nanak, I give thee My pledge. Let this be thy life's mission.

Nanak's voice rose in praise of his Maker:

> There is One God.
> He is the supreme truth.
> He, the Creator,
> Is without fear and without hate.
> He, the Omnipresent,
> Pervades the universe.
> He is not born,
> Nor does He die to be born again.
> By His grace shalt thou worship Him.
>
> Before time itself,
> There was truth.
> When time began to run its course
> He was the truth.

Even now, He is the truth.
And evermore shall truth prevail.

(Japjī)

Nanak is said to have received the robe of honor from the hands of God Himself.

He was missing for three days and nights and it was assumed that he had drowned. He reappeared on the fourth day. …

People said, "Friends, he was lost in the river; from where hath he emerged?" Nanak came home and gave away all he had. … Crowds began to collect. [The local administrator] also came and asked, "Nanak, what happened to you?" Nanak remained silent. The people replied, "He was in the river and is out of his mind." The Khan said: "Friends, this is very distressing," and turned back in sorrow.

Nanak went and joined the fakirs[, or Sufi mystics]. With him went the musician Mardana. One day passed. The next day he got up and spoke. "There is no Hindu, there is no Mussalman." Whenever he spoke, this is all he would say: "There is no Hindu, there is no Mussalman."

This incident probably took place in AD 1499 when Nanak was in his thirtieth year. It marks the end of the first phase of his life: the search for the truth was over; he was ready to go forth to proclaim it to the people of the world.

There is some uncertainty about the exact itinerary of Nanak's travels in the years following. All sources are, however, agreed that he did travel extensively to different parts of India and abroad as far west as Baghdad. Wherever he gained adherents he set up a centre of worship. In all probability the first extensive tour was to the east, when he went through Hindu places of pilgrimage[.] He spent some years traveling in the Punjab, paying more than one visit to [a] Sufi establishment. His next tour was southwards. … He is said to have come back along the western coast through … Bombay, and Rajasthan. The third tour was in the Himalayan regions [to the east].

The Guru's last journey was his pilgrimage to Mecca and Medina. He went farther westwards to Baghdad, where he spent some time with the local fakirs. On his way back home he passed through Saidpur when the town was sacked by Babar. He went around preaching in different towns of the Punjab, and then settled down with his family in a new township that he had built earlier on the banks of the Ravi and named Kartarpur (the abode of the Creator).

Although there is some uncertainty about the exact itinerary, the [prevailing reports] are agreed about the incidents that took place during the travels. They go into great detail about the outlandish garb that Nanak wore on his journeys. It was always a combination of styles worn by Hindu sadhus and Muslim fakirs. The people were constantly asking him, "Art thou a Hindu or Mussalman?" On two of his long journeys, he took the

Muslim Mardana as his companion. On the others he was accompanied by Hindus of lesser castes. While visiting Hindu places he had long discourses with the local pandits. He also spent many days with Shaikh Sharaf, Shaikh Ibrahim, and other Sufi saints at Pak Pattan and Multan. The substance of these discourses was later put in verse by the Guru.

When Nanak was on his way to Mecca, he stayed in a mosque and fell asleep with his feet towards the *Kā'bā* – an act considered of grave disrespect to the house of God. When the mullah came to say his prayers, he shook Nanak rudely and said: "O servant of God, thou hast thy feet towards *Kā'bā*, the house of God; why hast thou done such a thing?" Nanak replied: "Then turn my feet towards some direction where there is no God nor the *Kā'bā*."

Nanak spent his last years at Kartarpur, where large crowds flocked to hear him preach. He made them observe a strict routine, which set the pattern of daily life for his followers, who by then had come to be known as his Sikhs (presumably derived ultimately from the Sanskrit *śiṣyā*, or disciple, or *śikṣā*, instruction – Pali, *sikkhā*), i.e., disciples ….

Nanak not only founded a new religion and started a new pattern of living, he also set in motion an agrarian movement whose impact was felt all over the country. To get a comprehensive picture of his achievements, it is necessary to know the religious and secular aspects of his teaching.

We will first refer to some salient points of his faith.

Conception of God

Nanak was a strict monotheist. He refused to accept any compromise on the concept of the unity of God. In this he disagreed with the Bhaktas, who, despite their profession of monotheism, believed in the reincarnation of God and of His avatars. Since God was infinite, argued Nanak, He could not die to be reincarnated, nor could He assume human form which was subject to decay and death. Nanak disapproved of the worship of idols because people tended to look upon them as God instead of symbolic representations. Nanak believed that God was *sat* (both true and reality), as opposed to *asat* (falsehood) and *mithyā* (illusion). He thus not only made God a spiritual concept but also based principles of social behavior on the concept. If God is Truth, to speak an untruth is to be ungodly. Untruthful conduct not only hurts one's neighbors; it is also irreligious. This principle is stated categorically by Nanak in the opening lines of his most celebrated morning prayer, the *Japjī*, and is the *mūl maṅtra* or basic belief of Sikhism.

Nanak believed that the power that was God could not be defined because God was *niraṅkār* (formless). All of his descriptions of God were consequently admissions of an inability to define Him.

> Thou hast a million eyes, yet no eye hast Thou.
> Thou hast a million forms, yet no form hast Thou.
> Thou hast a million feet, yet no feet hast Thou.
> Thou art without odor, yet millions of odors emanate from Thee.
> With such charms, O Lord, hast Thou bewitched me.
> Thy light pervades everywhere.
>
> (Dhanāsarī)

Despite the difficulty of definition, Nanak used a variety of names for God. He was the Father (*Pitā*) of all mankind; He was the Lover (*Prītam*) and Master (*Khasam*) of his devotee; He was also the Great Giver (*Dātā*). Nanak did this to show human dependence on God rather than invest Him with anthropomorphic qualities. Although Nanak used both Hindu and Muslim nomenclature for God, Ram, Govinda, Harī, Murārī, Rab, and Rahīm, the attribute he usually ascribed to Him was that of the True Creator (*Sat Kartār*) or The True Name (*Sat Nām*).

In equating God with the abstract principle of truth, Nanak avoided the difficulty met by other religious teachers who describe Him only as the Creator or the Father: if God created the world, who created God? If He is the Father, who was His father? But Nanak's system had its own problems. If God is truth, what is the truth? Nanak's answer was that in situations when you cannot decide for yourself, let the guru be your guide.

The Guru

The Bhaktas and the Sufis had emphasized the necessity of having a spiritual mentor; Nanak went further and made the institution of the guru the pivot of his religious system. Without the guru, said Nanak, there could be no salvation. He was the guide who prevented mankind from straying from the straight and narrow path of truth; he was the captain of the ship which took one across the fearful ocean of life. But the guru, insisted Nanak, was to be regarded as a guide and not a god. He was to be consulted and respected but not worshipped. Nanak accepted for himself the status of a teacher but not a prophet; in his writings he constantly referred to himself as the slave or servant of God.

The Ideal of Life: Purity among the World's Impurities

Nanak did not approve of ascetic isolation or torturing of the flesh as a step to enlightenment. His ideal was to have the detachment of the yogi while living among one's fellow beings – *rāj meṉ jog* (to achieve enlightenment in civic life).

Religion lieth not in the patched coat the yogi wears,
Not in the staff he bears,
Nor in the ashes of his body.
Religion lieth not in rings in the ears,
Not in a shaven head,
Nor in the blowing of the conch shell.
If thou must the path of true religion see,
Among the world's impurities, be of impurities free.

(*Sūhi*)

Nanak believed that one of the essential requisites for the betterment of individuals was *sādh saṅgat* (the society of holy men) and righteous conduct towards one's neighbors.

Sacoṉ ore *sabh ko*
Upar sac ācār

Truth above all,
Above truth, truthful conduct.

Casteless Society

The Bhaktas had paid only lip service to the ideal of a casteless society; Nanak took practical steps to break the vicious hold of caste by starting free community kitchens – *guru kā laṅgar* – in all centres and persuading his followers, irrespective of their castes, to eat together. Nanak's writings abound with passages deploring the caste system and other practices which grew out of caste concepts, particularly the notion held by Brahmins that even the shadow of a lower-caste man, on a place where food was being cooked, made it impure. Said Nanak:

Once we say: This is pure, this is unclean,
See that in all things there is life unseen.
There are worms in wood and cowdung cakes,
There is life in the corn ground into bread.
There is life in the water which makes it green.
How then be clean when impurity is over the kitchen spread?

Impurity of the heart is greed,
Of tongue, untruth,
Impurity of the eye is coveting
Another's wealth, his wife, her comeliness.
Impurity of the ears is listening to calumny.

(*Āsā dī vār*)

The Gentle Path of Nām and Sahaj

The Hindus had advocated three alternative paths to salvation: that of action (*karmamārga*), of knowledge (*gyānamārga*), and of devotion (*bhaktimārga*). Guru Nanak accepted the path of *bhakti*, laying emphasis on the worship of the Name (*nāmamārga*). "I have no miracles except the name of God," he said.

> As hands or feet besmirched with slime,
> Water washes white;
> As garments dark with grime,
> Rinsed with soap are made light;
> So when sin soils the soul
> The Name alone shall make it whole.
>
> Words do not the saint or sinner make.
> Action alone is written in the book of fate.
> What we sow that alone we take;
> O Nanak, be saved or forever transmigrate.
>
> (*Japjī*)

Nanak believed that by repetition of the *nām* one conquered the greatest of all evils, the ego (*haumaiṉ* – literally, I am), because the ego also carries in it the seed of salvation which can be nurtured to fulness [*sic*] by nām. Once the power of the ego is properly canalized, the conquest of the other five sins – lust, anger, greed, attachment, and pride – follows as a matter of course. The wanderings of the restless mind are stilled and it attains a state of divine bliss (*vismād*). It is in that state of super-conscious stillness (*divya driśṭī*) that the tenth gate, the *dasam dvār* (the body having only nine natural orifices), is opened and that one receives a vision of God and merges one's light with the light eternal. For such a one the cycle of birth, death, and rebirth is ended and he attains salvation.

Nanak believed in the triumph of human will over fate and predestination. He believed that all human beings have a basic fund of goodness which, like the pearl in the oyster, only awaits the opening of the shell to emerge and enrich him. But most human beings are as ignorant of the goodness in them as the deer is of the aromatic *kastūrī* in its navel; and just as the deer wanders about in the woods to fall in the snares of poachers or becomes a victim of the hunter's darts, so man falls in the snares of māyā (illusion). The chief task of the Guru is to make men aware of the treasure within him and then help him to unlock the jewel box.

A method advocated by Nanak was the gentle one of *sahaj*. Just as a vegetable cooked on a gentle fire tastes best because its own juice gives it the proper flavor, so a gradual training of the body and mind will bring out the goodness that is inherent in all human beings. There is no general rule applicable to everyone; each person should discipline himself according to his physical capacity and temperament. Ascetic austerity, penances, celibacy, etc. had no place in Nanak's religion. In addition to self-imposed discipline of the mind, he advocated listening to kīrtan (hymn singing). Nanak's verses were put to music in *rāgas* or modes best suited to convey their meaning. He advised his followers to rise well before dawn and listen to the soft strains of music under the light of the stars. He believed in the stillness of the ambrosial hours (amrit-velā) one was best able to have communion with God.

What Nanak taught was not startling in its originality. Different Bhaktas and Sufis had stressed one or another aspects in their writings. Nanak alone made all these into one system and started instructions with traditions to nurture this eclectic creed. In addition, what he said was said with utter simplicity which could be understood by the rustic as well as by the sophisticated. He himself summed up his message in three commandments: *kirt karo*, *nām japo*, *vaṅd cako* – work, worship, and give in charity. That is why the names of other saints of the time passed into the pages of history books while that of Nanak was kept alive by a following which increased day by day.

The way of life adopted by Nanak's disciples was somewhat different from that of the Hindus or the Muslims from whom they had sprung. Since Nanak had emphasized the role of truthful companionship (*sat saṅg*), his disciples naturally interpreted it as being constituted of those who accepted Nanak as their guru. The breakaway from the parent communities started in the guru's lifetime. It began with a different place and mode of worship. The Sikh no longer chanted Sanskrit *ślokas* to stone idols or murmured Arabic of the Koran while genuflecting towards Mecca; he sang the hymns of Nanak in his own mother-tongue, Punjabi. He ate with his fellow Sikhs at the guru's kitchen, which he helped to organize by collecting rations and in which he took turns to serve as a cook or scrubber of utensils. To greet people he no longer used the Hindu's *namaste* or the Muslim's *salām alāikum* but the guru's Sat Kartār (True Creator). All this resulted in building a community of people who had more in common which each other than with the communities to which they had belonged.

As important as the religious and communal aspects of Nanak's preaching were the political. He was the first popular leader of the Punjab in recorded history. And even though the number of his actual disciples was not perhaps very great, the number of those belonging to other communities who paid homage to the ideal of "there is no Hindu; there is no Mussalman," was considerable[.]

* * *

Guru Nanak's transformative message of religious harmony and universal brotherhood sought to bind Hindus and Muslims, men and women, high-caste and low-caste under the single umbrella of the Creator. Nanak advocated strongly on behalf of gender equality – a concept that still eludes civilized societies today and that was comparatively unfathomable during Nanak's time. Nevertheless, he pressed the notion that man and woman were the same in the eyes of God. Indeed, under Nanak's leadership, men and women sat together during worship and meals, and performed community service without distinction between them. Sikh feminist scholar Nikky-Guninder K. Singh writes:

> From the very beginning of the tradition, Guru Nanak took special care to give women a position of equality with men in matters religious as well as mundane …. His was a new positive attitude towards women, who had long been relegated to a low place in social life and mythicized as the agent of sin and evil …. He sees them as active partners in furthering goodwill, general happiness, and the collective moral values of society …. At the Court of the True One, there will be no distinctions made on the grounds of sex or creed. Those who repeat the praise of the One will prove acceptable. That tongue alone will be blessed that utters words of devotion, be it man's or woman's.[2]

Guru Nanak died in 1539. Prior to his death, he appointed one of his closest devotees, Lehna, to serve as the propagator of the Sikh teachings Nanak had set forth. Guru Nanak renamed Lehna, "Angad," derived from the word "ang" or hand – in other words, according to Nanak, Angad was essentially an extension or part of Nanak. This began the line of ten Gurus, starting with Nanak and ending with Guru Gobind Singh. While they are certainly not reincarnations, each is considered to carry the same message and enlightened thinking as Nanak himself. Still, each of the ten gurus made unique contributions to the faith.

During his tenure, Guru Angad formulated the *Gurumukhi* (literally, "from the mouth of the Guru") script that is used in the Sikh holy text. He also gathered Guru Nanak's hymns and added his own to the compilation, thus forming the beginning of what would become the Sikh holy text. He established centers where Guru Nanak's teachings could be passed on and where physical exercise, not just spiritual advancement, was encouraged. Guru Angad dictated that Guru Amar Das was to serve as his successor upon his death.

Guru Amar Das, the third Sikh guru, assumed the guruship in 1552, when he was in his early-seventies. He formalized the practice of *langar*, a free community kitchen for anyone of any faith. The only condition to partake in langar was that everyone would sit together on the floor, regardless of caste, age, gender, faith or social status. *Langar* endures today as one of the most important institutions in Sikhism. Guru Amar Das appointed Guru Ram Das to be the fourth Sikh guru.

2 Nikky-Guninder K. Singh, *The Feminine Principle in the Sikh Vision of the Transcendent* (Cambridge: Cambridge University Press, 1993), pp. 30–31.

Guru Ram Das began his service as the head of the faith in 1574. He ordered the construction of a religious tank of water – a pool of nectar – in Amritsar that would later became part of a religious focal point of Sikhism. He also penned the hymns that are used for the Sikh marriage ceremony. Guru Ram Das emphasized the suggestion that Sikhs are to obtain enlightenment not solely through reflection, but also through active service to his fellow man. He called upon his son, Arjun, to be the fifth Sikh guru.

Other than Guru Nanak and Guru Gobind Singh, Guru Arjun is perhaps the most pivotal figure in Sikh history. His notable contributions to the development of Sikhism include overseeing the planning and construction of the Harimander Sahib (colloquially called the "Golden Temple") in Amritsar, the holiest shrine in the faith. The land upon which construction took place was donated by the Mughul Emperor, Akbar. To help defray the costs of the building and other projects, he asked Sikhs to donate a fraction of their funds to these charitable causes. He also took great pains to collect the original hymns composed by the previous gurus. He added to this collection the works of Hindu bhagats and Sufi saints, most notably Kabir and Farid, respectively. He also authored his own hymns, which would come to make up a vast majority of the collection. Guru Arjun's efforts amounted to the first edition of the Adi Granth, the Sikh holy text, which was placed in the Harmandir Sahib in 1604. It was a collection that impressed Akbar, the Mughul ruler of the time who himself sought to understand humanity and encouraged cross-religious conversation.

Akbar, however, died in 1605. He was replaced by the Mughal Emperor Jahangir, who was the diametric opposite of the open- and pluralistic-minded Akbar. Jahangir, upon learning of Guru Arjun's growing influence, summoned Guru Arjun. Jahangir ordered Guru Arjun to disavow his teachings and convert to Islam, which the Guru refused to do. Guru Arjun was jailed and subsequently tortured for several days with hot irons, boiling water, and other such treatment. He died in 1606, less than a year after Akbar himself passed.

The brutal manner in which Guru Arjun died was a critical turning point in Sikh history. Guru Arjun resisted non-violently the threats and harm of the Muslim leadership. He gladly and peacefully accepted death. His successors, however, adopted an alternative response and extended Nanak's message of equality into a more active fight for justice.

Chapter 3
Fighting Against Injustice

Around the turn of the seventeenth century, Guru Arjun's son, Guru Hargobind, assumed command of the Sikh people. A young boy of around 11 years of age, he would become the sixth Sikh guru in a time of religious tension and continued growth of the Sikh community.

Upon living through his father's torture and death, Guru Hargobind thought that the saintliness exhibited by his father and the previous Gurus must be supplemented by a rigorous defense of the faith and active protection against the tyranny of religious oppression. He therefore instructed Sikhs to be saint-soldiers – those who would not only adhere to Guru Nanak's underlying message of remembering God's name, but who would also fight for justice. This duality manifests itself in what Guru Hargobind called the *miri* (secular) and *piri* (spiritual) aspects of the faith. It is also reflected in the Harimander Sahib complex, where Guru Hargobind built the Akal Takht, a place at which Sikh affairs would be conducted and managed – it was the secular head of the faith, which faced the spiritual center of the faith, the Harimander Sahib.

Guru Hargobind took his new role as defender of the faith seriously – he trained in the martial arts and asked followers to donate horses and other items to be used in the formation of a Sikh cavalry. Jahangir ultimately imprisoned Guru Hargobind upon learning of his military preparedness. Guru Hargobind was ultimately ordered released, but he refused to leave unless a group of fifty Hindu prisoners was allowed to go with him (their collective release is celebrated by Sikhs during the Indian festival of Diwali). Although the guru eventually established peaceful relations with Jahangir, Jahangir's successor, Shah Jahan, was not fond of the Sikhs. Guru Hargobind and his followers battled Shah Jahan's army, with mixed results. The guru died in 1644, having left a legacy of *miri-piri* that continues to this day.

Guru Hargobind's eldest son, Har Rai, took over his father's duties and was installed as the seventh Sikh guru. He embraced his father's call to arms and maintained the Sikh martial tradition as a complement to the pacifist teachings of Guru Nanak. For example, it is said that Guru Har Rai's cavalry consisted of approximately 2,200 saint-soldiers. Despite his martial behavior, Guru Har Rai was known to be a compassionate man, refusing to kill hunted animals and sending medicine for the Emperor Shah Jahan's ill son. A momentous change in Sikh history took place during Har Rai's guruship – Emperor Aurangzeb won control of the Mughul Empire when his father, Shah Jahan, was unable to rule due to his failing health. Guru Har Rai died at the young age of 31, and passed the mantle of Sikh leadership to his five-year-old son, Har Krishan.

Har Krishan became the eighth guru of the Sikhs in 1661. Aurangzeb summoned Har Krishan to Delhi for a meeting, and over the objections of some close to him, Har Krishan traveled from Punjab to Delhi for this purpose. There, he met with large groups of devotees who sought the blessings of the guru. At the time, a smallpox epidemic was raging through Delhi. Guru Har Krishan ministered to many of those infected, and himself contracted smallpox in the process. He died at the young age of eight. Before his death, he called upon his great-uncle and Hargobind's father, Tegh Bahadur, to assume control of the Sikhs.

After Guru Har Krishan passed away in 1664, there was some uncertainty as to the identity of the next true guru. Guru Tegh Bahadur resolved any ambiguity and soon flocks of devotees went to him for spiritual guidance. In doing so, Tegh Bahadur ensured the Sikh faith was under one umbrella when there were opportunists intent on being recognized as the guru and possessing the authority and reverence that came with the role.

Nonetheless, Guru Tegh Bahadur had to contend with Aurangzeb, whose mission it was to spread Islam through conversions (some forcible or coerced). Aurangzeb ordered a group of northern Hindus to convert, though they refused and claimed they would do so only if Tegh Bahadur would accept Islam. Aurangzeb ordered that Tegh Bahadur be arrested, which he was, and imprisoned in Delhi. There, Aurangzeb gave Tegh Bahadur a choice – convert or be killed. Tegh Bahadur gladly opted for the latter, and was executed in 1675 at a spot now enshrined as the temple Sis Ganj in Delhi. Prior to his death, he appointed his son, Gobind, to be the tenth Sikh guru.

Guru Gobind Singh was a transformative figure in Sikh history, matched only by Guru Nanak in this respect. His story embodies the call to fight against injustice and religious oppression. It is during his tenure that the Sikh identity becomes formalized, and thus during which the Sikh turban takes a central place in Sikhism. Gobind Singh would also install the collection of hymns, the Adi Granth, as the "living" guru from his death on. To describe Gobind Singh's contributions and life, we turn again to Sikh historian Khushwant Singh.

* * *

Khushwant Singh[1]

> [Before establishing the Sikh brotherhood and dispensing with the succession of human gurus,] Gobind decided to abolish the institution of masaṅds which had become a fertile cause of disruption in the community. Many masaṅds had set themselves up as gurus in their own districts and had begun to nominate their own successors. Instead of propagating Sikhism and forwarding their collections they made to the Guru, many of

1 From Khushwant Singh, *The Illustrated History of the Sikhs* (New Delhi: OUP India), reproduced by permission of Oxford University Press India, New Delhi.

them engaged in moneylending and trading on the 'offerings' they extorted from the poor peasants. Gobind realized that the abolition of the masaṅds would for some time deprive the central exchequer of its only source of income. Nevertheless, he felt that the risk was worth taking and might in the end prove beneficial.

Gobind had to give his people something positive to replace what he had destroyed. He had created a martial atmosphere and an expectancy of military action. His father's murder was still unavenged, and the persecution of religious minorities continued as before. …

Early in 1699 he sent messages inviting his followers to make a special effort to come to Anandpur for the festival of the first Baisakh[, in which Punjabis celebrated the Spring harvest]. He specifically exhorted the Sikhs to come with their hair and beards unshorn.

The crowd that collected at Anandpur is said to have been great [and specifically around 50,000–80,000 people]. After the morning service, the Guru appeared before the congregation, drew his sword out of its scabbard, and demanded five men for sacrifice. After some trepidation, one rose to offer himself. He was taken into a tent. A little later the Guru reappeared in front of the throng with his sword dripping with blood and asked for another victim. In this manner five men were taken for a 'sacrifice' into the tent. Then the Guru came out with the five 'victims' (he had slaughtered goats instead) and announced that the *paṅj piyāre* (five beloved ones) were to be the nucleus of a new community he would raise which was to be called the *Ḵẖālsā*, or the pure.

He baptized the five men in a new manner. He mixed sugar in plain water and churned it with a double-edged dagger, to the recitation of hymns, including some of his own compositions. The five who had until then belonged to different Hindu castes (one was probably a Brahmin, one a Kshatriya, and the remaining three of lesser castes) were made to drink out of one bowl to signify their initiation into the casteless fraternity of the Khalsa. Their Hindu names were changed and they were given one family name 'Singh,' for thenceforth their father was Gobind Singh (so renamed after his own baptism), their mother Sahib Devan, and their place of birth Anandpur. The baptism symbolized a rebirth, by which the initiated were considered as having renounced their previous occupations (*krit nāś*) for that of soldiering; of having severed their family ties (*kul nāś*) to become the family of Gobind; of having rejected their earlier creeds (*dharma nāś*) for the creed of the Khalsa; of having given up all ritual (*karm nāś*) save that sanctioned by the Sikh faith.

Five emblems were prescribed for the Khalsa. They were to wear their hair and beard unshorn (*kes*); they were to carry a comb (*kaṅgā*) in their hair to keep it tidy; they were always to wear a knee-length pair of breeches (*kach*), worn by soldiers of the times; they were to carry a steel bracelet (*kaṛā*) on their right wrist; and they were to be ever armed with a sabre (*kirpān*). In addition to these five emblems, the converts were to observe four rules of conduct (*rahat*): not to cut any hair on any part of their body (this was a repetition of the oath regarding the *kes*); not to smoke, chew tobacco, or consume alcoholic drinks; not to eat an animal which had been slaughtered by being bled to death, as was customary with the Muslims, but only *jhaṭkā* meat, where the animal had been despatched with one blow; and not to molest the person of Muslim women.

At the end of the oath-taking, the Guru hailed the converts with a new form of greeting:

> *Vāh guru jī kā k̲h̲ālsā*
> *Vāh guru jī kī fateh*
>
> The Khalsa are the chosen of God
> Victory be to our God.

Having initiated the five Sikhs, Gobind asked them to baptize him into the new fraternity. The Guru was no longer their superior; he had merged his entity in the Khalsa.

Gobind Singh is said to have explained these innovations in a lengthy address to the assemblage: "I wish you all to embrace one creed and follow one path, obliterating all differences of religion. Let the four Hindu castes, who have different rules laid down for them in the *śāstras* abandon them altogether and, adopting the way of cooperation, mix freely with one another. Do not follow the old scriptures. Let none pay heed to the Ganges and other places of pilgrimage which are considered holy in the Hindu religion, or adore the Hindu deities, such as Rama, Krishna, Brahma, and Durga, but all should believe in Guru Nanak and his successors. Let men of the four castes receive baptism, eat out of the same vessel, and feel no disgust or contempt for one another."

The turbulent period that followed this baptismal ceremony did not give the Guru much time to explain the significance of the symbols he made obligatory for his followers. But they are not very difficult to understand. The chief symbol was the wearing of the hair and beard unshorn. This had been customary among aesthetes in India from time immemorial. There is reason to believe that all the gurus after Nanak and many of their disciples had abstained from cutting their hair. (The injunction did not surprise the Sikhs, since it was not really an innovation.) By making it obligatory for his followers, Gobind intended to raise an army of soldier-saints who would wield arms only in a righteous cause, as would saints if they were so compelled. The other emblems were complementary to this one and the profession of soldiering.

A more important question than the significance of the new forms was: did Gobind mean to change the faith of Nanak? Yes, and no. In its essential beliefs Gobind introduced no change. His Sikhism was that of Nanak, believing in One Supreme Creator who was without form or substance and beyond human comprehension. He condemned the worship of idols. He gave the institution of Guruship a permanent and abiding character by vesting it in the immortality of the Granth and in the community of the *Khālsā Paṅth*. Being the author of so many traditions, he was particularly conscious of the danger of his followers imposing divinity on him.

For though my thoughts were lost in prayer
At the feet of Almighty God,
I was ordained to establish a sect and lay down its rules.
But whosoever regards me as Lord
Shall be damned and destroyed.
I am – and of this let there be no doubt –
I am but the slave of God, as other men are,
A beholder of the wonders of creation.

(*Bicitra Nāṭak*)

Like Nanak, Gobind Singh believed that the sovereign remedy for the ills of mankind was *nām* – a life of prayer. He did not alter the form of prayer – the Adi Granth remained the scripture; his own works were never accorded the same sanctity. He disapproved of asceticism and ridiculed the caste system. His motto was: *mānas kī jāt sab ek hī pahcānbo* – known all mankind as one caste. Like Nanak, he believed that the end of life's journey was the merging of the individual in God:

As sparks flying out of a flame
Fall back on the fire from which they rise;
As dust rising from the earth
Falls back upon the same earth;
As waves beating upon the shingle
Recede and in the ocean mingle
So from God come all things under the sun
And to God return when their race is run.

(*Akāl Ustat*)

The only change Gobind brought in religion was to expose the other side of the medal. Whereas Nanak had propagated goodness, Gobind Singh condemned evil. One preached the love of one's neighbor, the other the punishment of transgressors. Nanak's God loved His saints; Gobind's God destroyed his enemies.

* * *

Khushwant Singh's closing remarks touch upon a central topic in Sikh history – whether Guru Nanak's conception of humanity as told to his Sikh following is consistent with the evolution of the faith as culminated by Guru Gobind Singh's creation of a distinct brotherhood of saint-soldiers. On this point, Rajdeep Singh Jolly, the legal director of a Sikh civil rights organization and student of the Sikh military tradition, explains that Guru Gobind Singh extended – but did not change – the message of Nanak:

> In a social environment marked by inter-religious and intra-religious persecution, Guru Nanak envisioned a society in which human beings mutually embrace the common thread of divinity and reject the exploitative and unjust notion that some people are inherently inferior to others in virtue of religion, caste, social status, and gender. The social and political intuition of Guru Nanak predated many of the ideals regarding human equality that formed the basis of the American Revolution, the U.S. Constitution, and the American civil rights movement by several centuries, and laid the foundation for the Sikh tradition of fighting injustice …
>
> There is a widespread misconception that the early Gurus were apolitical and uncritical pacifists; that the adoption of militarism by the Sikhs during the time of Guru Har Gobind was a response to persecution by the Mogul empire; and that the development of a distinct Sikh identity by Guru Gobind Singh was calculated to unite the Sikhs against the Moguls. Although it is true that early Sikh history was shaped by the presence of the Moguls, the Sikh religion was conceived from its very beginning as a holistic way of life that not only incorporated but also *encouraged* social and political activism. Although it is true that the adoption of militarism and a distinct identity enabled Sikhs to withstand persecution by the Moguls, these phenomena cannot be viewed as an ad-hoc response to the contingencies of the day; they are more appropriately regarded as integral and inseparable extensions of the philosophy of Guru Nanak, which is timeless and as relevant now as it was five centuries ago ….
>
> Although Guru Gobind Singh fought numerous battles with the Mogul army, and although he and his family lost their lives in the turmoil of the times, the establishment of the *Khalsa* was not merely a response to persecution by the Moguls. Guru Gobind Singh crystallized the Sikh identity in a way that consolidated the teachings of his predecessors.

Following Guru Gobind Singh, the Guru Granth Sahib became the permanent, living guide of the Sikhs. It is revered due to the fact that it is the principal source of spiritual enlightenment and guidance for Sikhs, and that it contains the written words of the gurus themselves. Because it holds such a special place in modern Sikhism, it is necessary to explore its contents and character further. For this task, we turn to a Sikh scholar and the chair of Sikh studies at the University of California, Santa Barbara, Gurinder Singh Mann. Please note that the Adi Granth, a term used by Mann, refers to the actual text, whereas the Guru Granth Sahib refers to the status as guru conferred upon the Adi Granth by Guru Gobind Singh.

* * *

Gurinder Singh Mann[2]

The Sikhs consider the Adi Granth as the highest authority within the community, and it plays a central role in Sikh devotional and ritual life. Sikh belief in the authority of the Adi Granth is based on two fundamental assumptions: that its text is revealed and hence immutable and unchangeable, and that answers to all religious and moral questions are available in it. Both in its concept and its role in day-to-day living, the Sikh understanding of scripture comes close to the Jewish and Muslim treatment of their respective sacred texts. By according the Adi Granth the status of the manifest guru (Guru Granth Sahib), the Sikhs have in one sense taken their conception of the sacred book farther than that of Jews and Muslims. As a result, Sikh belief in the status of their scripture has strengthened through the years.

The Adi Granth consists of approximately 3,000 hymns of carefully recorded authorship. Over 2,400 of these hymns were written by the six Sikh gurus who lived between 1469 and 1675 in the Punjab. The remaining hymns are attributed to 15 or so bards associated with sixteenth-century Sikh court in the Punjab and 15 non-Sikh saint-poets known in Sikh tradition as Bhagats (literally, "devotees"), who lived between the twelfth and the sixteenth centuries in the northern and northwestern region of the Indian subcontinent.

The compositions in the Adi Granth celebrate the unity and uniqueness of God, a primal being (Adi Purakh) who is the lord of the universe (Sahib). The theology propounded in these hymns is monotheistic, with absolute insistence on the non-incarnate nature (*ajuni*) of the deity. The world came into being in historical times as a result of the divine command (*hukam*), and God maintains the course of human history and individual destinies by means of the twin principles of justice (*nian*) and grace (*karam*).

The hymns in the Adi Granth also state the way human beings should live in this God-created world so as to attain liberation, the ultimate goal of human life. This liberation is achieved through meditating on the divine name (*nam*) and cultivating a relationship of love (*bhau*) and fear (*bhai*) for the creator. In its mystical ascent, the human soul rises through the stages of duty (*dharam*), knowledge (*gian*), humility (*saram*), grace (*karam*), and finally effable state of truth (*sach*). Nonetheless, the Adi Granth sets forth a view of spirituality that rejects asceticism of any kind and instead

2 From Gurinder Singh Mann, *Making of Sikh Scripture* (Oxford: OUP, 2001). By permission of Oxford University Press, Inc.

mandates an effective fulfillment of the routine obligations of our lives within society. Liberation is attained by living actively as an individual who is also part of a family and a community and is guided by a strict code of ethical conduct (*achar/rahit*) built on the values of hard work, charity, and service to humanity.

In addition to the praise of God and a statement of the ethical demands that human beings should meet, some hymns appeal for divine help to fulfill personal and collective Sikh aspirations. Still others express gratitude for divine blessings bestowed on the Sikh gurus and for the success of community ventures like the establishment of cities and the construction of *gurdwaras* (Sikh temples). A set of hymns composed by the bards glorify the Sikh gurus and present them as the representatives of God or earth.

The text of the Adi Granth is divided into three parts. The opening section is liturgical and includes three daily prayers. The *Japji* (Meditation) by Guru Nanak consists of thirty-eight stanzas and two couplets. The *Rahiras* (Supplication) contains nine hymns: four composed by Guru Nanak, three by the fourth guru, Guru Ramdas (born 1534, guru 1574–1581), and two by the fifth guru, Guru Arjan. The *Sohila* (Praise) consists of five hymns: three by Guru Nanak, and one each by Guru Ramdas and Guru Arjan. The Sikhs recite *Japji* at sunrise, the *Rahiras* at sunset, and the *Sohila* at the end of the day just before going to sleep.

The hymns in the main body of the Adi Granth are divided into thirty-one separate subsections according to the music mode (*rag*) assigned for their singing. Each subsection begins with hymns of four stanzas (*chaupadas*) and goes on to include hymns of eight stanzas (*ashtpadis*), four stanzas of six verses each (*chants*), and other longer compositions containing a sequence of couplets and stanzas (*vars*). These smaller units within each subsection open with the hymns of Guru Nanak and include the compositions of his successors and those of the Sikh bards and the Bhagats. The hymns of the Bhagats are treated as distinct units but follow the same principle of organization based on the number of stanzas.

The final section of the text of the Adi Granth is composed of miscellaneous hymns not set in any musical code. These compositions include couplets authored by Guru Nanak, Guru Arjan, Guru Tegh Bagadur (born 1621, guru 1644–75), Kabir (d. 1448), Farid (d. 1265), and a set of panegyrics (*savaiye*) by the bards. The text closes with the *Ragmala* ("Garland of musical modes"), a hymn of 12 stanzas grouping rags prevalent in the medieval Indian system of music into six families.

The language of the hymns recorded in the Adi Granth has been called "Sant Bhasha," a kind of lingua franca used by the medieval saint-poets of northern India. But the broad range of contributions to the text produced a complex mix of regional dialects. The Sikh gurus themselves used Punjabi in many of their hymns, but like other contributors they also used elements of Apabhramsha (a later dialect of Sanskrit), Braj Bhasha (the language of the Braj region around Mathura), Hindui (the language spoken around Delhi), and a heavily Persianized Punjabi. All this makes the Adi Granth a rich repository of dialects that were prevalent in medieval northern India.

From the outset, the Sikh manuscripts were recorded in a distinct script, Gurmukhi (literally, "from the mouth of the guru," but in the context "of the Gurmukhs/Sikhs"), which contains 35 characters. The script existed in an elementary form before the Sikhs appropriated it to record their writings and in the process modified the shapes of several of its characters and developed a complex system for its usage. The Sikhs assigned to it a high degree of sanctity. For Guru Nanak, the status of Gurmukhi for the Sikhs corresponded with that of Arabic and Devanagari, the sacred scripts of the Muslims and the Hindus, respectively.

Given the centrality of scripture in the tradition, almost all the Sikh chronicles refer to the compilation of the original text and its eventual expansion into the Adi Granth. These authors constructed their accounts primarily around oral traditions, using them with varying degrees of ingenuity. By the middle of the nineteenth century, there emerged a common narrative of the history of the Adi Granth, one that holds sway in both popular and scholarly circles within the Sikh community.

* * *

Chapter 4
Sikh Migration to the West

As noted above, it was the sixth Sikh Guru, Hargobind, who first framed physical defiance as a necessary and honored pursuit for Sikhs. Himself a respected warrior, Hargobind gradually changed the Sikh outlook to include a reverence for valor and skill when confronted with aggression, oppression, or injustice. The first Sikh standing army came into being during this time, originating as little more than a local police force before evolving into a coordinated body capable of defending the entire Sikh community against hostile entities.

No doubt, it was under the direction of Guru Gobind Singh that the military focus of the Sikhs was taken to new heights. While the martial spirit of the Sikhs under Hargobind grew out of pragmatic and largely secular concerns, it began to take on loftier connotations and was solidified as a spiritual exercise under Gobind Singh. His father's bravery and commitment to his faith in the lead up to his execution inspired Sikh followers, and Gobind Singh subsequently altered the Sikh faith by enlisting an army of Sikhs and establishing the Khalsa *panth*. Gobind Singh's militia turned out to be a formidable one, and he quickly proved himself a skilled commander and passionate defender of the Sikh faith. When he died in the year 1708, he left the Sikhs strong in faith and arms – a legacy that remained with the Sikhs throughout their progression.[1]

The Sikh commitment to righteousness, and the willingness to take up arms on behalf of such ideals, is well known. Sikh skills and devotion to fighting on the side of conscience have been praised by friend and foe alike, from their Afghan and Mughal enemies of centuries past to their European allies during World Wars I and II.[2] The Sikh Regiment of the Indian Army has long been one

1 See Gen. Sir Charles Gough and Arthur D. Innes, *The Sikhs and the Sikh Wars* (London: A.D. Innes, 1897), pp. 20–21: "By the energy of the great Guru, the Khalsa had been developed into a far from contemptible military force; differing from that of ordinary chiefs in its extraordinary recuperative capacity, since the rallying power remained so long as the Faith survived."

2 See, for example, Sir John James Hood Gordon, *The Sikhs* (Edinburgh: W. Blackwood, 1904), pp. 225–26: "As military material they are admirable. Possessing a strong individuality inured to hard labour and exposure from their early youth leading a healthy open air life in their hamlets and villages for they do not affect towns their home training is one to develop physical powers and to fit them for the hardest service in the field as soldiers. They combine a fine physique with energy …. [This has] undoubtedly stamped them with a national character a marked trait in which is their reserved and self respecting pride. Like Britons the fighting spirit is built into them and they do not lose it by years of peace. They still stand preeminent for military spirit and enterprise proud of their order."

of the most respected and decorated segments of the Indian Army. As Madra S. Amandeep and Parmjit Singh, authors of *Warrior Saints*, note:

> The reputation of the Sikh soldier as one of the world's finest has its origins in the creation of the *Khalsa* in 1699 by Guru Gobind Singh. The Khalsa, literally meaning the 'purified ones or the Guru's own,' are the Sikh men and women who choose to publicly affirm their commitment to their faith by taking *Khande di Pahul*, initiation by double-edged sword. Three hundred years ago, Guru Gobind Singh's dramatic founding of the Khalsa was attended by tens of thousands of Punjabi farmers, traders, artisans, untouchables and trained warriors who became the brothers and sisters of an unprecedented people's army of India.
>
> The original Khalsa initiates were never "belly-soldiers" or mercenaries; soldiering was part of their spiritual make-up as defenders of religious freedom for all faiths at a time when Mughal rulers of India were engaging in forcible and brutal conversions to Islam.
>
> "*To uphold right in every place and destroy sin and evil; that right may triumph, that good may live and tyranny uprooted from the land*" Guru Gobind Singh said. With this, he set out to "*teach the sparrow how to hunt the hawk and one man to have the courage to fight a legion.*" What the Guru succeeded in doing was to convert the Sikhs from humble peasantry of the Punjab into some of the greatest and most noble warriors in world history.[3]

Around the turn of the eighteenth century, Banda Singh Bahadur, a Sikh warrior, stepped up in the leadership void created by Gobind Singh's death. He established what would be the basis for a continuing Sikh authority in the region and mounted impressive resistance against the Mughuls. A Sikh federation of autonomous Sikh constituents emerged during this time. Maharaja Ranjit Singh built upon the successes of Banda Singh Bahadur and, with the downfall of the Mughul Empire, ruled over an expansive Sikh Empire that stretched from the Khyber Pass to present-day China, and down through Delhi. The Empire gave way to the British Raj, which asserted control of the Indian subcontinent from 1858 to India's Independence in 1947.

During the Raj, the Sikhs established themselves as an integral and highly respected part of the British armed forces. They contributed to the advancement of freedom and liberty in various wars and the Sikh Regiments in British Forces, were widely recognized as constituting the fiercest and most loyal warriors known on the battlefield. For example, in 1896, 21 members of the Sikh Regiment defended a British post against roughly 10,000 enemies. This military encounter, the Battle of Saragarhi, has drawn comparisons to the Battle

3 Amandeep Singh Madra and Parmjit Singh, *Warrior Saints: Three Centuries of the Sikh Military Tradition* (London: I.B. Tauris, 1999), p. viii.

of Thermopylae and has been designated by the United Nations Educational, Scientific and Cultural Organization as one of eight events exemplifying human bravery. It is during the Sikh participation in the armed forces of the British Raj that Sikh emigration to other parts of the world began in full swing (a topic to be discussed at greater length in Part III).

A major reason for Sikh migration to the West has historically been the Sikh participation in the British armed forces during the period of British rule. To be sure, the reasons for the Sikh exploration and settlement of Western areas are not monolithic – some left due to a political climate in India that was hostile towards religious minorities especially Sikhs, others due to where their military commitments had taken them, and yet others for the desire to provide a better quality of life for themselves and their families. To assist us in discussing the Sikh entry into the Western world, we turn to Gurharpal Singh and Darshan Singh Tatla, experts in the field of Sikh emigration.

* * *

Gurharpal Singh and Darshan Singh Tatla[4]

Before 1945

Among Sikhs the tradition of migration is in danger of becoming a culture. Beginning with integral migration in the eighteenth century and expanding through mass movements in the nineteenth and twentieth centuries, the tradition has developed a lore and economy of its own, becoming ingrained as part of the modern Sikh psyche. Sikhs, it seems, are permanently on the move, for ever in search of better pastures, restlessly seeking out different countries. The patter of going abroad to better oneself might well be the natural outgrowth of Punjab's highly competitive frontier society; it might also have deeper psychological roots that go beyond conventional social science explanations. "Each time a Sikh … leaves his homeland," as the popular saying goes, "it is a return to his most permanent tradition – that of roaming." Punjab's folklore mingles tales about migration and its attendant loss with the longing to be reunited. Sometimes migration has been an adventure, sometimes a necessity; always it has been the mark of an open community with few physical or spiritual barriers restraining a readiness to explore the modern world. Thus migration often has no end; instead it becomes a staging post for further movements and explorations.

Estimates of the Sikh diaspora suggest that today nearly 1 million, or about 5 percent of the total Sikh population of about 20 million, live outside India and Punjab. By far the largest community is settled in Britain, with

4 From Gurharpal Singh and Darshan Singh Tatla, *Sikhs in Britain: The Making of a Community* (London: Zed Books, 2006), pp 31–42. (Used with permission).

Table 4.1 Global Sikh population, 2005

Country	Population	Main Areas/Characteristics
Europe		
UK	336,179	London, West Midlands
Germany	25,000	Frankfurt, Heidelberg
Italy	20,000	South
Belgium	20,000	Luxemburg
Ukraine	8,000	
Cyprus	7,000	
Greece	5,000	
France	4,000	Paris
Spain	3,000	Barcelona
Denmark	2,000	Copenhagen
Sweden	2,000	Lund
Switzerland	2,000	
Americas		
Canada	278,415	BC & Ontario
United States	250,000	California, Mid-West, New York
Mexico	5,000	
Argentina	1,000	
Far East		
Australia	40,000	Woolagoogla, Sydney
Malaysia	36,000	Kuala Lumpur, Penang
Singapore	32,000	City
Philippines	20,000	Manila and suburbs
Thailand	12,000	Major cities
New Zealand	8,000	Auckland
Indonesia	5,000	
Middle East		
Gulf states	60,000–175,000*	Bahrain, Oman, Dubai
South Asia		
Afghanistan	7,000	Kabul
Pakistan	5,000	Nankana Sahib, Lahore
Sri Lanka	1,000	Colombo
Burma	1,000	Rangoon

Punjab and India		
India	19,923,000	
Punjab	14,592,387	Mainly rural
Rest of India	5,331,000	Delhi, Haryana, Uttar Pradesh, Maharashtra, Rajasthan

Note: * The number of Sikh migrants in the Middle East has varied dramatically due to wars and other factors.

Sources: For Canada and the UK figures are derived from Census 2001. For European countries, estimated numbers are calculated from national statistics. For Far Eastern countries, data is derived from Census reports using reasonable interpolation.

significant historic settlements in Canada, the United States, Australia and the Far East (see Table 4.1).

The first wave of Sikh migration began spanned the 1860s and 1890s, when the favored position of Sikhs in the Indian army attracted them to foreign lands. Many had served in Central Asia, Africa, and the Far East or had acted as security auxiliaries for British firms. Some Sikhs accompanied their fellow officers on tour and were recruited by British companies in the rubber plantations of Malaysia. From South East Asia these individuals then explored the Far East or made their way to the Pacific Coast, Australia, New Zealand, and Fiji. The first contingent reached the Pacific Coast in 1905, and from there some ventured into Mexico, Panama, and Argentina.

The second phase of migration began in the 1880s and lasted beyond World War II. This period is characterized by incorporation into the system of indentured labor and then free labor. Most migration from India in the mid-nineteenth century was in the form of indentured labor to colonies in Mauritius, British Guyana, Natal, Trinidad, Fiji, East Africa, the Transvaal, Cape Province, Ceylon, Malaya, and Jamaica. Because of Punjab's late incorporation into colonial rule, few Punjabis went abroad as indentured laborers. In 1895, 350 Punjabi workmen were contracted to work on Ugandan railways, a figure which rose to 31,895 six years later. After the rail project some 6,000 decided to stay on in East Africa. Some Sikhs went as indentured laborers to Fiji and the West Indies but they often rebelled against the appalling conditions, prompting authorities to ban further recruitment.

By the 1920s, Indians could enter most British colonies but access into the White Dominions was restricted. Entry into Britain could be secured on the production of a passport, and the British Nationality Act of 1914 greatly extended the scope of British citizenship by conferring common citizenship on all subjects of the Crown. Despite this legislation, admission into the Dominions remained difficult, especially after the first wave of migration to Canada by 1910 triggered the imposition of strict controls. The United States soon followed suit by limiting Asian migration, and many Sikhs who had already arrived and acquired U.S. citizenship were deprived of the status. Although these entry barriers successfully limited any further mass migration during the inter-war years, by the end of World War II, Sikh colonies had been established throughout the globe to become magnets for future migrants.

After 1945

Following the end of colonial rule a different set of conditions began to determine the patterns of Sikh migration. Among the pull factors were the growing demand for labor in the Western economies, more liberal migration policies, and the development of the Gulf states. Among the push factors were the impact of the partition, regular political instability in Punjab, the collapse of the rural economy from the 1990s onwards, the indigenization policies in countries such as Fiji, Kenya, Uganda, and China (Hong Kong). These sets of factors have operated in mutually reinforcing ways, a process hastened by the emergence of globalized networks within the Sikh diaspora.

The post-war reconstruction boom in Western economies fuelled by Keynesian economic policies created an insatiable demand for labor as shortages developed and governments increasingly turned to the former colonies to secure new recruits. In Britain this recruitment from the New Commonwealth countries of India, Pakistan, and the Caribbean region was officially encouraged, with particular emphasis on public sector workers, but also on general unskilled labor. In the early 1950s, British government policy was aimed at overcoming labor shortages. In these conditions, Sikhs were easily able to secure employment and the new workers quickly communicated this message to kith and kin at home, triggering large-scale chain migration.

The post-war demand for labor was also accompanied by liberal immigration policies. In Britain the Nationality Act of 1948 theoretically gave every citizen of the Commonwealth the right to settle, but in practice this right was circumscribed by informal restrictions such as the control over the issuing of passports and informal diplomatic pressures. Nonetheless, migrants from India proved particularly resourceful in circumventing some of these restrictions. For instance, in the 1950s, when the government of India was pressured into limiting the issue of passports, many Sikhs crossed the border and secured passports from Pakistan with Islamic names. It was not until the Commonwealth Immigrants Act of 1962 that the "liberal regime" came to an end.

Liberal immigration policies were also adopted by Canada and the United States. In Canada, the push towards a multicultural society was accompanied by a policy that opened the door wider to non-white settlers. Over the last four decades this has encouraged significant primary emigration from Punjab, with Canada's Sikh population increasing from 7,000 in 1960 to nearly 278,415 in 2001. Similarly, in the U.S. the 1960s saw the repeal of much of the restrictive immigration legislation that had been put into force in the 1920s to curtail Asian immigration. While the bias of U.S. immigration policies has been towards attracting professionals, the 1990s witnessed a significant influx of Sikh non-professionals who gained access as asylum seekers or through illegal means. This change is also reflected in the size and social composition of the Sikh U.S. population.

The oil boom of the early and mid-1970s provided the next major demand-led Sikh migration. Awash with petro-dollars, the Gulf states launched major infrastructure and building programs that attracted millions of Indian workers on the pattern of "neo-indentured" laborers who worked on fixed-term contracts without any rights. Precise figures for Sikh migration are unavailable, but it is estimated that currently there are 60,000–175,000 Sikhs in the Gulf states. The number of those who have been in the Gulf states at any time since the 1970s is considerably higher, for the average period of the contract varies from several months to a few years. This migration has created a substantial remittance economy and contributed further pressures for migration, as the returnees have often sought more permanent locations once their contracts have expired. The Middle East has often constituted the transition zone between India and further migration to the West or the Far East.

In the 1970s and the 1980s, the onset of recession together with the rise of anti-immigration policies seriously curtailed the flows of Sikhs to the West. In Britain, Thatcherism destroyed the manufacturing economy, the mainstay of Sikh employment, while imposing strict controls that all but curtailed primary immigration. As a result Sikh migrants from Punjab increasingly made North America and other countries their main destination. But as the economy in Britain in the 1990s revived, fuelled by the dot.com boom, Sikh migration also witnessed something of a revival, though this was not professional-led, but allied to supporting labor shortages on the back of asylum and refugee settlement. Recent measures to allow for more flexible and temporary workers from South Asia to meet skill shortages in key areas have added significantly to the temporary Sikh population as a whole. These changes in policy suggest that Sikh migrants are highly knowledgeable about migration opportunities and are always primed to exploit them as they arise.

Push Factors

Of all the factors that have contributed to Sikh (and Punjabi) migration the partition of India in 1947 was perhaps the single most dramatic. The division of the historic province of Punjab led to unprecedented ethnic cleansing with the accompanying transfers of population that made West Punjab a homogeneous Muslim territory and East Punjabi a province of mainly Sikhs and Hindus. For Sikhs and Hindus of the former Canal Colonies, resettlement in East Punjab was a traumatic event: the settlement process dragged on an in many cases inferior and inadequate landholdings were allocated in exchange for those they had relinquished. In fact, the partition threw the whole economy of East Punjab into turmoil, generating excessive demographic pressure on agriculture and the need to accommodate and resettle several million refugees who were often compelled to eke out an existence for several years. Many of these refugees, particularly the urban Sikhs, moved to Delhi or other states within the Indian Union. Many more saw the despair of the partition as an opportunity to build their lives abroad on the back of post-war reconstruction. The "Third Punjab" or the "diaspora Punjabi," as it has been argued, arose directly from the "ashes of the partition." For some of the migrants, even Delhi seemed an impermanent, insecure place to construct the "new home."

Since 1947, political instability in Punjab has also played a major part in Sikh emigration to Britain and other countries. [Political tensions between the Sikhs and the Indian government] in 1984 probably triggered the largest wave of Sikh migration to the West since the 1950s and 1960s. Young Sikh men, either to avoid persecution in Punjab or to exploit the opportunities for migration, sought political asylum in Western states in their thousands. The exact figures for the post-1984 refugee outflow will probably never be available but the numbers were not insignificant. From 1984 to 1992, 5,900 Indian citizens, excluding dependants, applied for political asylum in Britain and most of these were Sikhs. European countries with recognized asylum policies also received large numbers: Germany, France, the Netherlands, Norway, Denmark, Italy, and Switzerland now have sizeable Sikh settlements that date from the post-1984 overspill as the "Punjab problem" became internationalized. The European influx was extended to Canada and the United States, where large numbers of asylum applications were reluctantly granted. Immigration authorities in these states had to tread a fine line between granting asylum and maintaining controls. Several actually sent out their own missions to India to check the veracity of the asylum seekers' claims that brutal repression had driven them overseas. Asylum applications tailed off only with the rising asylum population in Western countries in the late 1990s. The end of the militancy in Punjab has effectively undermined the legitimacy of any further claims for asylum, though it would be premature to suggest that this mode of migration has now been closed permanently.

Sikhs, like other Indians, have also been the victims of indigenization policies in some decolonized states. In East Africa, the Far East, Hong Kong, South Africa, the Caribbean and, most recently, Afghanistan, small and large Sikh populations, often resident in these countries for several centuries, have increasingly relocated themselves to Western states because of such policies. This relocation has obeyed a natural bias towards places where the largest Sikh populations are centered, thereby invoking the immigration obligations of former imperial rules. Interestingly, it follows the overall pattern of movement of the Indian diaspora, from the traditionally low-income economies of the South to the North.

Of all the push factors, it is economic circumstances that have received most scrutiny from scholars .... Since the early 1990s the collapse of the rural economy in Punjab has created a vicious cycle of low growth, failing agricultural incomes and declining employment opportunities. Once again the local state is facilitating migration as a safety valve against the pressures created by the new circumstances, although increasingly this is articulated in the language of diaspora-led economic development. Today, as in the past, those most affected by the new squeeze are the marginal and poor farmers[.]

While economic factors have undoubtedly played a major part in Sikh migration, we also need to acknowledge the role of cultural factors. Migration from Punjab today is not only determined by the migrant's economic status: even well-established families have felt the need for "foreign connections," more so in the last decade as the pressures of globalization undermined agriculture while introducing Punjabis to global markets. The modernization of Punjab society over the last half-century, moreover, has created a large graduate population who prefer migration to commercial or agricultural employment, even though this often means taking up low-status employment in developed economies. One commentator has noted the famous "PhD taxi rank" in Sydney, run by alumni of Punjab Agricultural University. These alumni also proliferate in New York, Seattle, and Vancouver. But, paradoxically, while status compulsions lead Sikhs to outward migration, Punjab's Green Revolution [which modernized agriculture through the use of new, high-yielding seeds and technologies] has witnessed the large-scale immigration of almost three million agricultural laborers from other Indian states, most notably Bihar. For many Sikhs, migration in modern Punjab has become a compulsion to maintain the status differential, not least from India's own immigrants.

This culture of migration has been fuelled by the development of probably the most sophisticated migration industry in India, if not the whole of Asia. This industry began by enticing would-be migrants with information on the rich prospects in the West; it has now blossomed into a multi-billion-dollar enterprise that is singularly responsible for creating the current size of the Sikh diaspora. [S]ince the early 1950s [the travel] industry has established elaborate connections within the provincial and national state bureaucracy in India that have enabled it to develop complex networks of people-trafficking that extend to all regions of the globe. There is, indeed, nowhere in the world where the travel agents of Jalandhar [a major city in North Punjab] cannot deliver a migrant: the only constraint is the ability of the would-be migrant to raise the requisite funding. Over the years, several agents have developed reputations for delivering migrants that have been woven into the cultural folklore of the region. A recent visit to travel agents in Jalandhar highlighted easy access a potential migrant has to details of the migration and welfare policies of most Western states. The lobbying from this industry, with its networks in Punjab and overseas, especially Britain and Canada, has led to pressure for immigration procedures and airline travel to be made more accessible to its needs. In view of further plans to expand cheap airline travel to Punjab by most Western airliners, the size of this industry is likely to increase substantially in the near future ….

[In conclusion, s]ince the mid-nineteenth century almost a million Sikhs have settled overseas, creating a visible, dynamic and at times troublesome diaspora. Nearly a third of this diaspora is now based in Britain, an association that dates from the colonial encounter that dispersed the Sikhs across the globe in search of new opportunities opened up by travel and military service in the Indian army. These early pioneers contributed significantly to the development of a cultural tradition of migration that became much more pervasive throughout Punjabi society with the rise in demand for labor in the post-war boom and the liberalization of immigration controls. For Sikhs the global migration needs of Western and Middle Eastern economies have now supplanted the migratory mechanism provided by the Indian Army during colonial times. Sikhs are, in many ways, the premier migrants of South Asia.

At the same time we need to recognize that there were very specific reasons for some of the Sikh migration. Political dislocation – whether the partition or the "Punjab problem" of the 1980s and 1990s – has always played a major role in the movement of Punjabi and Sikh populations; economic pressures also have their own momentum[.] As political instability over the last few decades has undermined economic development, the Punjab, once the most prosperous province in India, has found itself reeling from an agricultural depression at a time when India's non-agricultural economy is making global waves. In these circumstances it is more likely that the culture of migration will become Punjabis' only culture – at least for the foreseeable future.

Finally, we need to note that Sikh migrants in the main were drawn from an agrarian society that was overwhelmingly traditional, patriarchal, conservative and hierarchically structured by caste rules[.] For most of these migrants Sikhism as a faith defined their outlook and behavior but it was also mediated by the everyday experience of living in broader Punjabi society, of which the village constituted the main social unit. In due course the *pendus* (villagers) would be supplemented by Sikh professionals from India, East Africa, the Far East and other parts of the Sikh diaspora, but it was the former group who were at the forefront in pioneering organizations

> of British Sikhs. In the traditions and culture of today's British Sikhs, the "remembered" village still occupies a pre-eminent position[.]

* * *

The Sikhs who entered the United States during these waves of migration arrived there as early as 1899. They settled mainly in the West "to build railroads, farm, or work in mills and foundries."[5] Sikh agricultural skills combined with the similarities between the fertile land of California and that of Punjab made the Western region of America a natural home for many Sikhs. Although there has been a vibrant Sikh community in Central California since the late nineteenth century, most of the Sikhs currently living around the country arrived after the 1965 immigration laws nullified immigration quotas: "After 1965 in the United States … immigration laws were revised to admit Indians in numbers equal to those for people of other countries."[6] As a result of the change in laws, which favored professionals, Sikhs were among the approximately "hundred thousand engineers, physicians, scientists, professors, teachers, business people and their dependents [who] had entered the United States by 1975."[7]

Although Table 4.1 cites a figure of 250,000, it is estimated that the actual number of Sikhs in the United States today is closer to 500,000. Despite the discrimination that Sikhs have faced in the United States, they have prospered in various aspects of American life, including politics and business.[8]

---

5 See U.S. Commission on Civil Rights, *Civil Rights Concerns in the Metropolitan Washington, D.C., Area in the Aftermath of the September 11, 2001, Tragedies* (June 2003), p. 8.

6 Joan M. Jensen, *Passage from India: Asian Indians in North America* (New Haven, CT: Yale University Press, 1988), p. 280.

7 Ibid.

8 *Civil Rights Commission Report*, p. 8, quoting Patwant Singh, *The Sikhs* (London: John Murray, 1992), p. 242.

Chapter 5
Contemporary Sikh History

In the early twentieth century, a group of Sikh religious leaders, academics, and others convened to formulate the Sikh Code of Conduct, or *Rehat Maryada*, which codified the rules of proper Sikh conduct that were promulgated by the Gurus.[1] These rules required Sikhs to complete daily prayers, adhere to the five articles of faith set forth by Guru Gobind Singh, proscribed Sikhs from consuming alcohol or tobacco, and enjoined them to otherwise live in accordance with the three principles of life provided by Guru Nanak – to remember God's name, to live honestly as a productive member of society, and to give back to society through charitable work. With respect to hair, it lists unshorn hair as the first article of faith, and lists "dishonoring the hair" as the first transgression.[2] It should be noted that some Sikhs have not been entirely faithful to the Rehat, despite the clear significance of the Sikh turban and unshorn hair to the faith. Explanations for this include an interest in assimilating into Western society or an interest in avoiding harassment and race violence.

There are three major events which form a fundamental part of Sikh history and of the modern Sikh identity. The first was the April 13, 1919 massacre of innocent Sikhs by British soldiers at Jallianwala Bagh. The Bagh is "an open plot of land about 225 by 180 meters in area … located a few hundred yards from the Golden Temple in Amritsar," as noted by respected Sikh historian Patwant Singh.[3] Over 20,000 people had peacefully assembled there that day to hear speeches on the growing political unrest between the ruling British and the locals. A large number had gathered in part because April 13 was Baisakhi, the day on which Sikhs celebrate Guru Gobind Singh's creation of the Khalsa.

In the afternoon, a British commander, Brigadier-General Reginald Dyer, "entered the Bagh which was completely enclosed by high buildings" and with no warning, "ordered his troops to fire into the densely packed crowd."[4] Within fifteen minutes the soldiers had emptied their rounds and killed an estimated 379 and

---

1 See Rahitnama Prahlad Rai and Bhai Nand Lal, "Sikh Code of Conduct No. 14152 bb2," translated in Trilochan Singh, *The Turban and the Sword of the Sikhs: Essence of Sikhism* (Amritsar: B. Chattar Singh Jiwan Singh, 1997), p. 303: "Cursed is a Sikh who goes out in the society without a turban or wears a cap instead of a turban."

2 See Sikh Reht Maryada, available at <http://www.sgpc.net/rehat_maryada/section_six.html>.

3 Patwant Singh, *The Sikhs* (New York: Knopf, 1999), p. 177.

4 Ibid., p. 178.

wounded over 1,000 innocent people in the Bagh.[5] The massacre was condemned even by Winston Churchill, who called for Dyer's dismissal. It was a moment that galvanized the Indian Independence movement and demonstrated the Sikh civilian sacrifice to the cause of India's freedom from British imperial rule.

The second historic moment is the killing of innocent Sikhs following India's independence in 1947. The partition of the British colony into a Muslim-dominant Pakistan and Hindu-dominant India drew a line that split Punjab in half, with thousands of Sikhs from Pakistan migrating to India and getting slaughtered in the process. The accounts of partition indicate that its effects on religious minorities, including Sikhs, were largely overlooked and that the boundaries themselves were hastily drawn, thus further complicating the lives of Sikhs who lived on both sides of the political line. Punjab, "the only state in which [Sikhs] were concentrated," was divided in two.[6] The results were predictable. According to Patwant Singh, "Sikhs stranded in Pakistan could be expected to be either killed or forced to leave their fertile lands, urban wealth, extensive properties and lucrative businesses ...."[7] All told, an estimated 600,000 Sikhs lost their lives in Punjab due to the sloppy and rash partition in the state, and even those numbers may be low.[8]

The third historical turning point for modern Sikhs took place in 1984. That year saw the storming of the Harimander Sahib by Indian Army forces, the retaliatory assassination of Indian Prime Minister Indira Gandhi by her Sikh bodyguards, and the anti-Sikh pogrom in Delhi that followed immediately thereafter. In April 1984, Indian Army forces charged into the Golden Temple complex. Their target was Jarnail Singh Bhindranwale, described by Patwant Singh as a "seminary preacher with considerable knowledge of the Sikh scriptures" and a "charismatic leader who eclipsed [the moderate Sikh political party] by utterances more fiery than their own."[9] As a result of his inflammatory political rhetoric, the Indian government sought to arrest him. In late 1983, Bhindranwale sought refuge in the Golden Temple complex.

In June 1984, following a large religious holiday, the Indian army – with soldiers and tanks – stormed the Golden Temple complex with the "ostensible purpose to flush out Bhindranwale."[10] Thousands of civilians died: "The use of massive power, resulting in the complete destruction of the Sikh seat of temporal power, the Akal Takht, and the loss of 5,000 civilian lives – for an entirely unconvincing purpose, simply to apprehend a 'handful of men,' – stunned Sikhs worldwide."[11]

The tension between Sikhs and the government culminated with the October 31, 1984 assassination of Prime Minister Indira Gandhi, who ordered the military

5 Ibid., p. 179.
6 Ibid., p. 194.
7 Ibid.
8 Ibid., p. 197.
9 Ibid., pp. 214–15.
10 Ibid., p. 215.
11 Ibid.

advance on the Golden Temple. She was killed by her two Sikh bodyguards. The retaliation by Indians and government authorities towards Sikhs was immediate and intense: "Eyewitness reports identified Congressmen and police personnel directing and often leading the [civilian Indian] killers in different areas of Delhi in which, by government's own admission, 2,733 persons were killed or burnt alive in those four days" after the assassination.[12] These official counts are disputed, and thought to be considerably lower than the actual death toll of innocent Sikhs.[13]

Many of those killed in all three of these events were targeted specifically because they could be identified as Sikhs. The turbans and unshorn hair that were made part of the Sikh uniform hundreds of years earlier gave them away. For thousands, it led to their deaths. So, one may ask, why would they continue to wear a turban in the face of persecution, violence, and possible death?

12 Ibid., p. 216.
13 Ibid.

Chapter 6
Spiritual Significance and Physical Aspects of the Sikh Turban

Although not specifically included as one of the five articles of faith, the turban holds tremendous significance for Sikhs. Indeed, some regard the turban as *part* of one's self. The question for our consideration is: Why?

First, it should be noted that the significance of the five articles of faith and the turban were not fully explored after the creation of the Khalsa. The wartime circumstances prevented Guru Gobind Singh from settling down and being able to expound on his reasoning for mandating these permanent items of Sikh identity.

Sikh historians and scholars have thus tried to fill in the interpretive gap by supplying their own explanations for why the Sikh uniform is what it is. Therefore, and perhaps unsurprisingly, historians have not reached agreement as to why these specific articles of faith were selected by Gobind Singh. Instead, they have propounded competing theories as to why the articles of faith are an integral part of the Sikh identity.

With respect to the turban, there are several suggestions. First, there is the practical justification that *kes*, one of the five Sikh articles of faith, should be kept tidy and that the turban may guard the hair from the elements.[1] Second, the turban ensures a common, visible identity for all Sikhs.[2] Third, the turban signifies equality.[3] It is not reserved for the aristocracy or social elite, as it had historically been worn in that part of the world. Fourth, as Sikhs may be identified on the basis of their turban,

---

1 See W.H. McLeod, "Sikhs and the Turban," in *Sikh: Forms and Symbols*, ed. Mohinder Singh (Delhi: Manohar, 2000), pp. 95, 103–4. In addition to providing such protection, W.H. McLeod, a pre-eminent British historian who studied the Sikhs during the British Empire, identifies a number of reasons why the turban is desirable for Sikh men today. These include: because the turban is hygienic, because it is comfortable in hot and cold weather, because it is easy and inexpensive to wear, because it is firmly fixed on the head, and because it is more suitable than the bare head for people dealing with food.

2 See Manvir Singh Khalsa, "Who Are Sikhs?," *Oxford Sikhs* (March 20, 2005), available at <http://www.oxfordsikhs.com/SikhAwareness/117.aspx>: "The turban and unshorn hair is part of the Sikh uniform."

3 See "Sikh Theology: Why Sikhs Wear a Turban," The Sikh Coalition, available at <http://www.sikhcoalition.org/Sikhism11.asp>: "The Sikh Gurus … sought to uplift the downtrodden and make them the equals of the highest of the high." See also Jeremy Waldron, "One Law for All? The Logic of Cultural Accommodation," 59 *Wash. & Lee L. Rev.* 3, 7 (2002): "[T]he Sikh's religious obligation is an obligation to present himself in public as a combination of saint and warrior."

the turban makes every member of the faith an ambassador of Sikhism.[4] Fifth, and related, the easily recognizable aspects of the turban and a Sikh's distinct appearance serve as "helpful deterrents against undesirable acts and behavior and keep [Sikhs] on the right path."[5] It is a reminder to the Sikh that he is to act in accordance with the teachings of the Gurus and that any transgressions may be easily noted by non-Sikhs, who can quickly spot a Sikh.[6] Sixth, as a Sikh is easily identifiable, anyone who is being persecuted and in need of help could quickly locate a Sikh who is obligated to help them. Seventh, the turban is an indication of the wearer's commitment to Sikhism, general discipline, and willpower to wear the turban in the face of persecution – particularly as Sikhs have encountered problems with turbans throughout the faith's history.[7] Sikhs with turbans may wear them for one or some combination of these reasons, though perhaps some Sikhs wear a turban simply to adhere to the religious mandate.[8]

In the aftermath of the 9/11 attacks, Sikhs often tried to offer a coherent explanation for why the turban was significant to them. This attempt was patently necessary as Sikhs in various settings were having their turban questioned, sometimes in ways that were offensive to Sikhs. For example, if an airport security official wanted to remove a Sikh's turban to determine if an object was being concealed therein, a Sikh needed to explain that the turban was no hat – it held deep religious meaning. Similarly, some non-Sikhs suggested to their colleagues and friends that they should opt for caps or wear their hair openly in a ponytail or a similar way to avoid the intrusiveness that invariably accompanied the turban in post-9/11 America. The Sikh, similarly, was in a position of having to state that this was not possible – the turban itself was important and irreplaceable.

To give non-Sikhs an insider's perspective on the significance of the turban, Prabhjot Singh penned the following essay in the weeks following the attacks. It was the first and perhaps most widely cited material issued on the subject after the attacks. The context of this writing must be appreciated. There was no opportunity to conduct extensive analysis of the different explanations, to traverse through the historical documents and accounts – time was of the essence as Sikhs were under the

---

4 See "Sikh Theology: Why Sikhs Wear a Turban." "[T]here is a great deal of responsibility accompanied by the turban. A person's actions are no longer just tied to him or her. Since Sikhs who wear the turban represent the Guru, their actions too reflect on the Guru and the Sikh Nation."

5 Ganda Singh, "Importance of Hair and Turban," in ed. Mohinder Singh *Sikh: Forms and Symbols* (Delhi: Manohar, 2000), pp. 39, 43.

6 See "Sikh Theology: Why Sikhs Wear a Turban." "[T]he turban serves to increase a Sikh's commitment to Sikhism and lends to him or her becoming a more disciplined and virtuous person."

7 See ibid.: "When many discarded their turbans, those that proudly adorned them in those times, even though it meant certain death, fully appreciated its significance. After all, it is in times of adversity that faith is tested and one must prove true to core values."

8 See ibid., claiming that "the reason all practicing Sikhs wear the turban is just one – out of love and obedience of the wishes of the founders of their faith."

gun as soon as the towers fell. This essay sought to advance a cognizable explanation for the Sikh turban under those tremendous time considerations and with a view towards mitigating the ignorance surrounding the Sikh turban.

* * *

Prabhjot Singh

The *dastaar*, as the Sikh turban is known, is an article of faith that has been made mandatory by the founders of Sikhism. It is not to be regarded as mere cultural paraphernalia.

When a Sikh man or woman dons a turban, the turban ceases to be just a piece of cloth and becomes one and the same with the Sikh's head. The turban as well as the other articles of faith worn by Sikhs have an immense spiritual as well as temporal significance. The symbolisms of wearing a turban are many from it being regarded as a symbol of sovereignty, dedication, self-respect, courage, and piety but the reason all practicing Sikhs wear the turban is just one – out of love and obedience of the wishes of the founders of their faith.

The turban's importance can be found in just about every culture and religion, starting with the ancient Babylonians to Western religions such as Judaism, Christianity, and Islam, as well as Eastern traditions. The Old Testament proclaims, "Once they enter the gates of the court," implying God's court, "they are to wear linen vestments. They shall wear linen turban."

Elsewhere in the Old Testament, the significance of the turban is further highlighted:

> He put the turban upon his head and set the gold rosette as symbol of holy dedication on the front of the turban as the Lord had commanded him. Moses then took the anointing oil, anointed the Tabernacle, and all that was within it and consecrated it. (Leviticus 8:9)

> Set the turban on his head and the symbol of holy dedication on the turban. Take the anointing oil, pour it on his head and anoint him. (Exodus 29:6)

The turban, since ancient times, has been of significant import in the Punjab, the land of the five rivers and the birthplace of Sikhism. There was a time when only kings, royalty, and those of high stature wore turbans. Two people would trade their turbans to show love or friendship towards each other.

At the time of Sikhism's birth, the majority of people in India, and even today, comprised the lower castes, mainly composed of peasants, laborers and servants. Many were literally owned by the upper castes and were severely maltreated. The Sikh Gurus (prophets/teachers) sought to uplift the downtrodden and make them the equals of the highest of the high. Guru Nanak, the founder of the Sikh faith, states in his divine revelation:

> Nanak seeks the company of the lowest of the low class, the very lowest of the low. Why should he try to compete with the great? Where the lowly are cared for, there lies the Grace of the Merciful Bestower.

The Sikh Gurus sought to end all caste distinctions, and vehemently opposed stratification of society by any means. They diligently worked to create an egalitarian society dedicated to justice and equality. The turban is certainly a gift of love from the founders of the Sikh religion and is symbolic of sovereignty that is of Divine concession. According to Sirdar Kapur Singh, a Sikh theologian and statesman:

> When asked by Captain Murray, the British Charge-de-affairs at Ludhiana in about 1830, for the captain's gallant mind was then wholly preoccupied with the Doctrine of Legitimacy, recently evolved or rediscovered by European statesmen at the Congress at Vienna, as to from what source the Sikhs derived their claim to earthly sovereignty, for the rights of treaty or lawful succession they had none; Bhai Rattan Singh Bhangu [a Sikh historian], replied promptly, "The Sikhs' right to earthly sovereignty is based on the Will of God as authenticated by the Guru, and therefore, other inferior sanctions are unnecessary."[9]

The turban has been an integral part of the Sikh Tradition since the time of Guru Nanak Dev. Historical accounts relay to us that all Sikh gurus wore turbans and their followers – Sikhs – have been wearing them since the formation of the faith.

The turban serves as a mark of commitment to the Sikh gurus. It distinguishes a Sikh as an instrument of the Guru and decrees accountability for certain spiritual and temporal duties. It is a mark of the Guru and declares that the Sikh wearing a turban is a servant of the Divine Presence.

Wearing the turban gives much inner strength as well. Sikhs take this gift of the Guru with them everywhere they go. Just by being exposed to this regal quality, their attitudes and psyche get shaped in a certain way. At the same time, there is a great deal of responsibility accompanied by the turban. A person's actions are no longer just tied to him or her. Since Sikhs who wear the turban represent the Guru, their actions too reflect on the Guru and the Sikh Nation. In this sense, the turban serves to increase a Sikh's commitment to Sikhism and lends to him or her becoming a more disciplined and virtuous person.

The turban certainly deepens the connection between the Sikh and the Guru. The turban proclaims the followers of Guru Nanak as Sikhs, but at the same time, it is not what makes them Sikhs. Prophet Mohammed in one of his hadiths states that the turban is a frontier between faith and unbelief. This aptly describes the significance of the turban for a Sikh as well. It is a true mark of sovereignty and a crown.

9 Kapur Singh, *Parasaraprasna* (Amritsar: Guru Nanak Dev University, 1989), pp. 130–31.

Due to its distinguishable nature, the turban has often been a target during times of persecution. There have been times in the relatively short history of the Sikh Nation that if one wore a turban, it was reason enough for his or her head to be cut off by the tyrannical regimes of the time. The collective response of the Sikh Nation was: "You may take off my head but not my turban." When many discarded their turbans, those that proudly adorned them in those times, even though it meant certain death, fully appreciated its significance. After all, it is in times of adversity that faith is tested and one must prove true to core values.

By adorning their turbans, Sikhs serve as ambassadors of the Sikh faith and commit externally to following the path laid down by the Sikh Gurus. True submission, of course, occurs internally.

The next time you see a Sikh, greet him or her and know that the turban you see is the same turban and stood up against oppression against those identified as lower castes in India, tyranny in World War I, the Nazi empire in World War II. As Sikhs tie their turbans each day, they should be heedful that it represents a very real commitment to the founders of the Sikh faith. The turban is deeply intertwined with the Sikh identity and is a manifestation of the mission given to all Sikhs – to act as a divine prince or princess by standing firm against tyranny and protecting the downtrodden.

* * *

As noted by Prabhjot Singh, while the turban has special importance in the Sikh community, the turban is by no means an exclusively Sikh piece of attire. Turbans have been worn in different parts of the world for at least the past 3,000 years.[10] Although it remains unclear when or where they originated, they were used in the Egyptian civilization, and depicted in Assyrian carvings – long before the advent of Christianity and Islam, let alone Sikhism.[11] The Old Testament has a number of references to turbans, including a turban worn by Moses as a symbol of his status as a prophet, holiness, and divine power.[12] Wearing turbans is also closely related to Islam. A specific hadith (Islamic tradition) tied to the Prophet Muhammad identifies turbans as being "a true mark of sovereignty and a crown."[13]

In South Asia, turbans were worn by a number of different groups for various reasons. The wealthy, for example, wore elaborate bejeweled turbans as a symbol of their power, prestige, and royalty.[14] Similarly, high-caste Hindus wore turbans

---

10 Eli Sanders, "Understanding Turbans: Don't Link Them to Terrorism," *Seattle Times*, May 27, 2003, available at <http://seattletimes.nwsource.com/news/nation-world/infocus/mideast/islam/understanding_turbans.html>.

11 Ibid.

12 See "Sikh Theology: Why Sikhs Wear a Turban."

13 Ibid.

14 See Sanders, "Understanding Turbans," describing Indian men as "sometimes wear[ing] turbans to signify their class, caste, profession or religious affiliation."

to differentiate themselves from lower castes.[15] More practically, men from the desert regions and rural farmers wore turbans to protect themselves from dust and the heat.[16] Men also swapped their turbans to show good faith and hospitality in a dealing or agreement.[17] Similarly, turbans may be worn by male members of bridal parties during Hindu wedding ceremonies.[18] Turbans have also been used to demonstrate one's political affiliation.[19]

But what makes Sikh turbans vulnerable is that they are the only form of turban that is absolutely mandated as a religious practice. In the United States today, 99 percent of those who wear turbans are Sikhs. Sensing the community's vulnerability, the media joined the effort to explain the turban. A guide published by the *Seattle Times* to help educate the public about Sikh turbans (called a *dastaar*, *pagh*, or *paghri*) after 9/11 illustrates the physical differences between the Sikh turban and turbans worn by others.

Figure 6.1 Sikh man's turban

Sikh men commonly wear a peaked turban (see Figure 6.1) that serves partly to cover their long hair, which is never cut out of respect for God's creation. Devout Sikhs also do not cut their beards, so many Sikh men comb out their facial hair and then twist and tuck it up into their turbans along with the hair from their heads. Sikhism originated in northern India and Pakistan in the fifteenth century and is one of the youngest of the world's monotheistic religions. There are an estimated 18 million Sikhs in the world, with some 2 million spread throughout North America, Western Europe and the former British colonies.

15 Ibid.

16 Ibid. "Desert peoples have long used the turban to keep sand out of their faces."

17 See, for example, "The Koh-i-noor Diamond," *BBC News*, June 6, 2002, available at <http://www.bbc.co.uk/dna/h2g2/A730801>, noting that in 1739, Nadir Shah of Persia obtained the Koh-i-noor diamond by "exchang[ing] turbans," which "would symbolise their close ties and eternal friendship."

18 See I.J. Singh, *Being and Becoming a Sikh* (Toronto: The Centennial Foundation, 2003), p. 56.

19 See "Why Turban Matters in Punjab Polls," CNN-IBN, February 7, 2007, available at <http://www.ibnlive.com/news/why-turban-matters-in-punjab-polls/32933-4.html>.

Figure 6.2 Muslim religious elders' turban

Muslim religious elders, like the man from Yemen shown in Figure 6.2, often wear a turban wrapped around a cap known in Arabic as a *kalansuwa*. These caps can be spherical or conical, colorful or solid white, and their styles vary widely from region to region. Likewise, the color of the turban wrapped around the *kalansuwa* varies. White is thought by some Muslims to be the holiest turban color, based on legends that the prophet Mohammed wore a white turban. Green, held to be the color of paradise, is also favored by some. Not all Muslims wear turbans. In fact, few wear them in the West, and in major cosmopolitan centers around the Muslim world, turbans are seen by some as passé.

Figure 6.3 Afghan men's turban

Afghan men wear a variety of turbans, and even within the Taliban, the strict Islamic government that controls much of the country, there are differences in the way men cover their heads. The Taliban member shown in Figure 6.3, for example, is wearing a very long turban – perhaps two twined together – with one end hanging loose over his shoulder. The Taliban ambassador to Afghanistan, on the other hand, favors a solid black turban tied above his forehead. And some men in Afghanistan do not wear turbans at all, but rather a distinctive Afghan hat.

Figure 6.4 Iranian leaders' turban

Iranian leaders wear black or white turbans wrapped in the flat, circular style shown in the image of Iranian supreme leader Ayatollah Ali Khamenei in Figure 6.4. The word "turban" is thought to have originated among Persians living in the area now known as Iran, who called the headgear a *dulband.*

Figure 6.5 Indian man's turban

Indian men sometimes wear turbans to signify their class, caste, profession or religious affiliation – and, as Figure 6.5 illustrates, turbans in India can be very elaborate. However, turbans made out of fancy woven cloths and festooned with jewels are not unique to India. As far away as Turkey, men have used the headgear to demonstrate their wealth and power.

Figure 6.6 Turban of Jordanians, Saudis, and Arabs of the Gulf

The kaffiyeh is not technically a turban. It is really a rectangular piece of cloth, folded diagonally and then draped over the head – not wound like a turban. Yasser Arafat, the Palestinian leader, made the kaffiyeh famous in recent times. However, the kaffiyeh is not solely Palestinian. Men in Jordan, Saudi Arabia, and the Arab Persian Gulf states wear kaffiyehs in colors and styles that are particular to their region. Jordanians, for example, wear a red and white kaffiyeh, while Palestinians wear a black and white one. And a man from Saudi Arabia would likely drape his kaffiyeh differently than a man from Jordan. The black cord that holds the kaffiyeh on one's head is called an *ekal.*

Figure 6.7 Desert peoples' turban

Desert peoples have long used the turban to keep sand out of their faces, as the man from Africa shown in Figure 6.7 is likely doing. Members of nomadic tribes have also used turbans to disguise themselves. And sometimes, the color of a person's turban can be used to identify his tribal affiliation from a distance across the dunes. This man's turban is a very light blue. In some parts of North Africa, blue is thought to be a good color to wear in the desert because of its association with cool water.

Source: Figures and accompanying text from Eli Sanders, "Understanding Turbans," *Seattle Times*, Thursday, September 27, 2001, E1.

Because Sikhs are not permitted to cut their hair, it can grow quite long. A Sikh male therefore ties his hair into a knot towards the front of his head; the knot and surrounding hair on the male's head are then covered by a turban.[20] Although there are a number of different ways of tying a turban, generally, a Sikh adult wraps the cloth around the sides of the head several times until the cloth covers all of the hair and is then fastened under a preceding layer.[21] This process generally takes between ten and fifteen minutes to complete.[22] The wrapping of the different layers will generally create a "V-shaped" or "peaked" look to the turban, whereas turbans worn by other groups will not have this peak.[23] The *Seattle Times* images demonstrate this point.

Although some Sikh women wear turbans to cover their hair, many choose not to. Generally, in the United States, female converts to Sikhism often wear turbans, while South Asian Sikh women tend to opt for a thin chiffon scarf, or *chhuni*, to cover their hair.[24] Sikh boys start wearing full turbans in their teenage years. Until then, they usually wear a *patka*, a smaller under-turban akin to a large bandana that is wrapped around the boy's knot and/or scalp.[25] Adult male athletes, such as popular cricketer Monty Panesar, may also wear a *patka* while they are playing sports or engaging in physically demanding activities.

* * *

Sikhs are members of a modern, monotheistic faith. They are a peaceful people who have espoused basic teachings – to remember the Creator, to live honestly in society, and to give back to others. They are a proud and loyal people who have contributed to the societies in which they live, through their labor and service in the armed forces. Sikhs happen to wear turbans. While individual reasoning may

---

20 See Karen McBeth Chopra, comment, "A Forgotten Minority – An American Perspective: Historical and Current Discrimination against Asians from the Indian Subcontinent," *Det. C.L. Mich. St. U. L. Rev.* 1269, 1275 (Winter, 1995), noting that Sikhs wear "turbans to cover their long hair."

21 For specific instructions on tying a Sikh turban, see "Learn How To Tie Different Sikh Turbans," SikhNet, available at <http://www.sikhnet.com/s/tyingturbans>.

22 U.S. Department of Justice, "Common Sikh American Head Coverings," available at <http://www.usdoj.gov/crt/legalinfo/sikh_poster.pdf>.

23 See commentary, "Reflections on September 11: Reconsidering Social Change in the Wake of Tragedy," 26 *NYU Rev. L. & Soc. Change* 431, 449 (2000–2001): "Sikh men are very distinct in appearance because they are required by their religion not to cut their hair. They often have long beards and gather their long hair in V-shaped turbans."

24 See I.J. Singh, "Sikhs and Sikhism: A View with a Bias," available at <http://www.sikh.net/publications/View/symbols.htm>: "certainly there is no bar to women wearing a turban and some Sikh women in India do; almost all of the Western converts to Sikhism do"; see also "Common Sikh American Head Coverings," providing pictures of a Sikh American convert wearing a turban and a South Asian Sikh wearing a headscarf.

25 The DoJ poster "Common Sikh American Head Coverings" provides a picture of a Sikh boy wearing a *patka*.

differ, it is nonetheless clear that the turban is a very personal and significant part of the Sikh identity.

It is their distinctive appearance that has come to define their identity and complicate their lives in the West – lands they went to in search of better opportunity and religious freedom. The extent to which Sikhs have been targeted on the basis of their turbans is the subject of Part II.

Part II

Targeting the Sikh Turban

I.J. Singh, a Sikh historian and commentator, writes of his own entry to the United States: "It was 1960, almost a half century ago and I remember being the lone Sikh in my travels across this vast land of the United States. Not many people knew that Sikhs wore long unshorn hair, neatly tucked away under a turban. And the turban attracted the most attention." The turbaned Sikh attracted such attention because of his turban, because he was visually so unique and identifiable in public space.

Prior to the terrorist attacks of 9/11, turbaned Sikhs often encountered negative reactions to their distinct appearance. For example, Singh recalls: "Questions were often raised at the job; most hospitals were loath to admit turbaned Sikhs in their operating rooms. Sometimes, one could explain the religious tradition and necessity that dictated our practice, and some managers understood." Serving as the collective forest to Singh's lone tree, legal scholar *Bill Ong Hing* notes that "turban-wearing Sikhs were victimized historically. When they arrived in the 1800s, Sikh men continued to wear turbans, because not cutting their hair is a requirement of their religion. As a result, they endured being called 'ragheads.'"[1]

September 11, however, dramatically intensified the frequency and severity of hostility against turbaned Sikhs.[2] "Times have changed," I.J. Singh himself observes. In 2003, the U.S. Commission on Civil Rights reported that "The attacks against the World Trade Center and the Pentagon on September 11, 2001 by terrorists from Middle Eastern countries led to a dramatic surge in hate violence and discrimination against people in the United States perceived to be of Arab or Muslim background." The report implicitly acknowledged that the pre-9/11 climate was not free of discrimination against these groups, while admitting such mistreatment had grown much worse in the aftermath of the attacks. A database created on 9/11 by the Sikh civil rights organization the Sikh Coalition contains 22 reported cases of bias incidents against Sikhs on the day of the attack alone.[3]

Turbans, as noted in Part I, are not an exclusively Sikh item of clothing. Still, according to community advocates, 99 percent of people who wear turbans in

---

1 See Bill Ong Hing, "Vigilante Racism: The De-Americanization of Immigrant America," 7 *Mich. J. Race & L.* 441, 446 (2002).

2 See District of Columbia, Maryland, and Virginia Advisory Committees, U.S. Commission on Civil Rights, *Civil Rights Concerns in the Metropolitan Washington, D.C., Area in the Aftermath of the September 11, 2001, Tragedies* (June 2003), p. 1, available at <http://www.usccr.gov/pubs/sac/dc0603/main.htm>.

3 Sikh Coalition Database, available at <http://www.sikhcoalition.org/ListReports.asp>.

America are Sikhs.[4] Those responsible for planning the 9/11 attacks, most notably Osama bin Laden, also wear turbans and long beards. This physical similarity resulted in a serious backlash against Sikhs, who were "conflated with bin Laden" and his cronies:[5] "Since the terrorist attacks of September 11, 2001, videos and images of Osama bin Laden have created an air of hostility towards Sikhs, with an uninformed American public equating the appearance of Sikh men with bin Laden's beard and Afghani-style turban."[6]

According to one survey, "nine out of 10 educated Americans identified Sikhs with Muslims."[7] This is despite the separate doctrinal views, different geographic homeland, different native languages, and distinct turban styles of Sikhs. What only mattered, it seems, is that Sikhs wear turbans, and so did bin Laden and his lieutenants: "Although the Sikh are from northern India, speak languages altogether different than Arabic, and are not Islamic, most people who look at a Sikh will associate that person with an Arab country because Sikhs wear turbans, and turbans are commonly associated with Muslims," wrote a South Asian lawyer.[8] Interestingly, none of the 19 hijackers wore turbans; instead, they were apparently selected for the mission precisely because they could blend into American society.[9] But since bin Laden and the top al Qaeda leadership wore turbans, it was the turban that became the identifier for the enemies of America and the ultimate perpetrators of the 9/11 attacks.

Part II presents examples of what turbaned Sikhs experienced in the aftermath of the 9/11 attacks. It describes incidents in which Sikhs were discriminated against on the basis of their turban. It also notes, where appropriate, the actual and possible legal resolutions of the incidents.

As a general matter, we recognize that not every adverse action against a Sikh is undergirded by hate or ignorance – the Sikh involved in an incident just may

---

4 See Amardeep Singh, remarks at the Commissioners Meeting Open Session, U.S. Equal Employment Opportunity Commission, December 11, 2001, available at <http://www.eeoc.gov/abouteeoc/meetings/12-11-01-transcript.html>: "I can say with great assurance that 99 percent of the persons who wear turbans in this country are Sikh Americans, and therein lines the very cruel irony of the Sikh American experience since the 11th."

5 Leti Volpp, "The Citizen and the Terrorist," 49 *UCLA L. Rev.* 1575, 1590 (2002), at 1590.

6 Mark Stromer, note, "Combating Hate Crimes against Sikhs: A Multi-tentacled Approach," 9 *J. Gender Race & Just.* 739, 740 (2006), at 740.

7 "Osama Becomes a Pain for American Sikhs," *The Financial Express*, July 10, 2006, available at <http://www.financialexpress.com/latest_full_story.php?content_id=133438>.

8 *Pratheep Sevanthinathan*, "Shifting from Race to Ethnicity in Higher Education," 9 *Scholar* 1, 36 (2006).

9 See Migration Policy Institute, "America's Challenges: Domestic Security, Civil Liberties, and National Unity after September 11" (2003), p. 7, available at <http://www.migrationpolicy.org/pubs/Americas_Challenges.pdf>: "al Qaeda's hijackers were carefully chosen to avoid detection: all but two were educated young men from middle-class families with no criminal records and no known connection to terrorism."

happen to be wearing a turban. In each of the cases in this part, however, there is evidence that the Sikh was selected for the mistreatment because of the turban.

These examples are presented by context – for example, profiling, or employment discrimination. They also span the time from the moments after the towers fell to the time of this writing, and cover instances from coast to coast. Accordingly, the reader should come away with at least three impressions. First, the backlash against turbaned Sikhs takes place in various forms and settings; second, the backlash is a continuous series of events that have not ceased even though the attacks giving rise to the hate violence occurred over eight years ago, and third, the backlash against Sikhs is not confined to any geographic region or type of region, such as a major metropolitan city – it is, by contrast, a facet of places large and small, urban and suburban, east and west, north and south.

It should be noted that the summary of incidents in this part is intended to serve as a representative sample of the climate that Sikhs encountered after 9/11, and is in no way an attempt to provide an exhaustive review of each incident (much less each type of incident) against a Sikh wearing a turban in the United States. That said, we decided to include these particular incidents because they are some of the most prominent that took place in the Sikh community. We consulted with several Sikh leaders and attorneys to identify those incidents that merited inclusion and that would best portray the forms and effects of the backlash as it pertains to Sikh Americans.

Interspersed throughout this part are interviews conducted by Valarie Kaur, a Sikh filmmaker, with Sikh victims of the incidents and/or their family members. Although we describe the incidents in factual form and rely on third-party accounts, these interviews provide those affected with an opportunity to discuss the incidents and their ramifications on their own terms and through their own voices. This part also contains reflections from Manpreet Anand on airport profiling of Sikhs.

We begin this part with an incident that took place literally minutes after the towers fell.

Chapter 7
Harassment

> Amrik Singh Chawla, 33, had been headed downtown on business on the morning of September 11, 2001, when he learned that the World Trade Center was on fire. He was leaving the island on foot when he saw the second plane hit. After climbing out from under the scaffolding and helping a woman out from under some debris, he began his panicked journey off the island. Suddenly, as he rounded a corner on Broadway, two men approached him. One pointed at him and yelled, "Hey, you f***ing terrorist, take that turban off!" They chased him into a subway station, where Amrik jumped on a train, narrowly escaping their angry threats.[1]

Once Chawla arrived in Brooklyn, "he slipped into a shop, stuffed his turban into his briefcase and wore his hair in a ponytail for the rest of the day."[2] Chawla offers his account of the incident and reflects back on that horrific day with the aid of Valarie Kaur.

* * *

> Amrik Chawla, a Brooklyn-raised Sikh American, … was probably the very first victim of a hate crime after 9/11. It happened only minutes after the second plane hit the Towers.
>
> That Tuesday morning, Amrik was in a cab three blocks south of the Towers, on his way to work when traffic stopped. He saw the family in the car next to him looking up at the sky, and Amrik followed their eyes to see the north tower on fire. He got out of the cab. There was a lamp post broken in half, and there embedded into the cement, a large tire wheel. It took him a few seconds to realize that this was the tire of an airplane. He heard a loud noise and looked up to see an airplane overhead.
>
> > The plane is loud and moving so fast, and I follow it right into the building. It's like the building just sucked up the plane. There's a huge explosion and fire and smoke on the other side. And the debris goes everywhere. There's already paper

1 Press kit, *Divided We Fall*, p. 32, available at <http://www.dwf-film.com/presskit/>.

2 Somini Sengupta, "Arabs and Muslims Steer Through an Unsettling Scrutiny," *New York Times*, September 13, 2001, available at <http://query.nytimes.com/gst/fullpage.html?res=9403E4DC1038F930A2575AC0A9679C8B63&n=Top/Reference/Times%20Topics/Subjects/S/Sept.%2011,%202001>.

> falling, because the wind blows in all directions. With papers falling everywhere, you see pieces of things burning in the air coming out of the building.
>
> I start running from the street to get underneath the scaffolding, and the debris is falling. I wait for the debris to fall. I wait to hear the noise all fall down. There's a lady crawling on her hands and knees, trying to get underneath the scaffolding, her legs bloodied up to her knees. I pull her underneath the scaffolding, and help her on her feet. I'm thinking, 'Head east, head south. Get off the island, get off the island.' I walk east. Everyone's in a walk-sprint, like a walking jog, because there are masses of people, and you can't run.
>
> I turn south onto Broadway. Now I'm south of the World Trade Center, going east. Broadway comes to a fork with another street. I'm crossing on the north side of the triangle to the next street, and I see two guys coming the opposite way, crossing from the west side of the street. They point at me.
>
> The first guy says, 'Hey, you better take off that f— turban!' The second guy says, 'You terrorist, you better take off that f— turban!' I look at them, ignore them, and continue walking south. A third guy trailing behind them yells, 'Hey you f— terrorist!' I turn left down the street and keep walking south. I look behind me and see them following fast. I break out into a run …."

Amrik ran for his life the second time in fifteen minutes. He escaped into a subway and made it out alive. This hate incident was the first of thousands that took place in the days and weeks and months and years that followed.

Today, Amrik told me that the trauma of that day has subsided. Immediately afterward, he would dream about it and wake up remembering it. But now he focuses more on what that event revealed about America's relations with the rest of the world, and Americans' relations with each other.

> 9/11 made us understand that from a national security standpoint, we underestimated the potential of our threat, and from a social and civil standpoint, how much we need to learn about each other …. Still when I walk down the street everyday, inevitably somebody is staring. They want to make a comment, it's just on their lips. People look at you. Even here in New York, it's anywhere you go, whether it's in a bar for a drink, a restaurant to eat, or on the path train. You know they want to say something. Sometimes it's 'Aren't you a Sikh?' and sometimes, 'Hey towel-head.'

* * *

No legal action was taken against the men who chased and verbally abused Amrik Chawla.

This incident is significant in at least three respects. First, the attack on Sikhs with turbans occurred almost immediately after the towers were struck, meaning the connection between turbans and "enemy" had existed and turbaned Sikhs were therefore imperiled as soon as the planes hit the towers. Second, and as a result, the Sikh community had to mobilize rapidly, in an already emotional and uncertain moment, to educate others, appeal for tolerance, and assert their rights. (These efforts will be described in greater detail in Part IV.)

Third, verbal harassment of Sikhs, such as being called "bin Laden," "raghead," or "towelhead," is commonplace, and generally happens without any formal legal consequence. For example, one turbaned Sikh claimed that being called "Osama bin Laden" or "terrorist" was "a normal occurrence after 9/11." However, his harassers were apprehended only when the verbal jabs escalated into a physical assault.[3] Offensive remarks, by themselves, however, escape any corrective legal measures due to expansive First Amendment protections. Indeed, in the context of the media, insulting comments directed toward Sikhs, like "bin Laden," take place with virtual impunity from the non-Sikh community. A trailer for a 2003 movie, *DysFunktional Family*, featured comedian Eddie Griffin pointing to a turbaned Sikh and saying, "there goes bin Laden."[4] No one, aside from Sikhs, raised any objections, suggesting that the general public finds such off-color humor unworthy of condemnation. Despite objections from Sikhs, the movie producers refused to issue a retraction or apologize, suggesting that they believed the general public would at least tolerate, if not enjoy, the humor.

Harassment of Sikhs is especially prone to occur where Sikhs come into regular contact with the general public, for instance where they are in the service industry or require interaction with clients or customers. For example, on September 14, 2001, Manga Singh, a cab driver in the New York City area, picked up a passenger who proceeded to reach through the open partition and tried to beat him with an umbrella while yelling, "I hate you, *I hate you and your turban.*"[5] Manga Singh's father, Surinder Singh, "recalled a rider who said to him, 'You do [*sic*] that, you attacked the World Trade Center!'" Surinder Singh responded, "No, I am an American Sikh … Osama bin Laden has a turban, but it's very different." There are no reports of legal action being pursued in this case either, again supporting the contention that verbal harassment alone, however hateful and hurtful, generally takes place without legal repercussions.

---

3 See, for example, Beth Velliquette, "3 Teens Held in Sikh Assault," *The Herald-Sun* (Durham, Chapel Hill, NC), April 2, 2004.

4 See generally "Smart Addressing Damaging Sikh Stereotype in Film *Dysfunktional Family*," Sikh Media and Resource Task Force, March 14, 2003, available at <http://saldef.org/content.aspx?&a=931>.

5 Chastity Pratt and Melanie Lefkowitz, "Arab, Shik [Sic] Cabbies Offer Free Rides, Volunteers Help Families, Hope to Avoid Harassment," *Newsday*, September 16, 2001, p. W33.

Dozens of reports of verbal harassment against Sikhs have been documented.[6] Although some incidents occurred just minutes or days following the 9/11 attacks, others took place in each of the eight years since. For example, in 2002 in California, a Sikh involved in a very common and innocuous activity – going to a Starbucks – was called "Osama" repeatedly after he left the store.[7] In 2003, two Sikhs on vacation in Tennessee were called "Osama bin Laden,"[8] while a Sikh in Texas observed in front of a Walmart another individual mimicking the Arabic language and laughing as the Sikh turned to him.[9] Also in 2003, a Sikh in Atlanta, Georgia was told, "fuck you," "Iraqi come here," in addition to being called "Saddam Hussein" and "Bin Laden."[10]

In 2004, a Sikh leaving a Circuit City heard an employee in charge of security saying that it would be "good idea" to check for stolen items in the Sikh's beard, as he might be hiding a bomb in it.[11] In 2005, a Sikh decided to move from Montana because the extent of the "off-color jokes" that connected him to bin Laden and Iraqis was much too much to bear.[12] In 2006, a Massachusetts man hurled ethnic and racial slurs at a Sikh convenience store clerk.[13]

In 2007 in Indiana, a Sikh storeowner and his employees were repeatedly insulted with slurs made against their perceived ethnicity and religion.[14] The store owner, Jaswant Singh Banwait, was labeled an "Arab/Muslim terrorist" and told to "go back to [his] country," among other insults that were hurled on multiple occasions. Even his non-Sikh employees were called "traitors" because they worked for a turbaned employer.

At times the verbal statements are coupled with simple assault and battery, where the Sikh is physically touched in inappropriate and unconsented to ways. For example, in January of 2008, in Hoboken, New Jersey:

---

6 See Sikh Coalition Database, Verbal Abuse category, available at <http://www.sikhcoalition.org/ListReports.asp?m=L&Cat_ID=2&>.

7 Sikh Coalition Database, Incident #275, available at <http://www.sikhcoalition.org/hatecrime.asp?mainaction=viewreport&reportid=275>.

8 Sikh Coalition, Incident #339, available at <http://www.sikhcoalition.org/hatecrime.asp?mainaction=viewreport&reportid=339>.

9 Sikh Coalition, Incident #364, available at <http://www.sikhcoalition.org/hatecrime.asp?mainaction=viewreport&reportid=364>.

10 Sikh Coalition, Incident #365, available at <http://www.sikhcoalition.org/hatecrime.asp?mainaction=viewreport&reportid=365>.

11 Sikh Coalition, Incident #438, available at <http://www.sikhcoalition.org/hatecrime.asp?mainaction=viewreport&reportid=438>.

12 Sikh Coalition, Incident #448, available at <http://www.sikhcoalition.org/hatecrime.asp?mainaction=viewreport&reportid=448>.

13 "Attorney General Reilly Obtains Civil Rights Injunction Against Billerica Man Accused of Attacking Sikh Store Clerk," *U.S. State News*, August 1, 2006.

14 "Editorial: Shop Owner's Tale of Prejudice a Jolt Of Reality," *The Herald Bulletin*, July 28, 2007, available at <http://www.theheraldbulletin.com/opinion/local_story_209210159.html?keyword=topstory>.

> a Sikh man was assaulted by a restaurant patron who tried to remove his turban in public …. While standing in the restaurant, a woman behind [the Sikh] grabbed a hold of his turban and attempted to pry it from his head …. [T]he woman remarked that she had a problem with "that stuff" on his head, and told him to "take it off."[15]

In these instances, which involve not only verbal remarks but a physical element, a Sikh may seek and obtain legal relief. For example, the Sikh in Massachusetts received not only verbal insults but was physically attacked – in that case, the state attorney general secured an injunction against the perpetrator, barring the man from threatening the Sikh again. Also, the Sikh man in the 2008 incident could press charges for simple battery and assault due to the touching of his turban.

In addition to verbal and physical harassment, Sikhs have also found themselves the victims of vandalism, an intrinsically overt act that publicly displays the perpetrators' animus toward the victims. The act of defacing another person's property or place of worship invariably contains the desire to harass, embarrass the victim publicly, and impart clear expressions of anger and intimidation in full view of the community as a whole, making such crimes particularly disconcerting and unsettling for the targeted groups.

In one instance, a Californian man was arrested and later charged with a hate crime after ramming a Sikh temple with a tractor he had stolen.[16] Police later reported the man had attacked the temple because "He thought they were Arabs."[17] In upstate New York, a Sikh temple was burned to the ground by three young arsonists just months after 9/11.[18] A documentary film chronicling the aftermath of the crime, including the arrest and sentencing of the perpetrators and the subsequent coalescing of the community in support of their Sikh neighbors, was released in 2004.[19]

Several remedies are available to victims of vandalism, including seeking damages for the property damage and trespass, and the perpetrators themselves may be guilty of criminal offenses, such as arson. As a general matter, however,

15 Sikh Coalition Database, Incident #600, available at <http://www.sikhcoalition.org/hatecrime.asp?mainaction=viewreport&reportid=600>.

16 Ryan Sabalow, "Man Arrested in Temple Damage," *redding.com*, March 14, 2007, available at <http://www.redding.com/news/2007/mar/14/man-arrested-in-temple-damage/>.

17 Jim Shultz, "Suspect to Stand Trial in Sikh Temple Attack," *redding.com*, April 12, 2007, available at <http://www.redding.com/news/2007/apr/12/suspect-to-stand-trial-in-sikh-temple-attack/>.

18 Tara Bahrampour, "3 Arrested in Arson at Sikh Temple," *New York Times*, December 18, 2001, available at <http://query.nytimes.com/gst/fullpage.html?res=9D06EED9143EF93BA25751C1A9679C8B63>.

19 Archana Ravinder, "How the Burning of a Sikh Temple Transformed Communities," *India Post*, October 3, 2004, available at <http://news.newamericamedia.org/news/view_article.html?article_id=0e9d8c7691c3cf1bbbd176fab80c985c>.

Sikhs subject to verbal harassment alone are without legal redress. This is troubling because of the frequency with which Sikhs are verbally harassed as a result of their appearance. Indeed, the limited examples provided here demonstrate that Sikhs in many different areas and in the period spanning the years after the attacks have been verbally abused. The First Amendment protections of free speech trump the Sikh concerns about offensive and insulting speech. Where, however, the harassment takes a tangible form, such as a physical attack or act of vandalism, the Sikh has the ability to obtain relief for these wrongs.

That speech alone may not give rise to a cognizable legal claim is not an absolute rule. As is often the case in the law, context matters. In the next chapter, we explore the harassment of Sikhs in the context of schools – a setting in which the general proclivity for childish remarks took a nasty turn in the aftermath of the 9/11 attacks.

Chapter 8
Bullying of Sikh Students

> A shy high school freshman, Harpal Singh Vacher, ended the school year last spring as the latest collateral damage in a citywide political tussle. What began as a childish argument with fellow students on May 24 ended with Harpal crouched on a bathroom floor at Newtown High School in Elmhurst, Queens, his previously unshorn hair littered on the ground around him.
>
> In keeping with his Sikh faith, Harpal had kept his unshorn hair tucked inside a dastaar, a religious turban. The police say that his attacker, a high school senior named Umair Ahmed, had removed Harpal's turban and cut his hair to punish him for making derogatory comments about Mr. Ahmed's mother – comments for which Harpal had apologized.[1]

As with harassment against adults, harassment against Sikh students occurred practically right after the attacks of 9/11. When a class watched the news the day of the attacks and bin Laden's image appeared on the television, students in a Maryland school started telling a Sikh student, "your [*sic*] probably a terrorist" and "you probably [have] a bomb in your book bag."[2] While the backlash immediately touched both Sikh adults and children, Sikh youth are particularly vulnerable to harassment and being bullied by their peers. For example, children may not have the same cultural sensitivity that adults have, and children are more prone to joke around and tease other children.

Given the importance of the turban to a Sikh, it should be evident that harassment of a Sikh on the basis of his hair or turban is not just like any other juvenile humor. In a seminal examination of Sikh students in American schools, Margaret A. Gibson characterized the harassment of turbaned Sikhs this way: for non-Sikh students, such harassment "seemed little more than a childish prank." For the Sikh, however, "it was a deliberate attack on their honor."[3] Similarly, following the 2007 hair-cutting assault in Queens, a Sikh lawyer summed up the importance of his unshorn hair and turban: "As a Sikh, if you could come to me and hit me in the face with a baseball bat, I could eventually forgive you, but if you cut my

---

1 Neha Singh and Khin Mai Aung, "A Free Ride for Bullies," *New York Times*, September 23, 2007.

2 Sikh Coalition Database, Incident #10, available at <http://www.sikhcoalition.org/hatecrime.asp?mainaction=viewreport&reportid=10>.

3 See Margaret A. Gibson, *Accommodation without Assimilation* (Ithaca, NY: Cornell University Press, 1988), p. 144.

hair, I don't think that I can personally forgive you."[4] What happened to Sikh students after 9/11 transcended the playful badgering that generally takes place among the youth. Sikh students, by contrast, were specifically targeted because of the association of the Sikh turban with terrorism. For example, in the *Vacher* case which is referenced in the opening of this chapter, the perpetrator of the assault was aware of the religious significance of the turban and unshorn hair for Sikhs, and therefore chose to make a deliberate attack on the articles of his peer's faith.

While Vacher was clearly harassed on the basis of his turban and was therefore very harmful to him personally and to the community as a whole, the damage was compounded by the disappointing response from the legal system. Due to the blatant disrespect for the victim's religious practices, the case was immediately classified as a hate crime. But the defendant avoided jail time despite being found guilty; instead, the 19-year-old perpetrator was sentenced to community service and instructed to write an essay for the judge.[5]

Similarly, in another case, an 18-year-old Sikh student was assaulted by a peer after enduring repeated taunts because of his turban and beard; the assailant in this incident was similarly sentenced to a light sentence of community service, despite being charged and convicted under hate crime laws.[6] In 2003, a Sikh New Jersey student was repeatedly called "Osama" and was hit on the head, resulting in contusions. The public school at which this occurred was later found by the New Jersey Human Rights Commission to have failed to meet its obligations in protecting the Sikh boy from the harassment. Such harassment has a profound impact – in this case, the family decided to move to Britain.

These incidents suggest that the harassment endured by the Sikh students was not sufficiently addressed by any supervisory agents or the legal system, which has at least two implications. First, if the schools and others do not take seriously the harassment of Sikh students, the members of the Sikh community may consider themselves to be inadequately protected by those responsible for ensuring classrooms and schools remain free of hate. For a Sikh student to have a sense that his civil rights are being minimally recognized is to imply that the positive and open learning environment required for educational and social development is not present for and does not extend to him and his Sikh brethren. Second, a perpetrator who receives a sentence that does not reflect the severity of the incident and/or does not match the crime for which the person was initially charged means

4 Christina Santucci, "Multi-faith Support for Sikh Teen Victim," *Queens Courier*, June 14, 2007, available at <http://www.queenscourier.com/articles/2007/06/14/news/news03.txt>.

5 Nicole Bode, "Teen Gets no Jail for Anti-sikh Hate Crime," *New York Daily News*, June 6, 2008, available at <http://www.nydailynews.com/ny_local/queens/2008/06/06/2008-06-06_teen_gets_no_jail_for_antisikh_hate_crim.html>.

6 Carrie Melago, "Punched Sikh Gets Apology From Joel Klein," *New York Daily News*, June 7, 2008, available at <http://www.nydailynews.com/news/ny_crime/2008/06/07/2008-06-07_punched_sikh_student_gets_apology_from_j.html>.

the deterrent effect of the punishment is itself limited. Thus the cost of a future incident of harassment against a Sikh student is reduced for the perpetrator. This further adds to the vulnerability of the Sikh from future incidents.

This is not to say, however, that school personnel have completely abdicated their respective role in addressing harassment of Sikhs. In Philadelphia, Mandeep Singh, a ninth grade student, was regularly harassed in school.[7] He was called "bin Laden" and "meatball head," and was told to go back to "turbanland," among other things. In this case, the Pennsylvania Human Relations Commission investigated the matter and in 2006 ordered an immediate end to the harassment, indicating that in some specialized institutional contexts such harassment may be effectively addressed through formal means. Overall, though, the legal response to harassment of Sikh students, at the local and state level, has been unsatisfactory.

One teenaged turbaned Sikh, Harkirat S. Hansra, took matters in to his own hands. Hansra was told to "go back to Afghanistan," among other things. The harassment he received compelled him to write a book explaining his faith and identity. In it, he writes:

> The anger from the community directed at Sikhs comes from the fear of the unknown, and I believe society will be stronger if we know about each other. When people understand Sikhs and our religion, prejudice against us will diminish.[8]

Ignorance and resulting harassment against Sikh students is regrettably widespread, Hansra's wishes notwithstanding. One of the main reasons for this, in the community's estimation, is the lack of information about who Sikhs are and what their articles of faith represent. For example, while Sikhism is the world's fifth largest religion, information about Sikhism is not generally included in World Religions courses in junior high or high schools. Even in areas like California, where Sikhs have been living for over 150 years, no mention is made of Sikhs in history textbooks or social science curricula. Only one California school system – Modesto City Schools – has included any information about Sikhs in its courses.

Over the past few years, Sikhs have been working to change that. Many Sikh families have a habit of going to go into their children's classrooms at the beginning of the school year to explain the significance of the turban, to help keep their children and other Sikh students from being bullied. A school district in the Seattle area has adopted a high school curriculum about post-9/11 backlash, which includes information on Sikhs. Education Boards in California and New Jersey are

7 "Coalition Helps End Student's Suffering from Bullying in School," Sikh Coalition, February 27, 2006, available at <http://www.sikhcoalition.org/advisories/student_hair.htm>.

8 Harkirat S. Hansra, *Liberty at Stake – Sikhs: The Most Visible, Yet Misunderstood, Minority of America* (Bloomington: iUniverse, 2007), p. 4.

currently in talks with Sikhs on including materials on Sikhs in its social studies curricula. Khalsa Kids, a website developed by the Sikh Coalition in response to the attack on Harpal Vacher, also makes available lesson plans and classroom resources for teachers willing to incorporate Sikhism into their courses.

Despite these efforts, the situation concerning Sikh youth reached the point where the Sikh Coalition conducted a study in 2007 to determine the scope of the harassment against Sikh students.[9] The report cited cases in which Sikh students from across the country had been harassed since the terrorist attacks. For example, two days after 9/11, a Sikh student in Georgia was called an "Afghani" and a "terrorist." In a separate incident, an eight-year-old Sikh was called "raghead" and "diaperhead."

To obtain a picture of how pervasive the harassment was, the Sikh Coalition focused on the treatment of Sikh students in New York City public schools. The report, titled *Hatred in the Hallways*, found:

- three out of four Sikh boys who go to school in Queens have been teased or harassed on account of their religious identity;
- more than half the over 200 Sikh students surveyed had experienced some form of harassment in school based on their religion or national origin;
- over 40 percent of Sikh students who wear turbans or *patkas* have been subjected to some form of physical harassment, either hitting, punching, or disrespectful touching of the head;
- although Sikh students often complain to school personnel, nearly a third of their complaints go unheeded, and nothing is ever done.[10]

In 2008, a short distance from New York, in Hightstown, New Jersey, a Sikh high school student had his turban set ablaze by a fellow student. This was followed soon after with two incidents in Queens, New York. In one case, Jagmohan Premi, a high school student who had been tormented all year by bullies who made fun of his *patka*, was beaten badly with a set of keys on his face. Within the month, an 11-year-old Sikh girl had her braid chopped off by a bully at school. These three events together were a tipping point for New York's Sikhs. In June 2008, they took to the streets in the hundreds, rallying for the Department of Education to better protect their children at school.

In response to both the outcry from the community and the Sikh Coalition's report, the New York City Department of Education created a regulation to help address the problem. The regulation would for the first time collect data on instances of bias-based harassment in New York City schools. It applies not just to Sikhs,

9 The report is available at <http://www.sikhcoalition.org/advisories/documents/HatredintheHallwaysFinal_000.pdf>.

10 See Sikh Coalition press release "City Council Members Join Coalition to Release Report and Letter to NYC Schools Chancellor," available at <http://www.sikhcoalition.org/advisories/HatredintheHallways.htm>.

but to students of all colors, races, genders, and religions, thereby impacting over 1.1 million students in the school system. What this means in practice, however, is still being worked out as civil rights groups monitor implementation of the new regulation in the upcoming school year.

Chapter 9
Violence

> [The five men] repeatedly punched the victim Khalsa in the face, knocking him to the ground where they kicked him until he lost consciousness. Khalsa was later treated at a hospital for multiple contusions, abrasions, swelling and substantial pain to his eye and face. A CAT scan revealed that Khalsa had sustained multiple fractures to the left orbital bone, as well as complex, obstructive fractures of the nose which required facial reconstruction surgery to enable him to breathe.[1]

In the first week following 9/11, 645 bias crimes were directed at those perceived to be Middle Eastern.[2] Human Rights Watch reported in November of 2002 that "anti-Muslim hate crimes in the United States rose 1700 percent during 2001."[3] In the first eight weeks after 9/11, over a thousand bias incidents were reported, including around 19 murders, assaults, harassment, and acts of vandalism.[4] One of those murders realized the Sikh American community's worst fears about post-9/11 sentiment towards turbaned Sikhs.

On September 15, 2001, Balbir Singh Sodhi, a Sikh gas station owner in Mesa, Arizona went to Costco to purchase an American flag and donated $75 to a fund established for the families of victims of the 9/11 attacks.[5] Back at his gas station, Sodhi was attending to the landscaping outside when Frank Roque drove by and fired five shots towards Sodhi.[6] Hit in the back by multiple bullets, Sodhi died

---

1 Press release, Queens County District Attorney's Office, DA Brown, "Five Sentenced to Incarceration in Bias-Related Attack on Sikh Man in Richmond Hill," December 22, 2005.

2 "South Asian American Leaders of Tomorrow, American Backlash: Terrorists Bring War Home in More Ways than One," November 2002, available at <http://old.911digitalarchive.org/documents/BiasReport.pdf>.

3 "'We Are Not the Enemy': Hate Crimes Against Arabs, Muslims, and Those Perceived to be Arab or Muslim after September 11," *Human Rights Watch*, November 14, 2002, available at <http://www.hrw.org/reports/2002/usahate/>.

4 See Muneer I. Ahmad, "A Rage Shared by Law: Post-September 11 Racial Violence as Crimes of Passion," 92 *Cal. L. Rev.* 1259, 1261–62 (2004).

5 See American Civil Liberties Union of North California, "Caught in the Backlash: Sukhpal and Balbir Singh Sodhi," available at <http://www.aclunc.org/issues/government_surveillance/asset_upload_file532_4380.pdf>.

6 See Nick Martin, "Sikhs Still Living in Shadow of Sept. 11," *East Valley Tribune*, September 16, 2006, available at <http://www.eastvalleytribune.com/story/48149>; Arizona Department of Corrections, Inmate Profile: Frank Roque, available at <http://

at the scene.[7] With his death, Sodhi became "the first murder victim of the 9/11-related hate crime backlash in America."[8]

After shooting Sodhi, Roque visited a nearby sports bar where he announced, "They're investigating the murder of a turban-head down the street."[9] On the day charges were filed against Roque, Maricopa County attorney Rick Romley noted: "Sodhi was apparently killed for no other reason than because he was dark-skinned, bearded, and wore a turban."[10] At trial, Roque's co-worker testified that Roque said he wanted to shoot some "ragheads."[11] Roque was later convicted of the racially motivated murder of Sodhi, and was sentenced to death. The Arizona Supreme Court, however, commuted the death sentence on August 14, 2006, citing Roque's "mental illness and low IQ [as] mitigating factors [that] should have resulted in the lesser sentence of life in prison with no chance of parole."[12]

Valarie Kaur reflects on Sodhi's death with those he left behind.

* * *

> Over the last four years, I have visited the Sodhi family several times, talking with them and filming their stories. The brothers and their wives and the children are all very close, and their togetherness and their spirit have always moved me.
>
> After the death of Balbir Singh, their private mourning was made public, and the brothers found themselves in the spotlight. They chose to speak out against hate crimes, so that "*no more innocent people would be killed.*"
>
> One year later, one of Balbir's brothers, Sukhpal Singh Sodhi, was shot and killed while driving his cab in San Francisco, just when plans for the Iraq war were emerging. Over the next months, his murder was followed by the shootings of three other turbaned Sikh cab drivers in the San Francisco Bay Area alone. Although the police had no hard proof for the motives,

---

www.azcorrections.gov/inmate_datasearch/results.aspx?InmateNumber=180333&LastName=ROQUE&FNMI=F&SearchType=SearchInet>.

7 "Man Questioned in Shooting Death of Sikh," CNN, September 16, 2001, available at <http://archives.cnn.com/2001/U.S./09/16/gen.mesa.shooting/>.

8 Federal Bureau of Investigations, "Protecting Your Civil Rights: Spotlight on Hate Crimes," October 30, 2003, available at <http://www.fbi.gov/page2/oct03/103003protectrights.htm>.

9 Southern Poverty Law Center, "The Forgotten: Balbir Singh Sodhi," available at <http://www.splcenter.org/intel/intelreport/article.jsp?pid=251>.

10 Alvin Powell, "Religious Consciousness Rises in U.s.," *Harvard Gazette*, February 14, 2002, available at <http://www.news.harvard.edu/gazette/2002/02.14/10-eck.html>.

11 *State of Arizona v. Roque*, CR-03-0355-AP (Ariz. 2006) (summary of oral argument).

12 Michael Kiefer and Jim Walsh, "9/11-tied Slayer Won't be Executed," *The Arizona Republic*, August 15, 2006, available at <http://www.azcentral.com/arizonarepublic/local/articles/0815roque0815.html>.

the families and larger communities have felt the repercussions of hate crimes.

When I visited the Sodhi family after the second brother was killed, I spoke with Daman Sodhi, their young nephew. When I asked him how he felt, he said that he didn't cry as much when his second uncle was killed. "Crying is not going to do anything," he said, "I already tried it. I guess I just cried enough."

On Thursday, when we visited their house, Daman was the first one we interviewed. He was in fifth grade the first time we met, and now he's starting high school. Always soulful, he shared memories of his uncle:

"He was killed because of the way he looked. It's so stupid. They call that guy a criminal, but I call him a terrorist. Terrorists kill innocent Americans and that's what he did … I used to call my uncle 'fatty' and chase him around the couch, laughing and stuff. For hours. We would just do that for hours …."

Daman began to cry. And I began to ache. How can I keep asking this family these difficult questions? How can I keep asking them to remember the darkest part of their lives and share it with me, over and over?

"I'm so sorry, Daman. I should just stop doing this."

"No, I'm glad you ask me these questions," he said. "Otherwise, how will anyone know what I'm feeling inside?"

I thought that on this visit, years after both murders, our interviews would show how things had improved in Phoenix. But when we talked with the brothers Harjit and Rana Sodhi, I realized that I was wrong.

"Just a week ago, after the London bombings, a man came to my gas station and yelled, 'Go back to your country!'" said Rana. "I told him that I would call the police unless he left. This discrimination is still here."

After the interview, the entire family gathered together for chai and biscuits in the living room – aunts and uncles and children spanning all ages, talking and joking and laughing. Then the widow of Balbir Singh Sodhi, whom I call "Auntie Ji" out of respect, joined us. She was wearing white, the color that widows wear. We embraced and sat together.

I didn't want to interview her. Every interview about her husband had always brought tears, and so this time we played with her grandchildren, who made her smile so much. It wasn't until we left that I realized it was August 4, the three-year anniversary of the murder of Sukhpal Sodhi.

On Saturday, we visited the gas station where Balbir Singh Sodhi was killed. As we approached, my body tightened. This place is like ground zero to me. It is ground zero for the epidemic of fear and hate against our communities. Inside the store, I look up to see a sign that has hung on the wall since the murder. It is the theme of our film.

Sukhwinder (Goldy) Sodhi now runs his father's gas station. The first time we met was soon after his father's death. What I remember most was his sadness when he said to me, "*My dad will never know his grandchildren.*" Goldy now has two young children, a girl and a boy.

Goldy walked me to the street and showed me the memorial they placed where his father fell. The plaque reads:

> In memory of all the souls who lost their lives on September 11, 2001 and all the backlash victims. "We don't want any other innocent people hurt." – The family of Balbir Singh Sodhi (1949–2001). On Saturday, September 15, 2001, Balbir Singh Sodhi, a Sikh, was shot here at this corner while planting flowers in front of this shop. In the tradition of the Sikh faith, he wore a turban and beard. He was killed simply because of the way he looked. Sikhs believe: in one God. That all religious paths lead to God. That all people are equal in the eyes of God. In peace, and love for humankind.

* * *

While the Sodhi murder took place four days after the attacks on New York, one of the most brutal attacks on a turbaned Sikh occurred almost three years after 9/11. On July 11, 2004, in Queens, New York, several men began taunting Rajinder Singh Khalsa and his brother, also a turbaned Sikh. The perpetrators made several remarks in reference to Khalsa's turban. One said, "Look, somebody stole my curtains. … Why did you steal my sheets from my house?"[13] Another joined in, "Give me my curtain."[14] Khalsa testified that he asked in response, "What do you mean, 'Give me my curtain?'" One of the men replied, "You still here?" "Go to your home. Go to your country." Khalsa's brother responded: "This is my country. This is my home, too."

After this exchange, the group of five men then began assaulting Khalsa. He lost consciousness, sustained multiple abrasions and fractures, and required surgery as a result. After the perpetrators finished beating Khalsa, "they took off his turban and threw it away,"[15] adding religious insult to significant physical injury. Assistant District Attorney Elizabeth Parke noted that the assault on Khalsa "was a truly vicious, despicable act of hate."[16] Khalsa shares his experience with Valarie Kaur.

* * *

We met Rajinder Singh Khalsa in front of his brother's restaurant, where he told us what happened to him on July 11, 2004. On the street, several men accosted him and his brother. "Give me that dirty curtain," they said.

---

13 Herbert Lowe, "5 Tried in Sikh's Beating: Prosecutors Call Assault an Unprovoked Hate Crime but Defense Attorneys Say Religious Leader Escalated Fight," *Newsday*, November 1, 2005, p. A14.

14 Herbert Lowe, "Sikh Testifies in Case," *Newsday*, November 2, 2005, p. A29.

15 Kenji Yoshino, "Uncovering Muslim Identity," *Toward Freedom*, November 23, 2005, available at <http://www.towardfreedom.com/home/content/view/674/54/>.

16 Lowe, "5 Tried in Sikh's Beating."

"I tried to tell them that it's not a dirty curtain, it's a turban," Rajinder Singh told us. "But another guy came and said, 'Go back to your country.' I said, 'But we are American, where should we go?' He thought that we were Iranian. So I told him, 'We are not Iranian. We are not Muslim. We are Sikhs from India.' He said, "Then go back to India.'

"Then they started beating my brother at once. I said, 'Don't do this; he's innocent!' They left him and everybody started beating me. They beat me and crushed my nose. They punched me in the nose, eyes, head, everywhere. They left me unconscious on the sidewalk. They threw my turban away."

People on the street watched as the men beat Rajinder Singh unconscious and left him for dead in broad daylight. Nobody intervened. His brother ran to get the ambulance. Although witnesses reported five men taking part in the beating, the next day, the police charged only one man with assault. Rajinder Singh's lawyer, Amardeep Singh, told us why the community protested.

"The community had suffered so many hate crimes without anyone being charged that the community just boiled over in rage. Only because of a spontaneous protest did the police re-open the investigation."

Rajinder Singh Khalsa became the first to file a civil suit against his perpetrators. This is not the first time that he has stood up against injustice. Back in India, he fought the Indian government for human rights atrocities against the Sikh community after 1984. He was tortured by the police. This is why he came to America in the first place

* * *

Following a five-week trial, Khalsa's five attackers were convicted: two were found guilty of second-degree assault, two were found guilty of second-degree aggravated harassment as a hate crime, and the fifth defendant was found guilty of harassment in the second-degree. The men received sentences ranging from five days in jail to two years, and which included community service for three of them.[17]

The federal hate crime statute "prohibits willful injury, intimidation, or interference or attempt to do so, by force or threat of force of any person because of race, color, religion, or national origin."[18] Hate crimes statutes generally are designed to punish those who attack or threaten individuals on the basis of an immutable characteristic, such as one's race or national origin.

"Sikhs are protected by hate crime statutes, even if the perpetrator believes the Sikh to be a Muslim terrorist," notes lawyer Marc Stromer.[19] But a substantial

17 DA press release, "Five Sentenced to Incarceration in Bias-Related Attack on Sikh Man in Richmond Hill."

18 18 U.S.C § 245 (1996).

19 Mark Stromer, note, "Combating Hate Crimes against Sikhs: A Multi-tentacled Approach," 9 *J. Gender Race & Just.* 739, 755 (2006) at 755.

difficulty in prosecuting hate crimes is obtaining evidence of hate. Thus, differentiating between a simple assault on an individual who happens to be Sikh and an assault on a turbaned Sikh where the perpetrator selected the Sikh because of his actual or perceived national origin is often difficult. The *Khalsa* case represents a rare instance in which the perpetrators verbalized their hate and thus provided authorities with colorable evidence of a hate crime.

Other examples where a bias-motive was revealed in the course of the incident include a 2007 case from Washington State, where a 21-year-old male was convicted of a hate crime and other assault-related charges after beating a Sikh cab driver while calling him an "Iraqi terrorist" and blaming him for the 9/11 attacks. In another, a Sikh leaving his temple in Queens, New York in January of 2008 was confronted and punched by a man who said, "Arab, go back to your country." The Sikh, Baljeet Chadha, suffered a broken nose and jaw, and his assailant was quickly apprehended and charged with a hate crime.

Elderly Sikhs, regrettably, are not spared from such hate violence. Standing outside his garage with his granddaughter, Iqbal Singh, a turbaned Sikh, was stabbed in the neck with a steak knife on July 29, 2006. He had been waiting to go to the temple near his home in Santa Clara, California.[20] According to the local prosecutor, Jay Boyarsky, the perpetrator, "wanted to seek revenge for Sept. 11 and attack a member of the Taliban."

Understandably, there is a renewed interest in hate crimes statutes in the post-9/11 world. Hate crimes statutes remain a vital tool in the legal system's arsenal of addressing criminal activity based on an impermissible motive of hate and bias against people of color or certain religions or national origins. Despite their obvious importance in combating hate violence against Muslims, Arabs, South Asians, and Sikhs, legal commentators have argued that federal hate crimes statues are "inadequate,"[21] "completely unworkable,"[22] and have "failed in [their] deterrent aspect."[23] Accordingly, to the extent that federal hate crimes statues are ineffective, a compelling case can be made that stronger hate crime enactments are needed. Several years on from the 9/11 attacks, the violence continues, lending credence to the suggestion that hate crimes laws are presently insufficient to deter hate crimes.

There are, however, important countervailing considerations that must be factored into any reasoned revisiting of hate crimes legislation. Perhaps chief

20 John Coté, "Hate Crime Alleged in Stabbing of Sikh: Santa Clara Suspect Could Face Life Term if he is Convicted," *San Francisco Chronicle*, August 2, 2006, available at <http://www.sfgate.com/cgi-bin/article.cgi?f=/c/a/2006/08/02/BAGBUK9HTO1.DTL>.

21 Frederick M. Lawrence, *Punishing Hate: Bias Crimes Under American Law* (Cambridge, MA: Harvard University Press, 1999), p. 157.

22 Jason A. Abel, "Americans Under Attack: The Need for Federal Hate Crime Legislation in Light of Post-September 11 Attacks on Arab Americans and Muslims," 12 *Asian L. J.* 41, 45 (2005).

23 *Stromer,* "Combating Hate Crimes against Sikhs," at 757.

amongst these is taking into account the concerns of First Amendment advocates who are worried that hate crimes statutes punish speech or thought. The First Amendment tradition remains strong in the United States and as such these objections should be respected and carefully incorporated into any conversation on the improvements or expansion of hate crimes statutes.

It seems to us, however, that hate crimes statutes aim to punish conduct. What someone says is often used as evidence in the legal system. For example, where a man states that he will kill someone else and then does this days later may show proof of premeditation and thus may call for a particular crime to attach to his action. The response would be that this statement does not call for a different crime based on viewpoint – whether the man is going to kill another has nothing to do with the man's thoughts on Sikhs, Jews, Christians, blacks, whites, and so on.

But the legal system does have an established tradition of relying on using viewpoint statements as the basis for a legal claim. For example, under Title VII of the Civil Rights Act 1964 an employer who says he does not like Muslims or that Muslims should pay for the 9/11 attacks provides direct evidence of an intent to discriminate against a Muslim employee who has suffered an adverse employment action. There would be no question that the use of such evidence is proper and consistent with First Amendment principles. The anti-Muslim statements distinguish a legitimate employment termination (not actionable) from an act of discrimination (actionable). Similarly, anti-Sikh statements can distinguish an assault where the victim happened to be Sikh (actionable as an assault) from a hate crime where the victim was assaulted because of his religion (actionable as a hate crime). We value Title VII and hate crimes laws due to the fact that in this nation, freedom of religion is a hallmark of individual rights safeguarded by the Constitution. These statutes do not degrade speech; rather, they help ensure a free nation by punishing hate-based conduct.[24]

---

24 See *Wisconsin v. Mitchell*, 508 U.S. 47 (1993), rejecting a First Amendment challenge to a sentencing enhancement for bias-motivated criminal conduct.

Chapter 10
Profiling

> I am a physician who lives in Rural Nebraska. I was on my home from Denver when I saw a vagrant on an isolated stretch of the rural highway. I turned my car around to check and as soon as I did I saw an Air Force truck which was pulling into a driveway of a fenced off area turn around and follow me. I stopped and pulled over and pointed out the person to the Air Force personnel who assured me that they would take care of the matter. But, a few miles later I was pulled over by 3 patrol cars and me, my wife and 3 year old son were made to wait in the blazing sun while they verified my information. Me and my wife were asked to put our hands on the dashboard and the officer took my driver's license. There was no response from the Air Force and 45 minutes later they called the sheriff of the town where I practice, who confirmed my being an upstanding citizen. I later learned that if he had not done so, we would have been in jail until they could communicate with Air Force.[1]

Profiling of those appearing to be Muslim, including Sikhs, is still prevalent in the United States.[2] Indeed, in 2008, a Sikh family who had called Harris County deputies to report a burglary in their Houston home found themselves handcuffed and kneeling in the middle of the street, being questioned about the terrorist bombings in Mumbai that had occurred on the same day. Sikh truck drivers continue to report being checked out by law enforcement officers on the road who see their faces and their turbans before pulling them over.

An obvious setting for discrimination against Sikhs with turbans after the hijacking of four airliners on 9/11 is airports. Accordingly, one of the most widespread problems for turbaned Sikhs after 9/11 has been airline racial profiling at the nation's airports. The concern of profiling at our nation's airports by the federal government and private airlines alike – colloquially referred to as "flying while brown" – has generated significant anxiety in the Sikh community. The Sikh American experience with respect to airport profiling is so prevalent that Sikh American clothier Rootsgear attempted to make light of the grim circumstances by designing a T-shirt with the slogan "100% Randomly Searched at the Following Airports" above a map of the United States dotted many times over with locations

1 Reported to the Sikh Coalition Incident Database by Jugroop Singh Brar on September 11, 2001; minor typographical errors corrected.

2 See, for example, Amnesty International U.S.A, *Threat and Humiliation: Racial Profiling, National Security, and Human Rights in the United States*, available at <http://www.amnestyusa.org/racial_profiling/report>.

of major American airports. The T-shirt is a hit with the Sikh community and has been worn by Sikh luminaries such as Sikh actor Waris Ahluwalia.

Gallows humor aside, the fact is that airport profiling "can be an utterly degrading and humiliating experience,"[3] especially for especially for Sikhs, who may be pulled aside because of their turbans and the manner in which security officials subsequently deal with them.. The case of Hansdip Singh Bindra is particularly illustrative of the mistreatment that Sikhs with turbans have encountered during air travel.

On November 26, 2002, Bindra was set to board Delta Airlines Flight 6237 from Cincinnati, Ohio to Dayton, Ohio.[4] As the passengers made their way to their respective seats, a stewardess told several passengers in the rear of the plane that there might be "trouble," and said of Bindra, who was seated towards the front of the plane, "See the man up front with the turban on, he's the one who is going to cause trouble." The stewardess later told Bindra to keep a "low profile," "stay seated," and not to "cause any problems." The stewardess also attempted to communicate her views of Bindra (and a passenger who came to his aid) to the pilots and others in the plane. Bindra filed suit against Delta in the U.S. District Court for the District of New Jersey. Despite motions to dismiss filed by the defendant airline, the case was eventually settled by the parties.[5] It is therefore unclear how a judge or jury would have viewed the allegations of profiling on the merits, for example if they would have been sympathetic towards the stereotyped and marginalized religious minority, Bindra, or whether they would have deferred to the judgment of the airline personnel who were operating in the tense post-9/11 climate.

That climate as a whole challenges the notion that turbaned Sikhs are treated equally or that searches of Sikh passengers are random – the *Bindra* settlement notwithstanding. For example, in February of 2008, one Sikh reported the following:

> On 27th Feb. 2008, I took a flight from Los Angeles to Seoul (Asiana Airlines). While passing through the security screening I have noticed that all the turbaned Sikhs were asked to stand in a glass tunnel and patted one by one. … On

---

3 See Charu A. Chandrasekhar, "Flying While Brown: Federal Civil Rights Remedies to Post-9/11 Airline Profiling of South Asians," 10 *Asian L. J.* 215, 224 (2003) at 224, offering examples of racial profiling incidents in the airline context as well as remedies being pursued by South Asians against the airlines.

4 *Bindra v. Delta Airlines* (DNJ, September 16, 2003) (complaint).

5 Paige Mudd, "Richmond brewpub shuts out turban wearer," *Richmond Times Dispatch*, November 25, 2006, available at <http://www.saldef.org/content.aspx?a=1611&z=8&title=RICHMOND%20Brewpub%20shuts%20out%20turban%20wearer>; four years later, Bindra was denied entry in a Virginia restaurant due to his refusal to remove his turban and comply with the establishment's "no-headgear" policy.

> enquiring security staff and their supervisors *told me* that they are instructed to screen every single Sikh passenger irrespective of any alarms going off.[6]

Today, Sikhs face unique obstacles in the course of trying to get to their planes, as airport security policies have become more restrictive since 9/11. In August of 2007, the Transportation Security Administration (TSA), the federal agency charged with the duty of overseeing airport security activities in the United States, altered their standing policies and began imposing secondary turban pat-downs for passengers coming through airport security, irrespective of whether a metal detector had been set off.[7] Sikh travelers were immediately singled out and affected by the change, though they received high-profile support when congressional leaders quickly wrote to the TSA questioning the efficacy of such a sudden modification.[8] Specifically, the group of lawmakers was unsettled by the fact that the previous policies had been carefully constructed with the aid of extensive consultations with minority communities, while the subsequent changes were implemented hastily and without explanation or training and guidance for TSA screeners. Previously, screeners had been instructed to conduct secondary searches only if a metal detector had been triggered, but the new policy removed that requirement and provided more leeway for screeners to conduct invasive searches of Sikhs and their turbans. In the wake of protests from lawmakers and Sikh rights groups, the TSA quickly reconsidered the change and worked directly with Sikh groups to modify its security policies.[9]

Manpreet Singh Anand, a Sikh, was a staff member on Capitol Hill as these policy changes were taking place. He was instrumental in engaging lawmakers to address the Sikh community's concerns. Here, Anand reflects on his own "flying while brown" experiences, how the federal government responds to Sikh American concerns, and the TSA policy changes.

* * *

---

6 Sikh Coalition Database, Incident # 605, available at <http://www.sikhcoalition.org/hatecrime.asp?mainaction=viewreport&reportid=605>; emphasis added.

7 "Sikh Turbans Will be Subject to Heightened Screening at U.S. Airports," Sikh Coalition press release, August 19, 2007, available at <http://sikhcoalition.org/advisories/TSARuleChange.htm>.

8 An electronic version of the letter, signed by five members of the United States House of Representatives, can be accessed at <http://www.sikhcoalition.org/advisories/documents/9-17-07TSA-headwear-screening-policy-Honda-Letter.pdf>. Another letter was subsequently sent from four prominent senators, including future president Barack Obama; it is available at <http://www.sikhcoalition.org/advisories/documents/TSALetteronSikhScreening.pdf>.

9 Sikh Coalition press release, "TSA Develops New Procedure for Screening Turbans at U.S. Airports," October 17, 2007, available at <http://www.sikhcoalition.org/advisories/TSADevelopsNewProcedure.htm>.

Manpreet Anand

The U.S. federal policy decision-making process is intended to be bureaucratic in nature. It is within this bureaucratic structure that various departments and equities are ensured a voice and input into decisions that could have wide-ranging implications. While this structure can be frustratingly slow at times, it helps to ensure that certain risks are mitigated, and this is especially true for issues that juxtapose national security and civil rights. This is an area in which Sikh American rights are particularly vulnerable and where a proper bureaucratic process is absolutely crucial.

Through my experience, however, the post-9/11 federal policy-making process has been ad hoc, inconsistent, and sometimes contrary to intended goals when implementing security policies that affect Sikh Americans. This has largely been due to a lack of sufficient understanding and respect for the way in which Sikhs practice their religion.

I do not believe that the U.S. federal government intends to target Sikh Americans because of who we are or for our belief system. Instead, policy decisions are sometimes made in a religious vacuum, or at least in a mode in which only those religions that are popularly known to Americans, such as Christianity, Judaism, and Islam, are taken into account. As a consequence, Sikh Americans who become subject to seemingly benign policy decisions are automatically put on the defensive by having to explain our beliefs, advocate for reforms, and defend our rights after a policy decision has already been made.

Having worked in the U.S. government for the past few years, I have had the opportunity to be a part of the oversight process for policy decisions that affect Sikh Americans. This has placed me in the somewhat rare position of being able to contribute to the policy reform process as well as experience the intended, and unintended, consequences of those very decisions.

Perhaps the best example to illustrate how misdirected policy goals coupled with uninformed staff of a federal government agency can lead to decisions that take away basic rights of Sikh Americans involves the TSA.

TSA Policy Changes

Background The TSA was formed after 9/11, in part to standardize, and hence strengthen, the way in which security at various ports of entry is handled. The TSA is most known for its agents at airports, who carry a bulk of the burden of making sure that security threats are neutralized before a plane leaves the airport.

From my personal experience, I remember keeping track of how many times I was "randomly" searched for the first two years after 9/11: I was stopped for a secondary "random" check 72 percent of the time. Many in the community termed this phenomenon "flying while Sikh." This tended to depend on the size of the airport, the frequency of turbaned passengers who went through the airport, and the disposition of the security agent. So I welcomed the inception of the TSA, hoping that it could serve a very useful purpose in standardizing the methodology of security screening so that less attention is focused on distractions (checking turbaned passengers because they are turbaned) and more on those who would actually do us harm. After the TSA took over security, the percentage of times that I was randomly stopped for secondary search dropped dramatically; it seemed to me that the system was working.

A sudden change in policy During the summer of 2007, the TSA instituted a new policy that required all passengers wearing certain types of headgear to be subject to additional screening at airports. In other words, even if a passenger did not set off the metal detector at an airport or trigger any other reason for a secondary search, that passenger would automatically be subject to additional screening solely because the passenger was wearing a certain kind of headgear. Specific types of headgear were even given as examples to TSA agents. Turbans and nun's habits were to be checked, but yarmulkes and baseball caps were not. "Flying while Sikh" had been institutionalized.

The policy change was not made public. There was no awareness campaign by the TSA to inform the passengers beforehand. Passengers were told, sometimes very rudely, at the airport itself that the rules had changed and that the turbans would have to be checked. In some cases, most notably at San Francisco International Airport, passengers were told that they had to remove their turban in public, which to Sikhs is akin to asking them to remove their pants in public.

Public backlash Sikh community groups, most notably the Sikh Coalition, and the U.S. Congress were outraged, and they decided to act. Letters from prominent members of Congress were written to the TSA Administrator as well as the Secretary of the Department of Homeland Security (DHS). The House Committee on Foreign Affairs (HCFA) and the House Homeland Security Committee brought in representatives from the TSA and DHS on several occasions to explain its policy and seek its remediation.

Evidently, the policy had changed, because a supervising TSA agent had randomly noticed a turbaned passenger go through security without having his turban subject to an additional screening, even though the passenger did not set off the metal detector. The TSA agent felt, for a reason that still eludes me, that allowing a turbaned passenger to pass through without being checked was not acceptable. So, instead of going through the proper bureaucratic process and checking with various civil rights offices that had been created for just such a purpose, TSA security officials moved quickly to change their internal procedures.

After the large public backlash, TSA regretted its hasty decision, especially since TSA agents were implementing the new policy inconsistently across the country. No coherent message was being delivered to passengers or the community groups, which added to suspicion about the motivation behind the new policy. Moreover, some turbaned passengers felt (justifiably) that they were being singled out because of their religion, creating de facto religious profiling from the TSA.

The security rationale While working on the HCFA, we investigated the issue and found, through multiple briefings from the administration, that the security impetus behind this policy mainly involved the threat of individuals bringing in components that could constitute an improvised explosive device (IED). Furthermore, the TSA believed that these non-metallic IED components could be hidden anywhere, including inside a turban. However, we also learned that these IED components could be as small as a pen cap. So the natural question that comes to mind is that if these components are as small as a pen cap, then why are we only checking items like a turban? Presumably, such a small device could be hidden in any number of places of someone's body. And the answer we learned, after much wrangling, was that doing a full check on every passenger would take too much time and was not practical. However, checking bulky clothing or other non-conforming headgear like turbans would not affect many passengers, and would therefore have minimal impact on security screening throughput.

When we found that this was the reasoning behind the change in policy, a number of questions came to mind: if the TSA cannot afford to stop everyone, what is the security rationale for choosing headgear, and specifically turbans, as a trigger for an automatic search? If the security gain of checking such items is minimal, and perhaps even counter-effective, then why focus valuable resources on such items? If those who are trying to harm us know that we are doing additional checks on say, turbans, do you think they will walk into airports wearing turbans? Shouldn't our TSA agents be more concerned with using their discretion to check unusual behavior or other security red flags rather than wasting their time with additional checks that are predictable and therefore avoidable by those who pose the real threats?

These were the questions that we posed to the TSA and DHS, but unfortunately to no avail. Without answers to these questions, the Sikh American community could easily believe that there exists an inherent level of suspicion regarding anyone who wears a turban within the federal security apparatus. As I mentioned earlier, I do not think that all policy-makers in the administration intended to single out turbans, nor do I believe that security officers believe this is the best way to screen for IED threats. However, one of the challenges of creating a federal bureaucracy is that once a decision is made, it is extremely difficult to walk that decision back, no matter the unintended effects.

After much pressure from the Hill and from community groups, the TSA did change its policy slightly. The policy now takes away the examples of headgear to be checked, institutes general guidance to check for all bulky clothing and non-conforming headwear, and is accompanied by a training video for all TSA agents to watch. In addition, passengers are given less embarrassing options when selected for additional screening: self-pat-downs of headgear and private rooms are to be offered to all turbaned passengers. In terms of a process, I was pleased that the TSA had recognized an issue with the current policy and had tried to remedy it. However, I was, and still am, extremely displeased that a policy that neither strengthens our security posture nor hinders religious profiling is still in effect. "Flying while Sikh" is still very much a reality.

Lessons Learned

There are a number of lessons to take away from this experience.

Security policy should enhance security First, a high priority for all Americans should be to support structures and policies that help to keep us safe. And, as the TSA case shows, the policy-making process fails all Americans, not just Sikh Americans, in this respect. It is our duty, therefore, to continue to pressure the TSA and the administration to remedy this security challenge. Profiling distracts our security agents from implementing a true security policy and is not in the best interests of the public.

Process matters Second, the inception of the policy and the way in which it is implemented matters a great deal in making sure that the best possible policy is put forward and that an acceptable level of credibility is retained. The bureaucratic process is vital to ensure that unintended consequences are mitigated. In this case, both the TSA and DHS have offices of civil rights charged with helping to prevent such problems from occurring. Unfortunately, they were not involved in the decision-making process and were only brought in after the public backlash to help with damage control.

In addition, the civil rights office representatives were brought in to liaise with advocacy groups, Congress, and other concerned parties. Often, the information that the civil rights office gave was incomplete and sometimes inconsistent with the information that I was getting from the security office, which led me to believe that they were either out of the loop or purposely providing misleading information.

It seemed that they were concerned more about damage control, which is disappointing because they could have been useful in helping to develop policies that upheld our collective national security priorities while addressing the community's religious sensitivities. Without that type of input into the decision-making process, the civil rights office was relegated to a public relations function, trying to coordinate between the decision-makers in the TSA and the advocacy groups, rather than as a true advocate for community groups.

Coordination counts Furthermore, it was unclear to what extent the Department of Homeland Security was actually involved *before* the policy decision was made. If the DHS was not involved, you have to question the coordination of the TSA with the DHS, and not just on issues dealing with civil rights. As citizens, we trust the TSA to provide us with the best security that they possibly can. I would expect that coordination with the DHS would be a prerequisite before significant policy decisions are made.

Federal policy should not discriminate The current policy infringes upon the civil rights of a select group of Americans largely because of the way in which they practice their religion. In the end, the TSA has excluded yarmulkes from additional screenings but has included turbans, and there is no compelling or coherent security rationale for that to be the case. Intentional or not, this creates a sense of religious discrimination and supports profiling, to say nothing about those passengers who have to live through the humiliation of being checked solely because of the way they practice their religion.

* * *

In more recent months, Sikh advocacy groups have monitored the behavior of TSA airport screeners by asking Sikhs to report their experiences while going through security. The results have been mixed. For example, at the beginning of 2008 nearly 100 percent of Sikhs traveling were additionally screened, but at the end of the year only one in three were screened.[10] At the other end of the spectrum, in December of 2008 100 percent of Sikhs were selected for secondary screening at Oakland Airport.[11]

Sikhs continue to encounter problems in airports, though at least some improvements may be noted. The community is continuing to work in tandem with the TSA officials to ensure that effective training takes places such that security screenings on the ground are administered equitably and in a respectful manner.

10 Sikh Coalition press release, November 16, 2008.

11 Sikh Coalition press release, January 29, 2009.

Chapter 11
Employment Discrimination

> Sukhbir Channa, 24, sued Disney … claiming that the theme park company refused to rehire him in 2006 because his beard, long hair and his turban, which he contends are religiously-mandated, did not conform with Disney's grooming and dress requirements known as "The Disney Look."[1]
>
> Once hired, [employees] have to maintain the "Disney Look," said Angela Bliss, spokesperson for Disneyland. "The Disney look is a fresh, clean and approachable look, ensuring that every guest feels comfortable with our entire cast," Bliss said.[2]

Employment discrimination against Sikhs became especially problematic in the immediate wake of the 9/11 attacks. Major companies such as Disney and Subway refused to employ Sikhs or harassed Sikh employees, apparently because turbaned Sikhs did not conform to their conceptions of what a presentable employee looks like. On the whole, Sikhs have faced discrimination both during the hiring process and on the job in various positions in the public and private sectors.

With respect to government jobs, Sikhs with turbans have faced marked difficulties in police departments in the United States after 9/11. Somewhat surprisingly, the most prominent examples of employment discrimination affecting the Sikh community, in the police or otherwise, are alleged to have occurred in one of the country's most diverse corners, New York City, and in one of the nation's most celebrated law enforcement offices, the New York Police Department (NYPD).

On his first day of work, September 21, 2001, Jasjit Singh Jaggi, was told by his employer, the NYPD, that he could not wear a turban on the job.[3] Jaggi claimed to have offered a compromise to his employer: to wear a white turban with the NYPD logo affixed to it, but the solution was rejected. Presented with the option of resigning or being terminated, Jaggi resigned.

He subsequently filed a complaint against the NYPD with the New York City Human Rights Commission. An administrative law judge ruled in favor

---

1 Scott Powers, "Sikh Musician Sues Disney World Over 'Disney Look,' Discrimination," *Orlando Sentinel*, June 16, 2008.

2 Janna Oberdorf, "The Secret Behind the Magic of Disney," *NYU LiveWire*, available at <http://journalism.nyu.edu/pubzone/livewire/archived/the_secret_behind_the_magic_of/>.

3 *Jaggi v. N.Y. City Police Department*, CHR Compl. No. M-E-C-02-1012382-E (NY City Commission on Human Rights, April 28, 2004).

of Jaggi, concluding that the petitioner sufficiently established that he was discriminated against in violation of Title VII, which generally requires employers to accommodate the reasonable religious needs of employees, unless the accommodation would present an undue hardship,[4] and recommending that Jaggi be reinstated and permitted to wear a turban while on duty. A settlement was reached in Jaggi's case, leading to his reinstatement.[5]

In early 2002, a turbaned Sikh New York City police officer, Amric Singh Rathour, was terminated for refusing to remove his turban only a few weeks after he had completed training and been inducted into the NYPD.[6] Despite widespread news coverage and several petitions to the NYPD, the city ignored his case. As a result, he filed suit under Title VII against the New York City Police Commissioner and the NYPD to regain his employment. The parties reached a settlement that paralleled the *Jaggi* settlement, and Rathour was reinstated.

Another New York public agency also made things difficult for its Sikh employees. Kevin Harrington, a turbaned Sikh train operator with the New York Metropolitan Transit Authority (MTA), was honored for driving his train in reverse on 9/11, away from the towers and towards safety.[7] Harrington had worked for the MTA for over twenty years.[8] Nevertheless, after the attacks, Harrington was informed by the MTA that he would have to either remove his turban or wear an MTA logo on his turban if he wished to work around passengers, otherwise he would be forced to work in the railyard.[9] Rather than accept a transfer to an inferior position in the railyard or be terminated for failing to comply with his employer's directives, Harrington eventually and reluctantly agreed to wear a logo on his turban.

Filmmaker Valarie Kaur spoke with both Rathour and Harrington after their respective post-9/11 experiences.

* * *

> Amric Singh Rathour was born and raised in Queens, New York, and his father was one of the first Sikhs to settle in Richmond Hill, now a thriving Punjabi community in New York. In 2000, Amric joined the NYPD, but was subsequently fired for wearing his turban. In his quiet Queens accent, he told us his story.

---

4 42 U.S.C § 2000e(j) (2007).

5 James Barron, "Two Sikhs Win Back Jobs Lost by Wearing Turbans," *New York Times*, July 29, 2004, available at <http://query.nytimes.com/gst/fullpage.html?res=9D07E4D6133DF93AA15754C0A9629C8B63>.

6 Sikh Coalition, "Sikh Coalition Challenges NYPD on Rule Disallowing Turbans," available at <http://www.sikhcoalition.org/amricsingh1.asp>.

7 Sikh Coalition, "Five More Sikhs to Resist MTA Turban Branding Policy," July 18, 2005, available at <http://www.sikhcoalition.org/advisories/mta_press.htm>.

8 Sikh Coalition, "Petition to MTA New York City Transit," August 16, 2004, available at <http://www.sikhcoalition.org/mta_sikh_petition.asp>.

9 *Harrington v. New York City Transit Authority et al.*, No. 05-CV-3341 (EDNY 2005) (Am. Compl.).

"In 2000, I went to the police department, wanting to serve the city I was born and raised in. I passed the exams and they hired me. I quit my other job and paid money for the uniform. But then they told me to take my turban off, or they would fire me. They trapped me.

"I had always felt that this was my home. This is the greatest city in the world. But after getting fired, the discrimination really disturbed me. I took it to heart. I got really depressed. I stopped having a social life. You think that you're not human. It may seem like nothing to someone who doesn't understand believing in something, but when you're judged like this, it really hurts."

Amric decided to fight the NYPD. Amardeep Singh and the Sikh Coalition took up his case, pointing out the long history of Sikh service in the army and civil forces. And after two-and-a-half years of litigation, they won. They won because of a court order, despite pleas to meet Mayor Bloomberg and the NYPD and to avoid going through the courts. Amric now wears his turban as a police officer on the streets of Manhattan.

"While I'm out there, directing traffic, people come up to me and shake my hand. It was a victory for our community. It feels really good."

Next, we met Kevin Harrington, a tall American of Irish decent who converted to Sikhism in his youth. His case against the MTA had also made news .... In June 2004, after 24 years as a train operator for the Transit Authority, Kevin was asked to remove his turban. He told us his full story.

"In 1981, the Transit Authority called me to work for them as a bus cleaner. It was hard to find a job as a Sikh with a turban. Because if you are an American [converted] Sikh, people think you're crazy. If you're an Indian, they assume it's heritage. But if you are a white American wearing a turban, they think you're nuts. As a result, most American Sikhs are self-employed. But I took the job and became a train operator.

"On 9/11 I was operating a Number Four train, and we lost signal power when the first tower fell. That meant the train could not move more than twenty feet at a time without being stopped by the emergency braking system .... So I would recharge the train, move it twenty feet, it would stop again, and I would redo it. I evacuated the people on my train to the Wall Street station."

Kevin was honored as a hero of 9/11. His passengers still come up to him and thank him for saving their life. In June of 2002, the superintendent of the Number Four train approached him:

"He told me that because I wore a turban, I wasn't allowed to work where the public could see me. I had to work in the yard. Or else I had to wear a MTA patch on my turban, if I didn't want to be fired. But to me, I felt that my turban was being used as a billboard."

* * *

The Sikh Coalition has filed suit on behalf of Harrington. The Department of Justice (DOJ) has also filed suit on behalf of Harrington. The case is still pending as of this writing.

What should the courts do in his case? Some legal scholars, including former circuit judge and current Stanford Law School professor Michael W. McConnell, have claimed that the courts have eviscerated religious rights in the workplace,[10] a situation that would ostensibly imperil turbaned Sikhs from bringing successful Title VII claims. For example, the Supreme Court has held that employers need not bear more than a de minimis cost to accommodate religious employees,[11] and that employers are not required to accept a particular accommodation suggested by the employee.[12] Courts have also allowed employers to defend themselves by claiming that the accommodation would negatively affect business operations,[13] impose on co-worker rights,[14] or endanger public health or safety.[15] Generally, it would seem that the protection Title VII affords to turbaned Sikhs is quite limited.

As a historical matter, the courts have not been kind to Sikh claims of employment discrimination. A 1998 case, *Kalsi v. New York City Transit Authority (NYCTA)*,[16] is one of the more discouraging cases for Sikhs with turbans in the public safety context. The case was brought by Charan Singh Kalsi, a Sikh car inspector trained by the NYCTA to work on subway cars, which involved working in pits under the cars, alongside the cars, and in other areas where there was a threat to his head. Kalsi was told to remove his turban and don a hard hat during the training session, and when he refused, was eventually fired. Kalsi brought

---

10 See Michael W. McConnell, symposium, "Religion in the Workplace: Proceedings of the 2000 Annual Meeting of the Association of American Law Schools Section on Law and Religion," 4 *Employee Rts. & Emp. Pol'y J.* 87, 98 (2000); see also Thomas D. Brierton, "'Reasonable Accommodation' under Title VII: Is it Reasonable to the Religious Employee?," 42 *Cath. Law* 165, 182–86 (2002), describing the ways in which the "courts have weakened reasonable accommodation rights in the workplace."

11 See *TWA v. Hardison*, 432 U.S. 63, 84 (1977): "To require TWA to bear more than a *de minimis* cost in order to give Hardison Saturdays off is an undue hardship."

12 See *Ansonia Board of Education v. Philbrook*, 479 U.S. 60, 68 (1986): "We find no basis in either the statute or its legislative history for requiring an employer to choose any particular reasonable accommodation. By its very terms the statute directs that any reasonable accommodation by the employer is sufficient to meet its accommodation obligation."

13 See *EEOC v. Sambo's of Georgia Inc.*, 530 F. Supp. 86, 91 (ND Ga. 1981), disagreeing that "customer preference is an insufficient justification or defense as a matter of law."

14 See *Weber v. Roadway Express Inc.*, 199 F.3d 270, 274 (5th Cir. 2000), finding that an accommodation is "more than a *de minimis* expense because [it] unduly burdens his co-workers."

15 See *Bhatia v. Chevron U.S.A., Inc.*, 734 F.2d 1382, 1384 (9th Cir. 1984).

16 62 F. Supp. 2d 745 (EDNY 1998).

claims against NYCTA alleging violations of the First Amendment, Title VII, and the New York State Constitution.[17]

The defendants moved to dismiss the case on the grounds that no reasonable jury would find in favor of Kalsi under the prevailing legal standards, even if Kalsi's factual allegations were accepted as true. The district court granted the defendants' motion and dismissed the case. The court noted, with respect to the Title VII claim, that Kalsi had failed to prove a prima facie case of discrimination or disparate impact: although he was a member of a protected group, he failed to show that his discharge occurred under "circumstances giving rise to an inference of discrimination."[18] Although Kalsi had a prima facie case for his reasonable accommodation claim, the court added, he could not be accommodated without undue hardship to the employer (and the employer's safety standards).

An oft-cited employment discrimination case, *EEOC v. Sambo's of Georgia*,[19] also produced a disappointing result for a turbaned Sikh. In this case, a Sikh man applied for a managerial position with the Sambo's chain of restaurants in Atlanta. His application was rejected from the very outset on the basis that if he were to obtain the position, he would not be able to shave his beard and moustache in compliance with Sambo's grooming policy. The company claimed that the wearing of a beard, moustache, and headgear was not permitted because they do not "comply with the public image that Sambo's has built up over the years,"[20] and that because Sambo's was a family restaurant, their customers would react adversely to a bearded and turbaned manager.

The court held, in part, that even if the refusal of an employer to hire a non-clean-shaven man was discriminatory, being clean-shaven is a bona fide occupational qualification for a restaurant that relies on the family trade, and therefore constitutes a Title VII exception:

> The requirement that Sambo's restaurant managers be clean-shaven is tailored to actual business needs, has a manifest and demonstrable relation to job performance, and is necessary to the safe and efficient operation of Sambo's Restaurants.[21]

The *Sambo's* case is significant because it considered important evidence "prov[ing] that a significant segment of the consuming public would not accept restaurant employees with beards."[22]

17 Ibid. at 748.
18 Ibid. at 753.
19 *Sambo's*, 530 F. Supp. at 89.
20 Ibid. at 89–90.
21 Ibid.
22 Brierton, "'Reasonable Accommodation.'"

Whether and to what extent appearance can serve as a legitimate basis for an adverse employment action is a question that is particularly salient in the post-9/11 context. In 2003, the Subway fast food chain, for example, began to "crack down" on Sikh men (many of whom were store owners) appearing in front of customers with their turbans on, saying that the turban did not "present a professional image," and requiring employees to wear black hats or visors instead.[23] Disney similarly barred a Sikh from performing in front of visitors to the theme park because the turbaned Sikh did not have the "Disney look" that would make people comfortable.[24]

Subsequent to *Sambo's*, however, several courts declared that preferences for personal appearance when an employee is dealing with the public are insufficient to defend against a Title VII claim. An attorney who specializes in employment matters observed that:

> a restaurant's customers' anxiety about the manager's Middle Eastern appearance cannot justify national origin discrimination, even with a clear link between the manager's Middle Eastern national origin and the loss of revenue. Although one may empathize with these employers, the law does not permit customers' bias to justify an employer's unlawful discrimination.[25]

Indeed, in a pamphlet published after 9/11, the Equal Employment Opportunity Commission (EEOC) clarified that employment decisions cannot be based on customers being uncomfortable with religious attire. In the pamphlet the EEOC noted:

> Narinder, a South Asian man who wears a Sikh turban, applies for a position as a cashier at XYZ Discount Goods. XYZ fears Narinder's religious attire will make customers uncomfortable. What should XYZ do?
>
> XYZ should not deny Narinder the job due to notions of customer preferences about religious attire. That would be unlawful. It would be the same as refusing to hire Narinder because he is a Sikh.[26]

---

23 See Jill Mahoney, "Sikh says Fast-food Boss Banned 'Diaper' on Head," *Globe and Mail*, December 11, 2003, available at <http://www.globeandmail.com/servlet/story/RTGAM.20031211.wturban1211/BNStory/National/>.

24 Oberdorf, "The Secret Behind the Magic of Disney."

25 See Bryan P. Cavanaugh, "September 11 Backlash Employment Discrimination," 60 *J. Mo. B.* 186, 192 (2004).

26 U.S. Equal Employment Opportunity Commission, "Questions and Answers about Employer Responsibilities Concerning the Employment of Muslims, Arabs, South Asians, and Sikhs" (2005), available at <http://www.eeoc.gov/facts/backlash-employer.html>.

Accordingly, to the extent that *Sambo's* stands for the proposition that discomfort with, or loss of business associated with public discomfort with, the Sikh turban or general appearance, *Sambo's* may no longer be considered a sound statement on Title VII's protections. Moreover, employers such as Subway and Disney may want to reconsider their employment decisions as they relate to banning or removing turbaned Sikhs from the public's gaze. (In determining what constitutes an appropriate "look" for their employees, these corporations also may want to keep in mind that the American "look" is not monolithic and in fact comes in many shades and forms. It would behoove these entities to embrace the increasing pluralism that is taking hold in this nation, rather than maintain and perpetuate the false notion that an American appearance is ultimately a homogeneous one.) On the other end of the spectrum, cases like *Kalsi* have firmly established that an employer may reliably defend a Title VII suit on the grounds that the accommodation will present a legitimate, non-discriminatory concern, such as one relating to health or safety.[27]

The *Harrington* case against the MTA does not appear to be one implicating health or safety, as Harrington was instructed to wear a MTA logo on his turban in the course of his saga: a logo hardly serves as a protective tool, but instead may have been a means to inform the riding public that Harrington indeed was an MTA employee and dissipate any concerns that the turbaned man at the helm of a New York City train was dangerous. The turban itself does not seem to present an undue burden since the employer required that a logo be affixed to the turban, not that the turban be removed or replaced with a hard hat or other headgear. In this respect, the *MTA* case should be adjudged under principles consistent with the EEOC guidance and not under the outdated *Sambo's* legal regime.

Aside from the "customer comfort" issue, overall, Sikhs facing alleged discriminatory conduct in the workplace with regards to their turbans may face difficulty in asserting their claims, particularly due to the de minimis undue burden test[28] and in the cases where public health or safety are at issue.[29] Accordingly, these Sikhs may turn to extra-legal remedies, such as the assistance of Sikh action

27 See Huma T Yunus, note, "Employment Law – Congress Giveth and the Supreme Court Taketh Away: Title VII's Prohibition of Religious Discrimination in the Workplace," 57 *Okla. L. Rev.* 657, 672 (2004): "Generally, cases that implicate public health or safety regulations have predictable outcomes. Courts have consistently held that any accommodation that requires employers to violate a state or business imposed health or safety procedure constitutes an undue hardship."

28 See *Cloutier v. Costco Wholesale Corp.*, 390 F.3d 126 (1st Cir. 2004), holding that requiring employer to permit an employee, a member of the Church of Body Modification, to wear numerous uncovered facial piercings would be an undue burden.

29 See Heather Payne and Norman Doe, "Public Health and the Limits of Religious Freedom," 19 *Emory Int'l L. Rev.* 539, 551 (2005), suggesting that "Sikhs may not enjoy legal protection to wear beards or turbans when an employer's rule is justified in the workplace on grounds of hygiene."

groups in encouraging employers to change their policies before an incident occurs, or to settle in case one does arise.

In other words, Title VII may be most effective for Sikhs when they are able to convince employers, without formal judicial proceedings, to accommodate the Sikh turban in the workplace.[30] The legal avenues available to Sikhs, though, may improve if a Workplace Religious Freedom Act, which would generally require employers to afford greater protections to religious employees, was finally passed by Congress.[31] Until then, with exception to the customer comfort issues, negotiations and settlements may be a more productive route than private litigation for turbaned Sikhs aggrieved by employment actions.

A final note with respect to employment discrimination: while each of the aforementioned incidents concerned turbaned Sikh males, turbaned Sikh females have also been discriminated against in the employment context. As noted in Part I, Sikh females generally opt for a chiffon scarf to cover their heads, but some females choose to wear turbans. In doing so, they become subjected to the same sort of prejudices and views that their Sikh brothers have encountered.

For example, Sukhvir Kaur's employment experience was a nightmare. For months, from the minute she stepped foot in the National Wholesale Liquidators Outlet in Queens, New York, Sukhvir had been forced to endure taunts and public humiliation. Her boss asked her to remove her religious turban, saying she would look more "sexy" that way. He called Sikhs "thieves" and "nasty people." When she complained, he stopped her from using the restroom during her shifts. Finally, Sukhvir Kaur broke. She left her job and spearheaded a class action lawsuit against her employer. It was then, she says, that she finally realized that "America's laws are the same for everyone." Nearly five years after the incidents began, Sukhvir, her fellow plaintiffs and her former employer agreed to a settlement in the case that awarded damages to the victim for their mistreatment at the hands of management. The case sent a loud message to corporations across the country that discriminating against Sikhs will cost them dearly.

---

30 See remarks of Amardeep Singh, Legal Director, Sikh Coalition, "Meeting of the U.S. Equal Employment Opportunity Commission, Employment Discrimination in the Aftermath of September 11," December 11, 2001, encouraging the EEOC to take steps to "inform employers on how they can conform their corporate behavior to the requirements of the law when a situation that may possibly involve unlawful bias occurs. [Such measures] can serve as a way to proactively prevent discrimination before it occurs."

31 See Debbie N. Kaminer, "Title VII's Failure to Provide Meaningful and Consistent Protection of Religious Employees: Proposals for an Amendment," 21 *Berkeley J. Emp. & Lab. L.* 575, 628–29 (2000), arguing that the Act would broaden Title VII protections for religious employees.

Chapter 12
Detention

On September 12, 2001, Sher Singh, a turbaned Sikh man, was taken off an Amtrak train, bound from Boston to New York, in handcuffs. Members of the crowd that assembled during the arrest were reported as shouting, "Kill him!," "Burn in Hell," and "You killed my brother."[1] The arresting officers joined in, asking Singh how bin Laden was doing. News stations replayed the video of his arrest in connection with its coverage of the attacks, thus associating Singh and other turbaned Sikhs with the planners of the attacks. As one Sikh remarked:

> The news that a possible terrorist had been arrested spread like wildfire, and national media outlets quickly picked up the story. Almost immediately, video clips of a young man with a green turban and a long, flowing beard being led away in handcuffs flooded the airwaves. CNN, Fox, and the Associated Press carried video and photos of Sher Singh.[2]

Thus any connection between terrorists and a turbaned male with a long, flowing beard was further embedded in the hearts and minds of emotional Americans. On the contrary, no media coverage followed news of Sher Singh's release, just three hours later.

Ultimately, it was announced that Singh was apprehended for carrying a concealed weapon – the Sikh kirpan – which was hidden under Singh's clothing and therefore would only have been discovered after the swarm of officials ejected Singh from the train. There was no reason – beyond the turban and long beard – for the public or law enforcement personnel to be concerned about his presence on a train. In other words, he did nothing to arouse suspicion, aside from looking the way he did and being in a public space. Singh reflects on this harrowing experience with Valarie Kaur.

* * *

Today we interviewed Sher Singh, who was arrested on September 12, 2001 as the first suspected terrorist after the 9/11 attacks. He was riding a

---

1 American-Arab Anti-Discrimination Committee, *Report on Hate Crimes and Discrimination Against Arab Americans: The Post-September 11 Backlash, September 11, 2001–October 11, 2002* (Washington, DC: ADC-RI, 2003), p. 43.

2 Jaideep Singh, "Confronting Racial Violence: Sikh Americans Have Been Targeted for Harassment and Attack More than Any Group Since 9/11," *Colorlines* (Spring 2003), pp. 23–26.

Boston-bound train when it stopped in Providence, Rhode Island. He was wearing a turban and kirpan, both articles of Sikh faith. His "suspicious" appearance had caught the attention of the FBI, who sent federal agents and local police with bomb-sniffing dogs to the station to intercept him.

Officers rushed the entrance of the train and pointed rifles at the man: "Get your f— hands up." They pulled him out of the train at gunpoint and handcuffed him. One officer said, "How's Osama bin Laden?" They led him onto the platform, where crowds of people had gathered, shouting profanities. Someone yelled, "You killed my brother." Others shouted, "Kill him."

Sher Singh was released within three hours of his arrest, because it was clear he was innocent. Authorities announced that he had no connection to the attacks. Yet the footage of his arrest was broadcast and published around the world for three days, showing a tall man with a turban and long black beard, eyes cast downward, led in handcuffs by black-uniformed officers believing they had apprehended the first terrorist.

We had first heard this story from Sher Singh in December 2001. Four years later, he reflected on his experience:

"I felt and sometimes feel a little estranged. I feel for a split second, maybe I'm not at home here. But then I tell myself it's all in my mind. If somebody has or had a negative opinion about my appearance or any Sikh's appearance, then it's in that person's mind. That person needs to open up. Home is where you are. No looking back." He smiles.

"After this happened, I got more involved in my community. I gave talks about Sikhism, attending rallies on civil rights, and talked to children on understanding different faiths. I felt that I had to give back a lot more than I had ever given back.

"I'm now a solution architect for EED; I develop solutions for the Navy and Marine Corps and help develop their information technology. I get to do very high level design and it's a new challenge every day."

* * *

In Sher Singh's situation, he should not have been detained in the first place, and surely not booted from the train in the manner he was. In other instances, Sikhs who may have been rightly detained have lodged complaints in response to their treatment after being taken into custody. Such was the case for Satnam Singh, a Sikh who had been arrested and sentenced to prison for two misdemeanor offenses in the state of Florida.[3] The strict laws in Florida regarding shaving and clothing for incarcerated persons would not have allowed Satnam to act in accordance with his faith, but quick action on the part of human rights groups facilitated his transfer

3 Toni Urquhart, "Prisoner bypasses Florida for Vermont," FSU College of Law Research Center Blog, April 8, 2006, available at <http://fsulawlibraryblog.typepad.com/fsu_college_of_law_librar/2006/04/prisoner_bypass.html>.

to Vermont, which had recently altered its regulations and is now one of the most accommodating and progressive states in America as far as the religious freedom of inmates is concerned.[4] An immigration detention center in New Jersey also reversed its policy of banning turbans in response to requests from human rights groups on behalf of three Sikhs being held at the center.[5]

Currently, regulations in federal prisons and jails in Kentucky, Vermont, and New York specifically allow for Sikh articles of faith in the list of permitted religious items for detainees. Other states and individual counties or townships do not have such permissions, and as such, attempts in these areas for relief to the inmate generally are secured on an ad hoc, reactive basis. In 2008, a Muslim woman sued San Bernardino County, CA for forcing her to remove her *hijab* while being held overnight for an expired train pass. She received monetary damages, indicating that change, however slow, may be on the horizon for Sikhs being denied their religious rights in custody.

4 Mark Connors, "Imprisoned Sikh secures religious freedom in Vermont," *India New England*, March 7, 2008, available at <http://www.indianewengland.com/ME2/dirmod.asp?sid=&nm=&type=Publishing&mod=Publications%3A%3AArticle&mid=8F3A7027421841978F18BE895F87F791&tier=4&id=00F37F4C83914996A814797447B6377A>.

5 "Immigration Detention Center Reverses Ban after Sikh Coalition Intervenes," Sikh Coalition press release, November 2, 2007, available at <http://www.sikhcoalition.org/advisories/DetentionCenterReversesTurbanBan.htm>.

Chapter 13
Denial of Entry into Public Places

> Like thousands of New Yorkers, Navdeep Singh liked to keep fit. That's why he joined Planet Fitness, a gymnasium in the Bronx, where he had worked out regularly for six months before his membership was terminated. It turns out that Planet Fitness had a "no bandanas" policy that they had applied to the tight cloth Navdeep wore around his head in lieu of a turban while he worked out. Planet Fitness gave Navdeep a choice between losing his membership or replacing his head covering with a hat instead. Though Navdeep explained that the Sikh faith explicitly prohibits wearing caps or hats instead of cloth turbans or patkas, the management at Planet Fitness kicked him out.[1]

The targeting of the turban after 9/11 has led to Sikhs being denied entry into various public buildings and places of public accommodation, such as courthouses,[2] higher education institutions,[3] and political events.[4] In many instances, the reason for the denial or ejection is the refusal of the location to exempt turbaned Sikhs from a generally applicable "no-hats" policy. For example, a Sikh reported the following to the Sikh Coalition:

> I am a resident physician in medical center in Houston and went out with my colleagues and friends to a club called "Pandora" on 06/07/2008 at 11:45 PM. I was wearing my turban and was otherwise dressed up appropriately for the club. When I was about to enter the club, I was stopped by the person (bouncer) at entrance and was told that I could not go in because of my turban. When I told him that it was part of my religion. He answered exactly as "I respect your preference for religion but we do not allow any kind of headgear in our club." I felt discriminated just because I was practicing my religion. My colleagues

---

1 Sikh Coalition, "Making Our Voices Heard: A Civil Rights Agenda for New York City's Sikhs," April 2008, p. 7, available at <http://www.sikhcoalition.org/RaisingOurVoicesReport.pdf>.

2 See, for example, Sikh American Legal Defense and Education Fund, "Georgia Court Apologizes for Denying Sikh American Man Entrance to Court," available at <http://www.saldef.org/content.aspx?a=1391>.

3 See, for example, Sonja Sharp, "Students Rail Scrutiny of Sikh," *The Daily Californian*, September 24, 2004, available at <http://www.dailycal.org/article.php?id=16228>.

4 See, for example, Ralph Ranalli, "Sikh Student Detained by Secret Service," *Boston Globe*, July 30, 2004, available at <http://www.boston.com/news/local/articles/2004/07/30/sikh_student_detained_by_secret_service/>.

> were all allowed in. It seemed as if I was a criminal just because I was wearing a turban.[5]

In certain instances, the "no-hats" policy only became an issue after the terrorist attacks of 9/11. Perhaps the most blatant example of this double standard took place on September 23, 2001, when Kabeer Singh was told to remove his turban or leave the Hard Times Café and Santa Fe Cue Club in Springfield, Virginia – despite the fact that prior to September 11, 2001, Sikh patrons, including Singh, had been permitted to wear turbans at this establishment.

The Department of Justice conducted an investigation and concluded that F & K Management, Inc., the owner and operator of the establishment, "had engaged in a pattern or practice of discriminating against Sikhs, Muslims, Indian Americans and other Asian Americans who wear certain kinds of head coverings, such as turbans, for religious or ethnic cultural reasons."[6] The DOJ found F & K in violation of Title II of the Civil Rights Act, which provides that "All persons shall be entitled to the full and equal enjoyment of the goods, services, facilities, privileges, advantages, and accommodations of any place of public accommodation … without discrimination on the ground of race, color, religion, or national origin."[7] The DOJ entered into a settlement agreement with F & K, which specified that the establishment was required, in part, to adopt a non-discriminatory dress code and apologize to Singh, his family, and to other Sikhs.

This appears to be a relatively "easy" case, as the same individual who went to this venue was only denied entry after the terrorist attacks. The settlement agreement could serve as a benchmark regarding the seriousness with which such discrimination in places of public accommodation may be viewed by the federal government given their involvement.

Cases involving turbaned Sikhs being denied entry to places of public accommodation are not, however, this straightforward. On January 25, 2007, a turbaned Sikh, Sanjum Paul Singh Samagh, was not permitted to enter the Pierce Street Annex bar in Costa Mesa, California on account of the establishment's "no hats" policy.[8] While Sikh groups consider the bar's actions to be blatantly discriminatory, others are not so sure. For example, UCLA law professor Eugene

5 Sikh Coalition Database, Incident #610, available at <http://www.sikhcoalition.org/hatecrime.asp?mainaction=viewreport&reportid=610>.

6 DOJ Settlement Agreement, United States and F & K Management, Inc., d/b/a Hard Times Café and Santa Fe Cue Club, February 28, 2003, available at <http://www.usdoj.gov/crt/legalinfo/discrimupdate.htm>.

7 42 U.S.C § 2000a (2007).

8 See Lisa Petrillo, "Sikh Wants Apology From Bar Owner," *Union-Tribune*, February 9, 2007, available at <http://www.signonsandiego.com/news/northcounty/20070209-9999-1mi9turban.html>.

Volokh, a leading constitutional scholar, did not think a federal case was a slam dunk for Samagh.[9]

Where, as with the *F & K* case, the discriminatory application of a "no-hats" policy is relatively clear, the ability of Sikh plaintiffs to achieve a favorable result or the likelihood that the government will intervene is surely greater. Indeed, the *F & K* case involved the same individual going to the same establishment both before and after 9/11. It is unlikely that other cases will be as clear-cut. Instead, they will resemble Samagh's, where a Sikh person may visit the establishment for the first time after 9/11 and there is no precedent regarding the establishment's previous treatment. Thus turbaned Sikhs like Samagh will have a greater burden to prove that that the application of the "no-hats" policy was discriminatory as applied to them, even though the *F & K* and *Samagh* cases both featured Sikhs being denied access to places of public accommodation after 9/11 on the basis of their turbans.

In 2007 alone there were additional instances at restaurants and nightclubs in Illinois,[10] Utah,[11] and California.[12] In the first two cases, as in the *F & K* and *Samagh* cases, a Sikh was denied entry to an establishment because management judged that his turban violated a "no-hats" policy. The California case differed, however, in that a Sikh was turned away from a nightclub after being told his turban fell under a policy to reject all "do-rags, beanies, bandannas and other head wear associated with street gangs." Placing a turban in the same category as items deemed to be informal fashion wear or to be "associated with street gangs" adds a novel and negative connotation to the Sikh turban.

In short, Sikhs who are denied entry to places of public accommodation due to the existence of a "no-hats" policy face an uphill battle in providing the evidentiary support that their denial was premised on discrimination and not a neutral application of the admission policy. The exception to this rule would be the *F & K* case, where the Sikh's patronage to the establishment both before and after 9/11 furnished colorable proof that the "no-hats" policy was not applied in a consistent or neutral fashion.

Cases where a Sikh attempted to enter a place only once after 9/11 feature an additional consideration, namely that a person who is denied entry to an

9 Jeff Overley, "'No Hats' Rule Protested," *Orange County Register*, February 8, 2007, available at <http://www.ocregister.com/ocregister/homepage/abox/article_1568186.php>.

10 Rupa Shenoy, "Nightclub Accused of Discrimination," *Chicago Journal*, August 8, 2007, available at <http://www.saldef.org/content.aspx?&a=1741&z=4&title=Nightclub%20accused%20of%20discrimination>.

11 "U.S. Club Owner Apologises to Sikh Man," *Times Of India*, August 30, 2007, available at <http://timesofindia.indiatimes.com/_U.S._club_owner_apologises_to_Sikh_man/articleshow/2321591.cms>.

12 Michael Burge, "Sikh Pursues Non-admittance to Club," *Union-Tribune*, August 24, 2007, available at <http://www.signonsandiego.com/news/northcounty/20070824-9999-1mi24sikh.html>.

establishment may not seek redress of their public accommodations rights because their desire to enter that public accommodation may be a one-time occurrence. For example, a Sikh who goes to one restaurant only to be barred from it may decide he will go to other restaurants from that point on and have no desire to eat at the apparently discriminatory restaurant. This is particularly the case if the first restaurant was visited on vacation or in a remote area, where the need to attain future entry is significantly minimized. Accordingly, these types of cases may be severely under-reported and therefore go without any formal legal consequence. Even if these cases are brought to court, the evidentiary issues may nonetheless preclude recovery.

* * *

In sum, while discrimination against Sikhs with turbans in America is nothing new, problems with Sikh turbans in various contexts have escalated rapidly since September 11, 2001. Because of the visual similarity between turbaned male Sikhs and the al Qaeda leadership, Sikhs appear to be singled out for hate crimes, racial profiling, and exclusion from public spaces, among other things, as a result of their appearance. Given the continuing nature of the backlash against Sikhs with turbans and the potential for residual hostility after 9/11 to increase with another terrorist attack, the need for legal protections for Sikhs with turbans has become exceedingly urgent, though the availability of legal remedies for Sikhs in various areas, including verbal harassment and most employment discrimination cases, appears limited. Sikh civil rights groups will need to continue to resolve cases through settlements, as the courts may not provide reliable protection where it is necessary due to the lack of evidentiary proof of animus or the narrow protections afforded by existing statutes and regulations.

The post-9/11 context has seen not only a direct attack on turbaned Sikhs, whether through violence or harassment in the public space or classrooms; the Sikh turban itself has been indirectly challenged as a sign of difference and extremism, and a failure to sufficiently assimilate. Accordingly, some Western nations, including those very nations for which Sikhs have laid down their lives, have called for Sikhs to surrender their turbans as a condition of working or going to school – a call that has been provoked by the 9/11 terrorist attacks. This more indirect attack is the focus of Part III.

Part III
Marginalization of the Sikh Turban

Sikh immigration to other parts of the world, particularly Europe and North America, has forced Sikhs to endure gawks, awkward questions, and negative attitudes directed at them. At the same time, native residents of those lands are compelled to make sense of these newcomers and to determine whether and to what extent their own customs, laws, and principles should absorb this new community and their turbans.

The attacks of 9/11 led not only to an increase in racial violence, harassment, and adverse employment actions against Sikhs with turbans; it has led to a more abstract questioning of the proper degree to which visible religious minority groups should be part of mainstream Western society. As two international legal scholars noted, in recent years in Europe and elsewhere: "Questions surrounding tolerance, multiculturalism, and the existence of 'parallel societies' have returned to the forefront of contemporary debates."[1]

Many Western democracies – some, like the United States, built on immigration – tout the separation of Church and State. They put an intrinsic value on the diversity of their citizens as a core principle of the nation. In the past, when it came to integration of non-Christian faiths and new immigrants, some emphasized the value of a "mosaic" or multicultural structure. In the aftermath of 9/11, however, Western nations have begun to change their model from integration to something more akin to a melting-pot of assimilation.

With terrorist activity occurring in the United States and throughout Europe, there is an increased call for visible minorities to integrate by way of adopting more of a national culture and secular appearance. More specifically, the pockets that are home to immigrants are no longer charming corners of America or Europe; they are considered by some to be isolated societies that serve as breeding grounds for "homegrown terrorists." Integration, it is argued, prevents a non-Western identity from festering and developing into "extremism."

Because many visible minorities are not only immigrants, but also profess a different faith from their largely Christian, Anglo-Saxon neighbors, the call for inclusion becomes multifaceted. On the one hand, these people are immigrants, and on the other, they are religious minorities. To be sure, certain immigrants are Christian, and sometimes natives do convert to minority faiths. When both identities are conflated in this way, however, visible religious minorities become the lightening rod for the reconsideration of immigration. Looking different –

1 See Helen Elizabeth Hartnell, "Belonging: Citizenship and Migration in the European Union and in Germany," 24 *Berkeley J. Int'l L.* 330, 339 (2006).

whether in appearance, skin color, or the way one worships – becomes a liability. These new citizens have become the scapegoats for everything ranging from terrorism and religious trends to the economic recession.

There are calls, therefore, for members of these self-segregating immigrant communities to sufficiently blend into mainstream society – to take on more of a Western identity and to consequently shed some of their cultural ties to their homeland and native beliefs. There is a mounting emphasis on the outer, superficial characteristics of citizens as being symbols of loyalty to a particular political regime, as though appearance is almost a proxy for allegiance. In short, there is growing discomfort not only with concentrated areas of immigrants, but also with the clothing of immigrants. Conspicuous articles of faith are manifestations of a "separate" people and are therefore under additional scrutiny.[2] These calls for assimilation represent a society in which religion is not viewed as an intrinsic part of the identity of an individual. While people are born with the color of their skin or their gender, religion is regarded as a choice or an interest that can be shed.

These Western attitudes are symptomatic of growing discomfort with orthodox Muslims and other visible minority groups. For example, a 2008 Pew Research Center report on European racial sentiments asserted that "[e]thnocentric attitudes are on the rise" across the Continent.[3] Indeed, the report found that negative feelings towards Muslims had risen since 2005,[4] and a number of recent court cases and incidents support the view that certain minorities have been faced with difficult decisions when trying to reconcile their cultural and religious traditions with contemporary Western societal norms. While the debate regarding whether conspicuous articles of faith are permissible in Western society is primarily focused on Muslims and Muslim religious clothing, Sikhs have often become collateral damage, sometimes without so much as a seat at the decision-making table.

Part III will offer a discussion of how the Sikh turban has been implicated by the growing Western interest in the assimilation of minority groups with visible identities. It will do so by surveying those countries in which this interest has been most manifest in the aftermath of the 9/11 terrorist attacks. As noted in Part I, it is the Sikh participation in military service that served as a major reason for the Sikh migration from South Asia to the West. Accordingly, this part will also note the initial treatment of Sikh soldiers by these countries, so as to provide a useful backdrop to the question of whether Sikhs' religious identity is welcome

2 See Mark Rice-Oxley, "Taking on the Veil: West Looks to Assimilation – From Britain to Australia, Unease Grows Over the Separateness of Many of the West's Muslim Communities," *Christian Science Monitor*, October 20, 2006.

3 Pew Global Attitudes Project, "Unfavorable Views of Jews and Muslims on the Increase in Europe," Pew Research Center, September 17, 2008, available at <http://pewglobal.org/reports/display.php?ReportID=262>.

4 Ibid.

in or compatible with particular Western societies. After all, participating in society as a law enforcement officer encourages not just civic engagement of new minorities, but builds their trust in government institutions.

We begin this discussion with a consideration of the nation where the assimilation question has been most fervent in recent years – France.

Chapter 14
France

Of all the European countries, the renewed debate regarding assimilation is most pronounced in France.[1] The French Republic was built on principles of separation of Church and State and religious secularism, known in French as *laïcité*.[2] *Laïcité* was at the base of the French Revolution, and has been a basic tenet of French government since the eighteenth century.[3] The separation of Church and State was formally declared in 1905, and the idea holds an almost militant sway over the French to this day.[4] Secularism implies not just neutrality, but is itself a government-mandated social norm,[5] leaving little space for identities that might clash with one's role as a politically French citizen. As one commentator noted: "The will of the state to avoid knowledge of citizens' spirituality is … a guarantee of liberty for the diverse religious confessions."[6] As another writer describes it: "The Republic has always recognized individuals, rather than groups: [a] French citizen owes allegiance to the nation, and has no officially sanctioned ethnic or religious identity"[7] – placing France squarely in the "melting pot" category of integrationists.

---

1 See U.S. Department of State, Bureau of Democracy, Human Rights, and Labor, *France: International Religious Freedom Report 2005*, November 8, 2005: "The [French] Constitution provides for freedom of religion, and the Government generally respects this right in practice; however, some religious groups remain concerned about legislation passed in 2001 and 2004, which provided for the dissolution of groups under certain circumstances and banned the wearing of conspicuous religious symbols by public school employees and students;" available at <http://www.state.gov/g/drl/rls/irf/2005/51552.htm>.

2 See Christine Langenfeld, "Germany: The Teacher Head Scarf Case," 3 *Int'l J. Const. L.* 86, 93 (January 2005), describing "the principle of laicism (*principe de laïcité*)" as a "core principle of the French Republic, that guarantees the peaceful and equal coexistence of different religions in French society" and which "demands a strict separation between the secular state and religion."

3 See ibid., noting that *laïcité* was "[m]entioned in France's 1789 Declaration of Human Rights."

4 See ibid.: "this principle was legally introduced in 1905 as the expression of a long tradition of separation of church and state and is now enshrined in Article 1 of the French Constitution."

5 Henri Astier, "The Deep Roots of French Secularism," *BBC News*, December 18, 2003, available at <http://news.bbc.co.uk/1/hi/world/europe/3325285.stm>.

6 Jacques Robert, "Religious Liberty and French Secularism," 2003 *BYU L. Rev.* 637, 643 (2003).

7 Ibid.

Sikhs have deep roots with the French that were first established when the Sikh Empire was still in bloom. Following Napoleon's final defeat at Waterloo in 1815, the Sikh ruler Maharaja Ranjit Singh welcomed a number of former French officers and generals into his employ.[8] These military leaders – Generals Jean-François Allard and Jean-Baptiste Ventura being the most prominent – upgraded the artillery and discipline of the Sikh army to make it one of the most formidable forces in the world.[9] At one point early in the nineteenth century, the Maharaja built a foundry and employed a Frenchman who made high-quality rifles for the Sikh soldiers.[10] In these ways, France contributed significantly to the modernization of the Sikh military in the days of Ranjit Singh and thereafter.

The military contributions of these few French individuals were repaid nearly one hundred years later when tens of thousands of Sikhs met their deaths in combat while defending French soil. At the outset of World War I, there were 35,000 Sikh soldiers enlisted in the British army, and that number had tripled by the time the war came to an end.[11] Sikh regiments were sent to the front lines in France and Belgium primarily, and they engaged in battles in Ypres, Neuve Chapelle, Festubert, La Bassée, Loos, Givenchy, and the Somme. In every theater of battle in which Sikh soldiers fought, one aspect was consistent: whether they were dislodging the Germans from their trenches at the front or defending Paris from German advances, the Sikh troops consistently refused to remove their turbans in favor of the standard-issue steel helmets. Instead, they chose to sign away the pensions their families would be entitled to should they fall in battle. In 1927, France dedicated a monument to the sacrifice of Indian – largely Sikh – soldiers at the site of the Neuve Chapelle battle, where three Sikh regiments fought valiantly and ultimately lost three-fifths of their personnel. Overall, 138,000 Sikhs fought to stop German advances in France and Belgium during World War I. In World War II, Sikh soldiers again turned out *en masse*, with a number of them once again fighting to protect French soil. As before, they fought proudly wearing their turbans. A total of 83,000 Sikhs lost their lives during both world wars, and over 100,000 were injured.

Despite these contributions to French freedom, the French attitude towards immigrant communities came down against Sikhs and their turbans after 9/11. In February 2004, French lawmakers passed a law prohibiting public school students from wearing articles of faith, including signs or clothes, "that exhibit

8 Charles Lowe, *Battles of the Nineteenth Century* (London: Cassell, 1897), p. 638.

9 Ibid.

10 Patrick Tuck, *Warfare, Expansion and Resistance* (London: Routledge, 1998), p. 153.

11 Amandeep Singh Madra and Parmjit Singh, *Warrior Saints: Three Centuries of the Sikh Military Tradition* (London: I.B. Tauris, 1999), p. 110.

conspicuously a religious affiliation."[12] The French aimed the law against those religious minorities who are most "visible" among them – those whose appearance itself manifests an alternative "political" identity.[13] The purpose of the ban was ostensibly to discourage the growth of Islamic fundamentalism and to promote secularism.[14] Although passed explicitly to prevent the wearing of headscarves by young Muslim women, the ban also prohibits Jewish skullcaps, "large" Christian crosses, and the Sikh turban in public schools.[15]

French Prime Minister Jean-Pierre Raffarin, commenting on the law, noted: "Today, all the great religions in the history of France have adapted themselves to [the principle of secularism] .... For the most recently arrived ... secularism

---

12 Law No. 2004-228 of March 15, 2004, *Journal Officiel de la République Française* (JO; Official Gazette of France) 5190, March 17, 2004.

13 Many of the French arguments for the law have been on the grounds that the presence of headscarves and yarmulkes in schools politicizes the school atmosphere and leads to political incidents between students. See Statement by M. Jean-Pierre Raffarin, Prime Minister of France, February 4, 2003, available at <http://www.ambafrance-au.org/france_australie/spip.php?article481>, noting in a speech entitled "Bill on the Application of the Principle of Secularity (Laïcité) in State Schools" that: "It has to be recognized that certain religious signs, among them the Islamic veil, are now becoming more frequently seen in our schools. They are in fact taking on a political meaning and can no longer be considered simply personal signs of religious affiliation."; see also *Stasi Commission Report*, <http://www.Assemblee-nationale.fr/12/dossiers/laicite.asp>; Sikh Coalition, "Chirac Endorsement – English Translation," December 17, 2003, <http://www.sikhcoalition.org/frenchban_chiracspeech.asp>; Caroline Wyatt, "French headscarf ban opens rift," *BBC News*, February 11, 2004, <http://newsvote.bbc.co.uk/mpapps/pagetools/print/news.bbc.co.uk/2/hi/europe/3478895.stm>.

14 See William J. Kole, "French Rue Religious Symbol Ban," Associated Press, February 15, 2004, describing the ban as "France's response to what many perceive as a rise in Muslim fundamentalism"; Christopher D. Belelieu, "The Headscarf as a Symbolic Enemy of the European Court of Human Rights' Democratic Jurisprudence: Viewing Islam through a European Legal Prism in Light of the Sahin Judgment," 12 *Colum. J. Eur. L.* 573 (2006), commenting on the "simplification of the legal debate through a representation of the headscarf as a symbol of Islamic fundamentalism"; Stefanie Walterick, "The Prohibition of Muslim Headscarves from French Public School and Controversies Surrounding the Hijab in the Western World," 20 *Temp. Int'l & Comp. L. J.* 251, 254 (2006): "While the new law reflects France's particular tradition of laïcité, the law can also be seen as a backlash against France's growing Muslim minority population."

15 See Walterick, "The Prohibition of Muslim Headscarves from French Public School:" "Although the new law contains neutral language that prohibits all religious garb, including large Christian crosses, Jewish yarmulkes, and Sikh turbans, the law was enacted with the specific intent to eliminate the Muslim hijab, or headscarf, from French public school classrooms."

is a chance, the chance to be a religion of France."[16] Secularism under this view implies not just neutrality, but is itself the "State religion" of sorts.[17]

Unsurprisingly, the ban on conspicuous articles of faith in public schools upset minority groups whose religious identities were challenged.[18] They are now required to choose between observing their faith and obtaining an education.[19] For example, Sikh boys with turbans are uniformly forbidden to enroll in public schools.[20] Accordingly, a number of students from these minority communities have been forced to find alternative forms of basic education, such as private or religious schooling, or home-schooling.[21] These individuals who rejected the ostensible call to shed religious attire believed that each culture adds to the identity of a nation by being able to express its own diverse characteristics, including, but not limited to, turbans.[22] As prominent Sikh scholar I.J. Singh points out: "the only

16 French Prime Minister Jean-Pierre Raffarin, quoted in Elaine Sciolino, "Debate Begins in France on Religion in the Schools," *New York Times*, February 4, 2004, available at <http://query.nytimes.com/gst/fullpage.html?res=9D0CE2DB153BF937A35751C0A9629C8B63&n=Top/Reference/Times%20Topics/Subjects/C/Church-State%20Relations>.

17 Henri Astier, "The Deep Roots of French Secularism," *BBC News*, December 18, 2003, available at <http://news.bbc.co.uk/1/hi/world/europe/3325285.stm>.

18 For example, demonstrations were held in response to the ban. See, for example, Delfin Vigil, "Worldwide Protests over Ban on Religious Symbols: French Proposal Would Apply to all its Public Schools," *San Francisco Chronicle*, January 18, 2004, available at <http://www.sfgate.com/cgi-bin/article.cgi?f=/c/a/2004/01/18/MNGCP4CJUT1.DTL>.

19 In the words of one 17-year-old Sikh student: "I'm 100 percent French, I speak French, I was born here." He continued: "But it's impossible for me to take off my turban. If they force me, I'll have to drop out, and never be able to do anything except a job that no one else wants"; Elaine Sciolino, "Bobigny Journal; French Sikhs Defend their Turbans and Find their Voice," *New York Times*, January 12, 2004, available at <http://query.nytimes.com/gst/fullpage.html?res=9E05EFDE1530F931A25752C0A9629C8B63&n=Top/Reference/Times%20Topics/Subjects/S/Sikhs%20(Sect)>.

20 Although the ban officially affects only primary and secondary education (elementary through high school), there have been reports that universities too are refusing to accept Sikh men with turbans. Karamvir Singh, a 19-year-old French-Sikh and French citizen, was rejected from five French universities in October 2003 in anticipation of the ban. He was told that they were willing to accept him, if he took off his turban. United Sikhs, "Right to Turban Petition," January 3, 2004, available at <http://www.unitedsikhs.org/us-eu/petitions/petition_eng.htm>.

21 See, for example, Emma Jane Kirby, "Sikh School Sidesteps French Ban," *BBC News*, September 15, 2007, available at <http://news.bbc.co.uk/1/low/world/europe/6996198.stm>.

22 See Robin Cook, "France Need Not Fear Schoolgirls in Headscarves," *The Independent*, December 19, 2003, arguing that the British form of multiculturalism has "judged that we are more likely to reduce friction and to promote harmony if we respect religious and cultural diversity and tolerate rather than suppress its outward expressions. While France has acted to ban headscarves, we adapted our law to permit Sikhs to wear

desirable integration for a small minority such as ours lies in a mosaic where our identity is sacrosanct."[23]

The Sikh perspective was completely overlooked in the lead-up to the French legislation.[24] When initially faced with Sikh objections after the bill's passage, one Ministry of Education official replied: "What? There are Sikhs in France? I know nothing about the Sikh problem. Are there many Sikhs in France?"[25] This is despite the fact that approximately 5,000–7,000 Sikhs live in France,[26] far more than the 1,200 veiled Muslim schoolgirls in the country.[27] Nevertheless, the Stasi Commission, appointed to investigate the possible repercussions of such a law, did not include even one Sikh in the more than 200 interviews it conducted.

In 2004, French Sikhs responded by seeking an exemption from the ban as applied, lobbying international support from Sikhs throughout the diaspora as well as the Indian government. Sikh groups in the UK and the U.S. argued their position through signing petitions, writing letters to the French president, marching in protests, and seeking comments from their own governments among other things. Their arguments included the following:

1. Sikhs were left out of the decision-making process, and repercussions on their community were ignored.
2. The Sikh turban is an article of cultural, ethnic, and social identity, and not purely religious. It should therefore not fall under the definition of "religious symbols" under the ban.
3. The rationale for excluding other articles of faith is that the mere wearing of them is in and of itself an act of proselytism that would undermine French principles of *laïcité*. Given that Sikhs do not believe in proselytism, however, their articles of faith should not be judged by the same standards.
4. Sikhs fought and died in France during World War I as soldiers in the British Army. French Sikhs are saying, "We fought for their freedom. Now they should respect ours."
5. Sikhs are willing to ensure that their turbans match the school colors and abide by school requirements for their appearance. However, any

their turbans when others may be required to wear helmets. … Our lives are enriched by the consequent diversity of cultures, heritage and, most popularly, cuisine."

23 I.J. Singh, *Sikhs and Sikhism: A View With a Bias* (Geulph, Ontario: The Centennial Foundation, 1998), p. 112.

24 "UK Sikhs Join 'Headscarf' Protest," *BBC News*, February 21, 2004, available at <http://news.bbc.co.uk/2/hi/uk_news/3508677.stm>.

25 Sciolino, "Bobigny Journal; French Sikhs Defend their Turbans and Find their Voice."

26 "French Sikhs Lambast School Ban," *BBC News*, September 7, 2004, available at <http://news.bbc.co.uk/2/hi/europe/3635768.stm>.

27 Elizabeth C. Jones, "Muslim Girls Unveil Their Fears," *BBC News*, March 28, 2005, available at <http://news.bbc.co.uk/2/hi/programmes/this_world/4352171.stm>.

> suggestion that they wear "transparent nets to cover their hair" would be considered "insulting."

In the four years since the passage of the law, Sikhs have used these arguments to appeal the decision to various domestic and international courts. Protests from Sikhs notwithstanding, France's highest administrative body, the Council of State, upheld the ban as it applied to Sikhs.[28] According to reports of the ruling, the Council of State concluded that the ban was "justified on the grounds of public security," an apparent allusion to the concern regarding the spread of religious fundamentalism, "and was not a restriction on freedom of faith."[29]

Thereafter, France's ban on the turban spread from public school to all forms of State-issued identification cards. For example, Shingara Mann Singh, a Parisian Sikh, had been a citizen of France for nearly fifteen years when the government refused to issue him a replacement passport in 2005. In 2008, the European Court of Human Rights dismissed a case pertaining to the turban in schools. Local Sikhs took both matters to the United Nations Human Rights Committee in 2008, where the case continues to date.

In France today, regulations governing the public sphere combine with the small size of the Sikh population to make a conspicuous and measurable Sikh presence virtually impossible in state institutions. The French concept of *laïcité* – a purely secular public sector – extends over all areas of civil service, from employees in public hospitals to those in the judiciary. Thus the same principle that now keeps turbaned Sikhs from enrolling in public schools also precludes them from serving as police officers or in other law enforcement capacities. The small Sikh population in France, despite the military ties of recent history, has little voice in the arenas of French public and military policy, often having to attempt an appeal either to the emotions of their French neighbors or to the international community, Sikhs and non-Sikhs alike, to raise their political capital and fight this injustice to their identity.[30] They are being slowly edged out of all facets of French society.

28 "French Sikhs Appeal On Turban Ban," *BBC News*, March 7, 2006, available at <http://news.bbc.co.uk/2/hi/europe/4782420.stm>.

29 Ibid.

30 See, for example, Tom Heneghan, "Sikhs Seek Exemption From Ban In France," *Washington Post*, January 3, 2004: "France's tiny Sikh community is seeking help from India's prime minister to have their traditional turbans exempted from a planned French law to ban Muslim headscarves and other religious symbols from schools."

Chapter 15
Britain

Sikhs have constituted a large ethnic minority in the British population and its armed forces since Britain's imperial era. First as citizens of the Commonwealth and servicemen from the British military, then as British citizens forced out by new African governments in Kenya, Uganda, and Tanzania after independence, and finally as enterprising immigrants from India and other countries around the world, Sikhs have been arriving and settling in the United Kingdom since the mid-19th century.

Today there are over 400,000 Sikhs living in the UK. They are active members of the community in all walks of life, including the armed forces and police departments, service and contracting sectors, and as entrepreneurs. Given the larger proportion of Sikhs in its population, as well as the long history of Sikh interaction with the British through its Empire, the UK has created a number of accommodations that make it easier for Sikhs to maintain the basic tenets of their religious faith – and especially the turban – while still manifesting their British identity.

Yet, in the new post-9/11 era, the row over integration and articles of faith raging in Europe has become ever more fervent across the English Channel in the UK.

The most significant and unusual protection for British Sikhs is their inclusion as a separate racial group for purposes of the Race Relations Act of 1976. For most of its history, the UK did not have a specific law proscribing discrimination on the basis of religion in any of its territories.[1] Thus, protections for religious minorities were rare, and generally required laborious interpretation of existing laws not passed for that purpose.[2] Sikhs and Jews, however, were granted special protection early on in UK civil rights history – they were protected as a race, rather than a religion – under the 1976 Race Relations Act. The Race Relations Act protects any "group of persons defined by reference to color, race, nationality or ethnic or national origins"[3] against both direct and indirect discrimination on racial grounds. The Act protects against discrimination by employers or public authorities in three

1 With the exception of Northern Ireland, which had such a law in place prior to 1998.

2 One author has even remarked: "But for the decision of the House of Lords in *Mandla v. Lee*, it is difficult to see how discrimination on religious beliefs could have been protected"; Vic Craig, "Discrimination: From the Particular to the General," *Emp. L. B.* 41, 2–5 (February 2001).

3 1976 Race Relations Act § 3(1).

major fields – education,[4] employment,[5] and the provision of goods, facilities, services, and premises,[6] although the recovery of damages is a rare remedy. A series of amendments to the Act in 2000 extended it to cover discrimination by the police and any other public authority.[7] Exceptions were originally granted to (among others) charities, seamen being recruited abroad, partnerships, acts done to safeguard national security, and employers discriminating on the basis of "genuine occupational qualifications", but the majority of these have been removed over time. The 2000 Amendments also contain a provision stating that all public employees have a positive duty to promote racial equality and tolerance, and can be punished for failure to fulfill this duty. With these protections, the Race Relations Act provides a number of broad protections for Sikhs and Jews, who have both been declared "racial groups" for the purposes of this legislation.

A 1983 case, Mandla *(Sewa Singh) v. Dowell Lee*,[8] applied the 1976 Race Relations Act directly to the protection of the Sikh turban. In that case, a father and son brought suit against a private school that would not permit the son to enroll in the school with long hair and a turban. Lord Fraser in this landmark case declared that the word 'race' in the Race Relations Act cannot have been intended only in a biological sense, and must be given a broad definition in the context of interpreting the Act. He identified a number of conditions that might constitute an ethnic group, including a long shared history, a cultural tradition of its own, common geography or descent, a common language (not necessarily peculiar to that group), a common literature, a common religion, and being a minority or dominating ethnic group. The case had two-fold significance for the Sikhs. One was to identify them as a distinct ethnic group, based on their common descendents from the Punjab, their shared history, language, religion, and culture, and their once having been the rulers of Punjab. The other was to clearly establish that, although Sikhs literally "can comply" with any rule if they're willing to give up their culture, this was not the purpose of the legislation. Lord Fraser held that "ethnic" to some extent does imply that a characteristic is "unalterable" and therefore that the school's behavior was in violation of the Race Relations Act. This ruling cemented the place of the Sikh turban as a protected and unalterable part of the ethnic Sikh identity in British law.

The British government has also explicitly shown support for Sikh turbans by affording them a right not available in other Western countries – the right to refuse to wear hard hats or helmets where they would otherwise be required.[9] Three separate pieces of legislation exempt Sikhs from hard hat or helmet requirements in spite of the public safety and health issues associated with this. These include

4 Ibid., § 17.
5 Ibid., §§ 4–15.
6 Ibid., § 20.
7 Race Relations Amendments (2000), §§ 1 and 4.
8 House of Lords, [1983].2 A.C. 548.
9 Craig (2001), 4.

laws that allow Sikhs to wear turbans while riding a motorcycle or horse, and in place of helmets on construction sites. A more recent piece of legislation exempting Sikhs from the same requirements holds that any provision requiring a Sikh to wear a helmet shall be "taken to be one which cannot be shown to be a proportionate means of achieving a legitimate aim."[10] This reinforces that not only can a British employer exempt a Sikh employee from this requirement, but it is required that he does.

Whereas France benefited from Sikh military prowess in the past and has now turned its back on turbaned Sikhs in various spheres of public life, Britain's general discomfort with visible minority groups has largely escaped Sikhs in the particular context of military or police service. The British recognized Sikh religious rights "even before a Sikh was legally considered the equal of an Englishman."[11] Sikhs have been active in the British military throughout its imperial conquests, often appearing in full uniform, including a turban and beard, on battlefields around the world. When the British Indian army first began to recruit Sikhs from Punjab, it insisted that Sikhs maintain a turban as part of their uniform at all times (including in battle). Each regiment enforced rules about the color, shape, and size of turban to be worn as part of the uniform dress code. A British Lieutenant who fought with the Sikh regiment in World War I – where Sikhs comprised one-third of the British Indian army[12] – recognized that if the British had even suggested that the Sikhs remove their turbans, they would have invited mutiny among some of their best soldiers. He also offered that, as far as he knew, no men in the regiment had died of bullet injuries to the head, although some have been saved by the bullet getting lodged in the turban instead.[13] In the Britain–Afghanistan War, Sikhs fighting for the British were asked to don tin helmets in place of their turbans while in battle. The Sikhs refused on the grounds of their religious beliefs, and fearing widespread mutiny, the British withdrew the requirement after having each soldier sign off on the equivalent of a current-day liability waiver.[14] After that, throughout the Sikh involvement in the colonial armed forces, they were never required to remove their turbans. Around the same time, Sikhs were also active in police forces throughout the British Empire – from Shanghai to Trinidad.

Although the British military's policies have seen some changes over time, the overall attitude has remained largely tolerant and accommodating as far as Sikh turbans are concerned. In the late part of the twentieth century, the British army adopted an informal rule allowing Sikh men to enlist and train in their ranks with

10 UK SI 2003/1660 Pt. IV Reg. 26.

11 Amarsect S. Bhachu, "A Shield for Swords," 34 *Am. Crim. L. Rev.* (1996), at 218.

12 Khushwant Singh and Raghu Rai, *The Sikhs* (New Delhi: Roli Books, 2004), p. 27.

13 Statements of Lt. General Sir Reginald Arthur Savory, as quoted in Trilochan Singh, *The Turban and the Sword of the Sikhs: Essence of Sikhism* (Amritsar: B. Chattar Singh Jiwan Singh, 1997), p. 306.

14 This story is partially recounted in ibid., p. 303.

their turbans as part of the uniform. Sikhs, however, are not permitted to enter combat with anything but a combat hat. It was justified by non-Sikh officers as "You can wear your five Ks … during training but in battle if I'm wearing a beret, you wear your turban."[15] This created tension between the Sikh community and the British, with some Sikh groups insisting on a boycott of the armed forces, and a trip to Delhi by the Queen was marred by questions and protests on the issue. Still, in 2009, the first two Sikh military officers were appointed to guard the Queen in a very public space – in front of Buckingham Palace.

Outside of the military context, Britain's leadership, like many of its European neighbors, has begun to express severe disapproval of its immigrant minorities. After 9/11, and especially after the London bombings of July 7, 2005, concerns regarding immigrant communities came to the forefront of British politics. Perhaps the most vocal stance against the minority groups came from the Prime Minister of the time Tony Blair's Foreign Secretary, Jack Straw, in response to the case of a young Muslim woman.

Twenty-three-year-old Aishah Azmi was a teaching assistant at a junior school in Dewsbury, West Yorkshire.[16] Azmi, who is Muslim, had filed claims of discrimination and harassment after being suspended from her position for refusing to remove her veil.[17] The Employment Appeals Tribunal subsequently denied her claims.[18] Moreover, on March 22, 2006, the House of Lords ruled that a Muslim girl's "right to manifest her belief in practice or observance" was not infringed when her high school excluded her for wearing a *jilbab* (a long, shapeless black gown), instead of the school's uniform.[19] The Lords reasoned, in part, that "there were three schools in the area at which the wearing of the *jilbab* was permitted …. There is, however, no evidence to show that there was any real difficulty in her attending one or other of these schools."[20]

Faced with this reality, Straw claimed that Muslim attire that covers women from head to toe, exposing only the eyes, hinders communication: "Communication requires that both sides see each other's face …. You not only hear what people say, but you also see what they mean."[21] Moreover, he stated that the Muslim veil

15 Amardeep Bassey, "Truth About Racism in the Army," *Sunday Mercury*, May 20, 2001, p. 16.

16 "Muslim Teacher Loses Veil Appeal," *Times Online*, March 30, 2007, available at <http://business.timesonline.co.uk/tol/business/law/article1593055.ece>.

17 Ibid.

18 Ibid.

19 *R. v. Headteacher and Governors of Denbigh High School* (2006) UKHL 15, available at <http://www.publications.parliament.uk/pa/ld200506/ldjudgmt/jd060322/begum-4.htm>.

20 Ibid.

21 Fareena Alam, "Beyond the Veil," *Newsweek*, November 27, 2006, available at <http://www.msnbc.msn.com/id/15789437/site/newsweek/>, noting also that "British Muslims immediately wondered how Straw's former cabinet colleague, ex-Home Secretary David Blunkett – blind since birth – ever did his job."

"separates people," suggesting that its use contributes to the erosion of British society.[22] He added:

> Simply breathing the same air as other members of society isn't integration. Britishness is thus an identity available to Anglicans, Catholics, Jews, Muslims, Sikhs, Hindus and those of other religions and none, and a central element of that identity is the principle that everyone has the freedom to practice their faith not as a matter of tolerance but of right.[23]

To wear a headscarf, therefore, is to refuse to adopt British identity – a decision Straw does not find acceptable. Following Foreign Secretary Straw's foray into the subject, Blair affirmed Straw's view that the veil is a "mark of separation" that makes "people from outside the community feel uncomfortable."[24]

David Davis, the Conservative Shadow Home Secretary at the time, observed that Straw had "touched on … the fundamental issue of whether, in Britain, we are developing a divided society."[25] He weighed in further by warning British Muslim leaders they were "risking voluntary apartheid" by refusing to compromise on certain religious traditions, also raising the question of whether Britain should continue to "allow the division of communities that will corrode our society."[26]

Sikhs have been subsumed under the larger national discomfort with visible Muslim attire, and as such have had to reaffirm their own unique space in the British populace. Sikhs began wearing shirts and logos with the phrase, "Don't Freak, I'm a Sikh," in order to identify themselves as Sikhs and arguably (and controversially) set themselves apart from Britain's multicultural makeup.

Notwithstanding any general animus towards visible immigrant communities in Britain, the British army continued to aggressively target people from ethnic communities, and especially males of South Asian descent, for recruitment into the armed forces. At present, Sikhs in particular are being actively recruited by the British forces and joining the ranks with their fellow citizens of other faiths. There has been some talk of setting up a Sikh regiment in the British army for the first time since India's independence. Sikhs are actively recruited by police forces throughout the country, and adopt turban styles in keeping with their uniform. In the Metropolitan Police, for example, they wear a black turban with

---

22 "Muslims Must Feel British – Straw," *BBC News*, November 2, 2006, available at <http://news.bbc.co.uk/2/hi/uk_news/politics/6110798.stm>.

23 Ibid.

24 Ibid.

25 "Veil Teacher 'Should Be Sacked,'" *BBC News*, October 15, 2006, available at <http://news.bbc.co.uk/2/hi/uk_news/england/bradford/6050392.stm>.

26 Tania Branigan and Vikram Dodd, "Muslim Leaders 'Risking Voluntary Apartheid' as Veil Row Escalates," *Guardian*, October 16, 2006, available at <http://www.guardian.co.uk/uk/2006/oct/16/religion.immigrationpolicy>.

a black-and-white checkered band around it to match any other police officer's hat.[27]

On the whole, while British attitudes, embodied by their leaders, may have been more hostile with respect to Muslims and those appearing to be Muslim, those negative thoughts have not reached Sikhs in respect of their service in British security or police forces. The longstanding Sikh military tradition in Britain has been largely immune from the growing disenchantment with easily identifiable minority communities.

27 To view this and other images of Sikh men in uniform with turbans, see <http://www.sikhpride.com>.

Chapter 16
Ireland

Ironically, just to the west of the UK, turbaned Sikhs in the military and police setting have fared far differently. Ireland, lacking the history and tradition of Great Britain with turbaned Sikhs, has taken a much harder stance on integrating Sikhs into its police force, the An Garda Síochána, or the Garda Reserve. Immigrants in the police force in Ireland are still a relatively new idea in that country. Recently, a Sikh member of the Garda was not allowed to wear his turban while on duty because it violated the uniform protocol. He had successfully completed three of his training stages while still allowed to wear his turban.[1] However, when he moved on to the fourth stage – which involved interaction with the public – he was no longer allowed to wear his turban. Reportedly, the man in question was a technology professional who joined the police force out of a sense of civic duty.[2]

The Irish Government has been supportive of the ban. Government officials have justified their stance by calling for minorities to visibly integrate into Ireland's largely white, Catholic population and expressing a belief in maintaining "impartiality" among religions, although no similar impartiality concern has been raised with regards to either gender or race, the other intrinsic parts of citizens' identities. Conor Lenihan, an official responsible for the country's integration policy, supported the Garda Síochána ruling, saying immigrants to Ireland must accept Irish culture, while at the same time he proclaimed that the civil service should actively recruit immigrants.[3] He added: "If we are to take integration seriously, people who come here must understand our way of doing things. When the President and Ministers travel to the middle-east, they accept cultural requirements of the country and the culture they are operating in. It is a vice versa situation with regard to Ireland."[4]

Many in Ireland agree with Minister Lenihan's view. In an opinion article in an Irish newspaper, one author, who is an Irish citizen living in the Middle East, sides with the ban.[5] The author, like Minister Lenihan, compares Ireland's ban on

---

1 "Irish Police to Review Turban Ban," *BBC News*, August 28, 2007, available at <http://news.bbc.co.uk/1/hi/world/europe/6966535.stm>.

2 Ibid.

3 See Fionnan Sheahan, "Sikh Member of the Reserve is Banned from Wearing Turban," *Independent.ie*, July 7, 2008, available at <http://www.independent.ie/national-news/sikh-member-of-the-reserve-is-banned-from-wearing-turban-1057548.html>.

4 Ibid.

5 Simon Lewis, "The Big Integration Question: Turban or Not Turban?," *Independent.ie*, August 21, 2007, available at <http://www.independent.ie/opinion/letters/the-big-

the Sikh turban with the "rules" he must live by in the Middle East: "My point is that the onus is on me to adapt to the society in which I find myself living, it is not up to that society to adapt to me."[6]

Furthermore, the Garda claims it is being impartial, not racist, by upholding the ban. Superintendent Kevin Donohoe said the police were not placing one religious belief over another, and that An Garda Síochána had an "effective intercultural policy;"[7] or "There is no doubt that the Garda uniform and dress standards present unique issues in accommodating cultural diversity."[8] He later said:

> These are challenges faced by all facets of Irish society as diversity and integration more and more become real issues. The Garda Síochána has, historically, been seen as providing an impartial police service, policing all sections of society equally. Accommodating variations to our standard uniform and dress, including those with religious symbolism, may well affect that traditional stance and give an image of An Garda Síochána which the [Police] Commissioner feels the public would not want."[9]

The Garda's policy has drawn some heated criticism by some in the government, members of the public and Sikh groups. Government official Teachta Dála (TD) Ciaran Cuffe, a member of the lower chamber in Parliament, has asked the Garda Commissioner Noel Conroy to lift the ban, stating: "In my opinion, the wearing of a turban would in no way impinge upon the operational effectiveness of a member of the force," and he also cited the use of the turban on other police forces worldwide as one of the reasons to reverse the decision.[10]

Likewise, an author of another opinion article takes the same approach and rejects the ban. The author condemns the logic of comparing this ban to the Middle East because Ireland is not, unlike many Middle Eastern countries, governed by any one religious belief or faction. Furthermore, the author calls the ban extremely racist, and rhetorically asks when in Irish culture did it forbid wearing religious insignia? The answer – never. Moreover, a letter which was apparently in the hands of that author called the turban the source of the London bombings. The author there says this shows Ireland's ignorance of other, non-Christian, religions which should be the real source of concern.[11] Sikh groups have also condemned the ban.

---

integration-question-turban-or-not-turban-1062964.html>.

6 Ibid.

7 See "Turban Ban Not Racist, Insist Gardaí," *Evening Echo*, August 23, 2007, available at <http://www.breakingnews.ie/ireland/turban-ban-not-racist-insist-gardai-324795.html>.

8 Ibid.

9 Ibid.

10 Deborah McAleese, "No Turban Ban For Sikh Psni Officers," *Belfast Telegraph*, August 23, 2007, available at <http://www.belfasttelegraph.co.uk/news/local-national/no-turban-ban-for-sikh-psni-officers-13469339.html>.

11 See Lewis, "The Big Integration Question."

The Metropolitan Sikh Association stated: "The question is not one of cultural integration, rather of religious rights and freedom to practice an individual's faith, regardless of jurisdiction."[12]

In 2007, the Irish Police Commissioner agreed to meet with prominent Sikhs to discuss the ban. However, the police say that if the ban was reversed, it would not be seen as impartial. A police spokesman told *BBC News* that they were looking into the issue of all religious insignia, including Christian crosses, on their uniforms. Yet Harpreet Singh, President of the Irish Sikh Council, stated that prohibiting turbans in the police force would effectually be "asking the whole Sikh community to stay out of the police force" because Sikhs are not religiously permitted to take off their turbans or cut their hair.[13] Harpreet Singh and the Irish Sikh Council have decided, however, not to press legal charges against the Garda. Instead, they hope to resolve the matter amicably with the Police Commission.

Given the lack of history of integrating Sikhs or other minorities into its civil service ranks, the current policy of Ireland is unsurprising. Furthermore, at present it is apparent there is general ignorance of Sikhism regarding the turban's religious significance. What the Integration Minister fails to recognize is that Sikhs are citizens of Ireland, not visitors to a foreign land; nor is Ireland governed, unlike some Middle Eastern countries, by a theocracy which regulates visible symbols of faith. Moreover, the entire integration discussion, according to Lenihan, places the focus on Sikh integration into Ireland, and not any accommodations Ireland can make for its religious minorities. By not making accommodations, the Irish government has unwittingly forced Sikhs to choose between their religion and the ability to work in certain sectors, and including and especially the government police.

---

12 "Anger at Irish Police Turban Ban," *BBC News*, August 22, 2007, available at <http://news.bbc.co.uk/2/hi/uk_news/northern_ireland/6957844.stm>.

13 "Irish Police to Review Turban Ban," *BBC News*, August 28, 2007, available at <http://news.bbc.co.uk/2/hi/europe/6966535.stm>.

Chapter 17
Other Western Nations

Sikhs may be found in various parts of the world, and as such they are amenable to the global reconsideration of the assimilation/integration debate that was provoked by 9/11. This chapter looks at how some of the relatively smaller players on the world stage have responded. Generally, it appears that several Western nations have empathized with the French position, and accordingly have threatened the wearing of religious articles of faith.

France's actions, which were examined at the outset of this part, have set an example for advancing a largely integrationist agenda in Europe. For example, Belgium imposed a similar ban in 2005, specifically disallowing Sikh turbans in public educational institutions.[1]

In the lead-up to Spain's 2008 general election, the primary opposition party proposed a French-style ban on Islamic headscarves in public schools and vowed to "require immigrants to sign a legally binding document obliging them to learn Spanish and observe Spanish social customs … in exchange for receiving the same rights as Spanish citizens."[2] This may not be as surprising, given the spectre raised by the Madrid train bombings in 2004.

The Netherlands is contemplating "a total ban on the wearing of burqas and other Muslim face veils in public, justifying the move on security grounds."[3] While Dutch lawmakers are "aware of the changes in Dutch society" and taking action to combat racism, according to a report published in December 2008 by the European Commission against Racism and Intolerance (ECRI), there has also been a lamentable deterioration in "the tone of Dutch political and public debate around integration and other issues relevant to ethnic minorities" since 2000.[4]

Germany finds itself in a similar situation, as it contends with the extent to which visibly identifiable immigrant groups may appropriately live in its society:

---

1 "Belgium Bans Turban in Schools," *The Tribune*, September 5, 2005, available at <http://www.tribuneindia.com/2005/20050905/punjab1.htm#10>.

2 "Spain's Conservatives Eye Headscarf Ban," Associated Press, February 8, 2008, available at <http://www.msnbc.msn.com/id/23072893/>.

3 Alexandra Hudson, "Dutch to Ban Wearing of Muslim Burqa in Public," *Reuters*, November 17, 2006 available at <http://www.reuters.com/article/topNews/idU.S.L17206206200611l7>.

4 European Commission against Racism and Intolerance (ECRI), Third Report on the Netherlands, Council of Europe, February 12, 2008.

> Amid heightened fears that wearing a veil is a symbol of fundamentalist Islam, the headscarf issue on another level also reflects sensitive topics such as the modern secular identities of European states, the compatibility of Islam with largely Christian Europe, the acceptance of immigrants, integration and religious rights.[5]

Accordingly, now half of Germany's states prohibit Muslim schoolteachers from wearing headscarves.[6] In 2007, the prohibition was upheld against a challenge in a Bavarian court, where the salient law requires teachers to dress according to "Western Christian" values.[7] In addition, a school in Berlin has not allowed "370 pupils … to speak in their native tongue" even though "[n]inety percent of the school's students have foreign-born parents … and each class features between eight and ten different languages."[8] The school's headmaster explained: "We have introduced this ban to enable our students to take part in German society through speaking and understanding the language properly."[9]

In 2007, Italy instituted a Charter of Values, Citizenship and Immigration in response to the "growing debate in Europe over integration standards for Muslim minorities."[10] The charter is a non-binding document asserting that immigrants should leave behind certain non-Italian practices, learn and speak the Italian language, and know "the essential elements of the national history and culture."[11]

To be sure, not all Western nations have responded to the terrorist activity and subsequent concern for the spread of fundamentalist Islam by clamping down on visible religious identities. For example, in 2005, the Australian government rejected a proposal "to ban Muslim girls from wearing traditional headscarves in state schools."[12] Indeed, an official speaking in opposition to the proposal said: "We're at war with terror, not young girls wearing scarves or crucifixes or skull

5 "German State Bans Hijab-clad Teachers," *Judeoscope*, June 1, 2006, noting that the hijab "has been the subject of growing debate in several parts of Europe for more than a decade. But it especially intensified following the Sept. 11 terrorist attacks in New York and Washington."

6 Ibid.

7 PR-Inside, "Court Upholds German State's Ban on Teachers Wearing Head Scarves," Associated Press, June 5, 2007, available at <http://www.pr-inside.com/court-upholds-german-state-s-ban-on-r144598.htm>.

8 Stefan Nicola, "German School Bans Foreign Languages," United Press International, January 26, 2006, available at <http://www.upi.com/Security_Industry/2006/01/26/German-school-bans-foreign-languages/UPI-78121138301029/>.

9 Ibid.

10 Silvia Aloisi, "No Face Veils, Italy Tells Immigrants," Reuters, April 24, 2007, available at <http://www.thestar.com/article/206512>.

11 Ibid.

12 Brendan Nicholson, "Pm Rejects Headscarves Ban," *The Age*, August 30, 2005, available at <http://www.theage.com.au/news/national/pm-rejects-headscarves-ban/2005/08/29/1125302511538.html>.

caps."[13] Just a year later, however, it was reported that in Australia, "multiculturalism is seen in an increasingly negative light."[14] For example, then Prime Minister John Howard talked of moving away from 'zealous multiculturalism' toward a reassertion of Australia's *national identity*."[15]

The Australian courts may exist as a healthy check against such a movement. For example, in 2008, a turbaned Sikh boy secured an out-of-court settlement and an apology from a private school in Queensland which had turned him away because his turban was regarded as a violation of the school's dress code.[16] The boy's lawyer relied upon Queensland's Anti-Discrimination Act 1991, which has counterparts in at least seven other territories in Australia, in making the case against the permissibility of the school's decision.

All of these rules, which focused largely on Muslim minorities, have affected Sikhs by proxy. At the end of the day, these regulations seem to be against any articles of faith outside of the Judeo-Christian traditions.

13 Ibid.

14 Mark Rice-Oxley, "Taking on the Veil: West Looks to Assimilation – From Britain to Australia, Unease Grows Over the Separateness of Many of the West's Muslim Communities," *Christian Science Monitor*, October 20, 2006.

15 Ibid.; emphasis added.

16 "Family Wins Case Over School's Turban Ban," *ABC News*, September 2, 2008, available at <http://www.abc.net.au/news/stories/2008/09/02/2352649.htm>.

Chapter 18
Canada

Today, Canada is known for advancing a very open approach to multiculturalism. Indeed, former Canadian Prime Minister Diefenbaker once said:

> Canada was not a "melting pot" in which the individuality of each element is destroyed in order to produce a new and totally different element. It is rather a garden into which have been transplanted the hardiest and brightest of flowers from many lands, each retaining in its new environment the best of the qualities for which it was loved and prized in its native land.[1]

This has not, however, always been the case. Sikhs first arrived in Canada over a century ago, in 1903, as British colonial subjects seeking to benefit from the global reaches of the Empire. They were met with fierce racism from the very start in a country that sought to keep itself white as it moved towards independence. There were anti-Asiatic riots, and an Asiatic Exclusion League formed in 1907 specifically to target the Sikh community. Sikhs were prohibited from voting in British Columbia until 1947. They were not permitted to move into certain neighborhoods because of widespread fear of the "tide of turbans," which many felt needed to be pushed back. They had difficulty getting jobs – professional or otherwise – and were paid less than white workers in mills around the country. Theaters would not allow them to watch shows on account of their turbans, hotels and pubs refused them entry (or forced them to sit in a separate part of the facility), and even shoe shiners refused to polish their shoes.[2] They were hated and resented by most of the locals, and those who were willing to give them jobs often did so only in honor of their representation in the British Indian army.[3]

Things changed in the aftermath of World War II, with increased Sikh emigration out of newly independent India. The Canadian government also had begun to reflect on its own racial policies when faced with the atrocities of Hitler's regime, and opened up immigration policies to allow in more and more Indian citizens after this period.[4] To complement the influx of immigrants, the

---

1 Bhagat Singh, *Canadian Sikhs: Through a Century* (New Delhi: Gyan Sagar Publications, 2001), p. 208.

2 Ibid., ch. 7.

3 Ibid., p. 181.

4 Narindar Singh, *Canadian Sikhs' History: Religion, and Culture of Sikhs in North America* (Nepean, Ontario: Canadian Sikh Studies Institute, 1994), pp. 71–73.

government stressed a policy of "multiculturalism" and recognized the diversity of its citizenship.

Former Prime Minister Pierre Trudeau instituted a policy of multiculturalism that sought to assist members of all cultural groups to overcome cultural barriers, promote encounters between different groups, and support all of Canada's cultures. Canadians and their government are increasingly willing to accommodate the 400,000 Sikhs that now live in their midst, but they also recognize the shortcomings of their system. Canada's commitment to multiculturalism has been hotly debated and opposed since the nation's inception. Opponents of the policy feel that it leads to the erosion of a unified Canadian identity. Despite the opposition, the government has sought to accommodate visible minorities into Canadian society.

A prime example of this tension was the path towards integrating Sikhs into the Canadian military and polices forces. Although there now appears to be a consistent view regarding active recruitment and involvement of Sikhs in official Canadian life, the road to integration in the military and police forces has been uneasy. First, the pre-World War II regulations in both the Canadian navy and air force restricted recruitment to those who were "natural British subjects" and of the "white race" or "pure European descent."[5] Emphasis on visible minority recruitment into Canadian forces came quickly on the heels of the announcement of the Multiculturalism Policy. In 1974, a task force created by the Ontario Police Force issued a recommendation regarding the inclusion of visible and ethnocultural minorities.

A specific task force was designated to step up their recruitment in 1980. The Metropolitan Toronto Police Force was already allowing Sikhs to join the ranks and keep their turbans by 1986.[6] In integrating these individuals into its ranks, however, the Metropolitan Toronto Police prohibited turbaned Sikhs from participating in certain duties, including going onto industrial sites where hard hats were required or performing jobs involving the use of a respirator or gas mask. Despite their willingness to accommodate members of visible minorities, however, groups covered by the Employment Equity Act (including religious minorities) are still under-represented in Canadian police forces.[7]

Furthermore, some criticize the police forces for "recomposing on the inside another diversity that causes tensions, breeds racializing relations within, while perpetuating on the outside the control of diversity, thus maintaining racializing social relations."[8] This criticism is based primarily on the idea that the integration of minority groups into the police services is less concerned with redressing inequities than with fulfilling a political project that serves to symbolize social

---

5 Surj Rattan, "The Slowly Changing Face of Canada's Military," *Mehfil* (August 2003), p. 62.

6 *Grant v. Canada*, [1995] 1 FC 158, § 33.

7 Mylene Jaccoud, "Ethnicization of the Police in Canada," 14 *SPG Can. J. L. & Soc'y*. 83, 88 (1999) at 88.

8 Ibid., at 100.

cohesion and reduce racial tension by "pacifying" the minorities.[9] Despite these criticisms, however, it remains a fact that most Canadian police forces have found some way to accommodate the needs of the Sikh community and have invited them to join the service.

Still, one police force in particular had an extraordinarily difficult time integrating Sikhs – the Royal Canadian Mounted Police (RCMP). The RCMP was originally created in 1874 by an Act of the British Parliament to police the Northwest Territories and to maintain friendly relations with the First Nation tribes in the area. In assisting the original settlers, it became a focus of national pride and tradition in everything from their saddles to their stetsons. Today, the RCMP is a federal, national, and provincial force throughout the country, and has even been deployed on international policing missions to places such as the former Yugoslavia and Guatemala. In March 1990,[10] in response to both the requirements of the Human Rights Act and applications by two Sikh men, the RCMP Commissioner formally addressed the issue of recruiting turbaned Sikhs into its ranks by amending the requirements to allow a uniform exemption for the Sikh turban. His actions created an unprecedented outcry among RCMP veterans and their families,[11] some of whom brought suits against the Commissioner in federal court.

In *Grant v. Canada*, a group of ex-RCMP officers supported by the RCMP Veterans Association brought suit challenging the regulation amendment on the grounds of infringement of their rights to freedom of religion, to fundamental justice (the need to preserve the neutrality of the police force), freedom from discrimination, and that the Commissioner's actions violated the Canadian Constitution. The court dismissed the action, thereby reinforcing the government's commitment to the Multiculturalism Policy and the diversity of the Canadian population, as well as the requirement to accommodate visible minorities wherever possible. It held that although the plaintiffs had public interest standing, having religious police officers neither constrained an individual citizen's chosen religious practice nor compelled

9 Ibid., p. 85.

10 The RCMP had informally allowed Sikhs to wear their turbans on duty since 1987. At that time, the policy was to allow the Sikh to join, but to tell him that the force had a long tradition of uniform and being clean-shaven and they hoped the new recruits would join in that tradition. See *Grant v. Canada*, § 39.

11 The two women who began the protest against allowing the turban into the ranks were relatives of former RCMP members. They started a petition to change the uniform, and received 210,000 signatures in total, as well as large amounts of funding. They maintain that they have nothing against wearing turbans per se, but that "The pride and 'Esprit de Corps' [of the RCMP] should not be jeopardized by any concessions to religious or ethnic minorities which result in changes to this truly great police force and its proud traditions and uniform;" *Grant v. Canada*, § 46. Their actions also spurred anti-Sikh sentiment in other parts of the country, where pins and calendars were distributed showing a Sikh in a turban with a line through it and the words "Keep the RCMP Canadian;" Narindar Singh, *Canadian Sikhs' History*, p. 138.

his or her participation in other religious practices. Furthermore, nobody had been deprived of liberty or security because of the two policemen wearing turbans. Most importantly, however, the court held that the change in uniform regulations was made specifically to protect against discrimination – to further the ability of those affected to exercise their religious freedom, to reflect the present-day multicultural composition of Canada, and to promote the more effective operation of the force – not to discriminate against others. In coming to these conclusions, the court effectively chastised those members of the public unwilling to accept their Sikh neighbors, and held up the normative principles enunciated by the government as to its own people. An appeal to the Federal Court of Appeals and an application for leave to appeal to the Supreme Court of Canada were both dismissed.

Thus, in some ways, the history of Sikh rights in Canada reflects the principle that "legislation in the absence of sincere education, either in the enactment or in conjunction with it, may be of little effect."[12] Since the early 1970s, the population has been subject to increasingly strict laws and governmental principles requiring the integration and inclusion of visible minorities in a "mosaic-" type conception of Canadian identity. However, public education and acceptance is often lacking, leading individual citizens to attempt to exclude Sikhs from private schools and jobs, and public traditions such as the RCMP. In those cases, legislative and judicial support for the visible minority has seemingly pitted the government against the will of the democratic majority, or at least an active segment of it.

After 9/11, the Canadian courts have ruled consistently with this approach. For example, the Supreme Court of Canada concluded that Sikh students can carry kirpans in school.[13] The court specifically held:

> an absolute prohibition against wearing a kirpan infringes the freedom of religion of the student in question under [Section] 2(a) of the Canadian Charter of Rights and Freedoms [hereinafter Canadian Charter]. The infringement cannot be justified under [section] 1 of the Canadian Charter, since it has not been shown that such a prohibition minimally impairs the student's rights.[14]

Similarly, a post-secondary student in Quebec, Canada, "was told to remove her *hijab* at College Jean-Eudes."[15] In response, the Quebec Human Rights Commission ruled that "religious schools admitting students from more than one faith must

---

12 Satwinder Gosal, *The Quest for Justice: Enforcing the Right to Wear the 5Ks* (Toronto: Ontario Society of Sikhs, 1993), available at <http://www.sikhcoalition.org/LegalCanada0.asp>.

13 *Multani v. Commission* scolaire Marguerite-Bourgeoys, Multani c. Marguerite-Bourgeoys, 264 D.L.R. 4th 577 (2006).

14 Ibid.

15 "Private Schools Can Reject Hijab," *Montreal Gazette*, October 5, 2005, p. A5.

make reasonable efforts to accommodate all their pupils' beliefs" – irrespective of whether they are public or private institutions.[16]

A 2006 shooting spree in French-speaking Montreal, Canada by an immigrant Sikh challenged Canada's multicultural ideal. On September 16, 2006, *Globe and Mail* columnist Jan Wong argued that the young man killed because of his alienation from Quebec's francophone society, which explained not only this rampage, but also others that occurred in Quebec's recent past.[17] The *Montreal Gazette* rejected Wong's argument in clear terms:

> The foolishness of her deduction was confirmed by the lack of evidence to support it. In none of the cases … was there even the slightest tangible hint that their actions were spurred by alienation from mainstream Quebec society. … In each case the ethnicity factor was purely incidental.[18]

Quebec itself has long struggled with the notions of identity and sovereignty in political, cultural, and linguistic contexts;[19] and in recent years, minority groups in the province have met with periodic resistance.[20] For example, the town of Herouxville, which is almost exclusively "white, French-speaking and Catholic," posted a code of conduct for immigrants wishing to move into the town.[21] The list was riddled with extreme stereotypes and generalizations, including provisions against "stoning women" and "pouring acid on them," and it specifically forbade Sikh students from wearing kirpans when attending school, despite the previous court rulings.[22]

Soon after this and other incidents in the province, Quebec held a series of public hearings on "reasonable accommodation" for immigrants and minority groups, with the goal of striking a balance between "harmonious integration" and preserving the Quebecois identity.[23] One panelist at the hearing in Montreal,

---

16 Ibid.

17 Jan Wong, "Get Under the Desk," *Globe and Mail*, September 16, 2006, p. A8.

18 Hubert Bauch, "Jan Wong Was Misguided, Maybe: But Why the Fuss?," *Montreal Gazette*, October 1, 2006, p. A15.

19 See, for example, Alain Gagnon, *Quebec: State and Society* (Peterborough, Ontario: Broadview Press, 2004).

20 Ibid., p. 18. See also the work of Canadian academics Jocelyn Maclure and Diane Lamoureux.

21 "Critics: Quebec Town's Conduct Code is 'Xenophobic,'" *CTV.CA*, January 29, 2007, available at <http://www.ctv.ca/servlet/ArticleNews/story/CTVNews/20070129/code_conduct_070129/20070129?hub=Canada>.

22 "Canadian Town of Herouxville Posts Controversial 'Norms' for Immigrants, Like 'No Stoning,'" *Fox News*, January 30, 2007, available at <http://www.foxnews.com/story/0,2933,248819,00.html>.

23 "Quebec to Reconsider Integration Of Immigrants," *CTV.CA*, August 14, 2007, available at <http://www.ctv.ca/servlet/ArticleNews/story/CTVNews/20070814/Quebec_immigration_070814>.

La Presse reporter Laura-Julie Perrault, asserted that "English Canada had less tension with the idea of accommodating especially religious differences, while in the francophone part, there are still more questions that are being asked."[24]

Nevertheless, the government position overall has been encouraging to the Sikh community in Canada, and has led to Sikhs being more actively involved as Canadian citizens. British Columbia has had a Sikh premier, and there have been at least five Sikh members of the legislative assembly and two Sikh members of parliament in recent years. Punjabi is taught in the British Columbia school curriculum, and Sikhism even has its own commemorative stamp, issued on the 300th birthday of the religion. These accomplishments were all possible only because of the Canadian government's commitment to wipe out the decades of religious intolerance at the beginning of the twentieth century. Its conscious policies have placed Canada further along the spectrum of integration of its visible minorities by affording them legal protections for the wearing of their religious garb.

24 "Montrealers Attend Forum On Reasonable Accommodation," *CBC News*, February 17, 2007, available at <http://www.cbc.ca/canada/montreal/story/2007/02/16/reasonable-accommodation.html>.

Chapter 19
United States

In the United States, "as in other industrialized democracies, we are seeing the 'return of assimilation.'"[1] The United States, home to hundreds of thousands of Muslims and Sikhs, is necessarily involved in the enterprise of determining where on the integration–passive multiculturalism spectrum its society lies – and consequently determining the extent to which the Sikh turban will be tolerated or challenged, not only as a symbol of terrorism, but as an assault on American identity and solidarity.

In contrast to France and other European nations, America's constitutional traditions dictate that turbaned Sikh Americans generally be permitted to practice their faith and enjoy the freedom of religion prescribed by the federal Constitution in public spaces, including schools. But whereas other nations, particularly Britain and Canada, recognized the loyal bravery and trustworthiness of Sikh soldiers and therefore largely exempted Sikh military service from the overall ambit of the renewed assimilation debate, the United States has recently barred turbaned Sikhs from joining its armed forces.

Sikhs' military ties with the United States have been robust in the past. Bhagat Singh Thind, a Sikh immigrant, joined and fought with the U.S. army in World War I. At the end of the war, he requested U.S. citizenship, but was refused. Nevertheless, more Sikhs joined the ranks of the U.S. military in World War II, and thousands of others fought alongside the United States as members of the Allied Forces. Sikh Americans participated in the Vietnam War and Operation Desert Storm. Today, Sikhs work hand in hand with U.S. forces as UN peacekeepers or soldiers assisting with the wars in Iraq and Afghanistan.

Still, twenty years before 9/11, the U.S. army formally rejected the Sikh identity by refusing to allow turbaned Sikhs to join. In 1981, the army decided that Sikhs' exemption from the army regulation that prohibited the wearing of religious or any other headgear while in uniform had opened the door too wide for religious communities. It began to enforce the policy across the board, with no exemption for religious headgear of any kind, and no safety or security justification for the move. Because there was no real security concern, those Sikhs already in the army were grandfathered in and permitted to retain their Sikh apparel.

In a 1985 decision involving a Sikh recruit, the army's decision to prohibit Sikhs from enlisting was upheld by the U.S. Court of Appeals for the Ninth

---

1 Kenji Yoshino, "Uncovering Muslim Identity," *Toward Freedom*, November 23, 2005, available at <http://www.towardfreedom.com/home/content/view/674/54/>.

Circuit in *Khalsa v. Weinberger*.[2] In this opinion, the circuit court held that army appearance regulations that would preclude the Sikh turban were not subject to judicial review, since these decisions are internal and only indirectly prevent civilians from enlisting. The court concluded that Khalsa's claims were "on the least significant end of the constitutional scale,"[3] since a "right to enlist" is not legally cognizable. As the army determined that permitting Khalsa to join would be a great disruption to its functions, the court held it was not free to second-guess that conclusion. This decision legally cemented the exclusion of Sikhs from the army, and has been a distressing one for many Sikhs, whose "illustrious legacy of army tradition"[4] has seen Sikhs serve in armies across the globe – from Singapore and India to Britain and Canada.

In 1986, a Jewish army doctor, S. Simcha Goldman, brought suit against the Secretary of Defense for prohibiting him from wearing his yarmulke under a similar air force regulation that forbade headgear from being worn indoors. He lost. By a narrow majority (5–4), the Supreme Court of the United States held that "to accomplish its mission the military must foster instinctive obedience, unity, commitment, and esprit de corps,"[5] which requires subordinating individual interests (in this case, religion) to the needs of the service. The majority deferred to military policies, citing the air force's need to maintain uniformity among its ranks as enough of a justification to infringe on Goldman's free exercise of his rights. Dissenting opinions, however, argued forcefully that citizens in uniform cannot be stripped of their basic rights simply because the armed forces have adopted a uniform,[6] that the Constitution requires that the greatest number of people possible be allowed to practice their faiths freely, whereas the current regulations only make it easy for majority religions,[7] that "favoritism based on how unobtrusive a practice appears to the majority could create serious problems of equal protection and religious establishment,"[8] and that the court should have attempted to articulate and apply an appropriate standard for a free exercise claim in the military context.[9] The opinions also mentioned the Sikh turban as being the next step if yarmulkes were allowed, and held that if that were to happen, the admissibility of the turban should be viewed separately.[10]

Partly as a consequence of the strong dissent, Congress passed 10 U.S.CA § 774, which allows members of the armed forces to wear an item of religious

2 759 F.2d 1411 (9th Cir. 1985).

3 Ibid., p. 1,415.

4 Christina Jewett, "Army Rules Deter Sikhs from Joining," *Sacramento Bee*, February 27, 2004, p. A1, quoting Gurinder Singh Mann.

5 *Goldman v. Weinberger*, 475 U.S. 503, 507 (1986).

6 Ibid. at 515, Brennan, J., dissenting.

7 Ibid. at 521.

8 Ibid. at 527, Blackum, J., dissenting.

9 Ibid. at 529, O'Connor, J., dissenting.

10 Ibid. at 519.

apparel while wearing their uniforms, except if the wearing of the item would interfere with the performance of their military duties and provided that the headwear is "neat and conservative," as per military uniform policies.. This law now governs the wearing of headgear in the armed forces, and has been used to permit Jewish yarmulkes, but has not extended to the Sikh turban. In 2009, two Sikh Army captains who had been recruited to join the military during medical school were prohibited from beginning active duty with their religious turbans and beards intact. The men filed legal complaints against the Army, asking that they be accommodated and that the broader policy excluding Sikhs from serving in the Armed Forces be changed. That case is still pending as of publication.

Even prior to the 1981 ban on religious headgear in the army, Sikhs had been prohibited from joining the navy or air force. In a 1980 decision, a federal appellate court judge concluded: "A turban does not meet [the] safety requirements necessitated by both the ordinary and extraordinary activities of the modern, mechanized Navy."[11] The plaintiff in the case, Ronald Sherwood, had been court-martialed as a result of his decision to become a Sikh and don a turban four years after joining the navy. The court upheld the navy's helmet requirements as being necessary to further the government's compelling interest in the safety of its recruits under the *Sherbert* test, and denied the Sikh the right to wear his religious headgear. This case reinforces the proposition that even if the new army regulation were to provide a way in for Jews wearing yarmulkes, it is unlikely that the same right would be afforded to Sikhs, primarily on safety grounds.

The significance of the United States armed forces' treatment of turbaned Sikhs is amplified by Rajdeep Singh Jolly, Legal Director of the Sikh American Legal Defense and Education Fund (SALDEF).

* * *

Rajdeep Singh Jolly

> The Sikh reputation for gallantry is rooted in the fundamental Sikh belief in promoting social justice and inexorably linked to the Sikh religious identity. It is precisely because the turban is a necessary component of an observant Sikh's religious identity, policies that preclude observant Sikhs from serving in the U.S. armed forces strike at the heart of what it means to be a Sikh – and an American ….
>
> Sikhs in the United States share an ideological kinship with those who uphold the highest ideals of Americana. The belief in human equality and spirit of self-reliance that inspired millions of people to migrate to the United States – and the related feelings of hope and optimism that motivate Americans to believe that anything can be accomplished through hard work

11 *Sherwood v. Brown*, 619 F.2d 47, 48 (9th Cir. 1980).

and trust in God – were foreshadowed and fully developed by the Sikhs hundreds of years before the United States came into being. If anything, Sikhs strengthen the fabric of American society because they are, ideologically speaking, among the most American of Americans.

It is ironic, then, that observant Sikhs are not allowed to join the U.S. armed forces. Although observant Sikhs were officially allowed to serve in the U.S. army between 1958 and 1981,[12] military officials gradually rolled back this accommodation after expressing concern that the presence of turbaned and bearded Sikh soldiers would undermine military discipline and jeopardize the safety of its personnel. Although observant Sikhs are permitted to serve in the militaries of other Western democracies – such as the United Kingdom and Canada – and although observant Sikhs were specifically permitted to serve in the U.S. army for more than twenty years, the torchbearers of the status quo in the United States believe that making religious accommodations for Sikhs will force it to make accommodations for others and lead its military down a slippery slope towards non-uniformity, loss of discipline, and operational ineffectiveness. Similar arguments were asserted in connection with the accommodation of women and people of color in the U.S. armed forces, and it is not clear why these arguments are any more compelling when applied to the question of accommodating observant Sikhs.

The argument against accommodating Sikhs on the basis of safety concerns is more compelling than those based on concerns about uniformity, but not insurmountable. According to American military officials, Sikhs cannot wear helmets because of their turbans and cannot wear gas masks because of their beards, and are therefore unable to comply with safety standards. It is not clear whether American military officials have promulgated these rules from an armchair or supported them with scientific findings, field research, and consultation with military officials in the United Kingdom and Canada, where observant Sikhs *are* permitted to undertake military service. With regard to helmets, observant Sikh soldiers and athletes are known to wear smaller head coverings – such as *patkas* – under their helmets, and should be allowed to do so when operational necessity calls for it in a military context. Similarly, many observant Sikhs secure their beards with elastic bands and may therefore be able to wear gas masks that form a proper seal. Significantly, in the course of hearing a case on the religious accommodation of bearded firefighters, a federal court heard evidence that some religiously bearded plaintiffs repeatedly passed safety tests for gas masks and that individuals

12 Captain Thomas R. Folk, "Military Appearance Requirements and Free Exercise of Religion," 98 *Mil. L. Rev.* 53, 62 (1982).

with shaved faces failed such tests with regularity.[13] The court also observed that certain types of gas masks can be safely worn by bearded individuals.[14] These findings reinforce the notion that the preclusive policy of the U.S. armed forces with respect to Sikhs is based on preconceptions about the extent to which Sikh religious practices can actually comport with military standards relating to safety. Apart from being unfortunate, it is also illegal – a violation of the Religious Freedom Restoration Act of 1993.

As a practical matter, in a post-9/11 era, and at a time when the U.S. armed forces expect to engage in protracted military and counter-terrorism operations in and around Afghanistan and Pakistan, observant Sikhs provide critical language and cultural competencies that can help – not hinder – the mission of the United States in that part of the world. Allowing observant Sikhs to serve in the U.S. armed forces would strengthen the ideological connection that Sikhs already have to the United States and give them the privilege of defending ideas and ideals that they have for so long considered their own.

* * *

In the aftermath of the 9/11 attacks, the U.S. has seen renewed efforts to keep visible minorities out of other aspects of public life as well. In Detroit, Michigan, home to a sizable Muslim population, a Muslim woman's case was dismissed after she refused to remove her veil.[15] The judge, Paul Paruk, explained that he needed to see the woman's face in order to assess her truthfulness,[16] an argument similar to the one made by Britain's Jack Straw, who claimed that the Muslim veil hindered effective communication. The Michigan case led to another suit, with the Muslim woman suing the judge who dismissed her case, but a court ruled there had been no violation of her First Amendment rights or her right to court access.[17] Certainly, the exceptional circumstances that inhere in a courtroom provide for a certain amount of departure from the rules that prevail in most public spaces, but there is mounting evidence of a trend in which American courts and public opinion favor assimilation.

---

13 *Potter v. District of Columbia*, No. 01-1189, 2007 WL 2892685 (DDC September 28, 2007).

14 Ibid.

15 Zachary Gorchow, "Veil Costs Her Claim in Court," *Detroit Free Press*, October 22, 2006, p. 1B.

16 Ibid., noting that the judge in question stated: "My job in the courtroom is to make a determination as to the veracity of somebody's claim …. Part of that, you need to identify the witness and you need to look at the witness and watch how they testify."

17 "Women's Veil Case Against Judge Tossed," *MSNBC*, May 13, 2008, available at <http://www.msnbc.msn.com/id/24600216/wid/7/>.

In 2008, Oklahoma lawmakers passed legislation prohibiting Sikh turbans and Muslim headscarves in drivers' license photographs. Departments of Motor Vehicles in Nevada are reportedly employing the same policy on an ad hoc basis. A court in Florida upheld a state law requiring an individual's full face to be shown on his or her driver's license photo.[18] A Muslim woman who wanted to wear her veil for her license photo sued, arguing in the main that the state law infringed upon her First Amendment right to free exercise of religion.[19] In ruling against the Muslim woman, the court wrote:

> We recognized the tension created as a result of choosing between following the dictates of one's religion and the mandates of secular law. ... However, as long as the laws are neutral and generally applicable to the citizenry, they must be obeyed. [Moreover, the law] did not compel [her] to engage in conduct that her religion forbids – her religion does not forbid all photographs.[20]

The case was especially notable because in February of 2001, the woman had been issued a driver's license picturing her with a veil, and it was only three months after the events of 9/11 when she received notice that her license would be invalidated unless she returned and posed for a new picture without her veil.[21] The noticeable change in American sentiments towards Muslim women who choose to keep their heads covered was also exemplified in a case that stemmed from the firing of an Arizona woman just four months after 9/11. The woman, a sales associate for a rental car company, was dismissed for refusing to remove her headscarf even though she had worked for the company for two years and had been allowed to wear the same headscarf previously.[22] The abrupt change in policy was acknowledged by the court and deemed to be discriminatory, and a jury ruled in the woman's favor.[23] Similar cases of discrimination against women who choose to continue wearing their headscarves have seen Muslim women barred

---

18 "Florida Appeals Court Won't Allow Veil in Driver's License Photo," Associated Press, September 7, 2005, available at <http://www.firstamendmentcenter.org/%5Cnews.aspx?id=15748>.

19 Ibid.

20 Ibid.

21 *Freeman v. Department of Highway Safety and Motor Vehicles*, So.2d, (Fla. App. 5 Dist. 2005).

22 *EEOC v. Alamo Rent-A-Car, LLC; ANC Rental Corporation*, CIV 02 1908 PHX ROS (2002).

23 Press release, "Phoenix Jury awards $287,640 to fired Muslim woman in EEOC religious discrimination lawsuit," Equal Employment Opportunity Commission, July 4, 2007, available at <http://www.eeoc.gov/press/6-4-07.html>.

from public buses,[24] dismissed from their jobs,[25] and denied the opportunity to participate in sporting events.[26]

On October 24, 2006, in one of the leading newspapers in the world, *The Washington Post*, a columnist argued that Muslim women in America should not wear a full-faced veil in public because "it [is] considered rude, in a Western country, to hide one's face."[27] While what is considered "rude" is inherently subjective (and thus may be based on bias, unfounded stereotypes, or class distinctions), the columnist nevertheless expressed the underlying notion that Western society is uncomfortable with certain articles of faith, and that it is therefore incumbent on religious minorities to shed this attire rather than continue insulting the host majority – a line of thinking again consistent with recent statements made by British leadership.

The editors of *The Washington Post* one day later struck a different tone. Responding to the European fixation on and discomfort with the Muslim veil, the editors noted:

> It's hard to believe that veils are the biggest obstacle to communication between British politicians and the country's Muslims; and it's even harder to imagine Mr. Straw raising similar objections about Sikh turbans or Orthodox Jewish dress. True, the Labor Party MP was reflecting – or maybe pandering to – the concern of many in Britain about the self-segregation of some Muslims. But veils … are not the cause of that segregation, much less of terrorism. Attacks on Muslim custom by public officials are more likely to reinforce than to ease the community's alienation.[28]

Indeed, there are promising efforts to bridge the gaps between certain immigrant populations and mainstream American society. The New York Police Department, for example, has a liaison to the Muslim community on staff.[29] The liaison, part

24 "Driver: Bus Policy Barred Muslim's Veil," *Washington Post*, January 20, 2007, available at <http://www.washingtonpost.com/wp-dyn/content/article/2007/01/19/AR2007011901421.html>.

25 "Philadelphia police can bar officer from wearing Muslim scarf," Associated Press, June 15, 2007, available at <http://www.firstamendmentcenter.org/news.aspx?id=18684>.

26 "Teen forced to sit out soccer game because of head scarf," WLS-TV/DT, October 15, 2007, available at <http://abclocal.go.com/wls/story?section=news/national_world&id=5708689>.

27 Anne Applebaum, "Veiled Insult," *Washington Post*, October 24, 2006, p. A19, available at <http://www.washingtonpost.com/wp-dyn/content/article/2006/10/23/AR2006102300976.html?nav=rss_opinion/columns>.

28 Editorial, "Europe's Muslims: A year after the French riots, their alienation is growing," *Washington Post*, October 25, 2006, p. A16, available at <http://www.washingtonpost.com/wp-dyn/content/article/2006/10/24/AR2006102401148.html>.

29 Robin Shulman, "Liaison Strives to Bridge Police, Muslim Cultures," *Washington Post*, January 24, 2007, available at <http://www.washingtonpost.com/wp-dyn/content/

of the NYPD's "New Immigrant–Special Outreach Unit,"[30] engages the Arab and South Asian communities of New York City in an attempt to "redeem the name of the police department to Muslims and the reputation of Islam to police officers."[31] Many Sikhs have taken into their own hands the task of educating their neighbors and integrating themselves into a community, on occasion rising to relatively prominent local positions. These efforts are only one part of the equation, however, as discrimination against Muslims, those perceived to be Muslims, and people of foreign heritage in general remains, and is even increasing, in some pockets of the nation even now, over eight years after 9/11. In many areas, Sikhs have chosen to remove their turbans and cut their hair in an effort to "fit in," often feeling burdened by the combination of those negative sentiments and the overt nature of the turban – which, ironically, is at least part of its purpose.

As noted in the previous section, Sikh Americans have struggled with the legal system to uphold their religious rights. What if Congress banned the wearing of conspicuous articles of faith, including Sikh turbans, in public schools? The Supreme Court has never ruled on such a question. While the legal remedies, particularly constitutional protections, available to Sikhs if legislation similar to that passed in France was enacted in the United States are unclear, there is reason for optimism following recent Supreme Court pronouncements.

The First Amendment of the United States Constitution provides that "Congress shall make no law … prohibiting the free exercise [of religion]."[32] The Free Exercise Clause has been interpreted to generally mean that, "the government is prohibited from interfering with or attempting to regulate any citizen's religious beliefs, from coercing a citizen to affirm beliefs repugnant to his or her religion or conscience, and from directly penalizing or discriminating against a citizen for holding beliefs contrary to those held by anyone else."[33]

In the 1963 case of *Sherbert v. Verner*,[34] the court identified "strict scrutiny" as being the appropriate standard by which to examine a free exercise claim.[35] Accordingly, for the government to prevail in a free exercise claim, it would have to prove that the law is supported by a "compelling state interest" and that alternative forms of regulation that are less restrictive of the free exercise right are unavailable.[36] It would therefore seem that Sikhs, who wear their turban as an

---

article/2007/01/23/AR2007012301330.html>.

30 Cara Buckley, "New York City Police Seek Trust Among Immigrants," May 31, 2007, available at <http://www.nytimes.com/2007/05/31/nyregion/31outreach.html?pagewanted=1>.

31 Robin Shulman, "Liaison Strives to Bridge Police, Muslim Cultures," *Washington Post*, January 24, 2007, p. A02, available at <http://www.washingtonpost.com/wp-dyn/content/article/2007/01/23/AR2007012301330_pf.html>.

32 U.S. Constitution, Amendment I.

33 Donald Kramer, 16A Am. Jur. 2d, Constitutional Law § 424 (1998).

34 374 U.S. 398 (1963).

35 Ibid. at 403.

36 Ibid.

expression of their religious identity, generally enjoy the highest level of protection under the First Amendment for the manifestation of their faith.[37]

After *Sherbert*, however, "the Court has started to move toward a narrower conception" of the free exercise clause.[38] In 1990, in *Employment Division, Department of Human Resources of Oregon v. Smith*,[39] the court upheld a state statute that prohibited the use of peyote for religious purposes by Native Americans, ruling in part that the law was generally applicable, neutral on its face, and evidenced no intent to discriminate against particular religious groups.[40] Although the court did not expressly overturn *Sherbert*, it limited *Sherbert*'s ruling to cases regarding the denial of unemployment compensation: "even if *Sherbert* possessed any vitality beyond the unemployment compensation field … we would not apply it to require exemptions from a generally applicable law."[41]

As one legal commentator noted, the *Employment Division* decision leaves "religious conduct little protection from the effect of a law that is neutral and generally applicable."[42] Since a ban on conspicuous articles of faith in public schools would not seem to intentionally target Sikhs, and Sikhs would thus be seeking an exemption from generally applicable policy, one would suspect that any First Amendment right that they could claim to allow them to wear the turban may fail under the *Employment Division* standard.

A state court case in which the appeal was dismissed by the United States Supreme Court, *Cooper v. Eugene School District*,[43] highlights the limitations of religious dress statutes enacted for public employees when applied specifically to Sikhs. Janet Cooper was a public school teacher who converted to Sikhism and began to wear a white turban and white clothes while teaching her sixth and eighth grade classes.[44] She was disciplined and her teaching license revoked as a result of a state statute that prohibited teachers in public schools from wearing any religious dress while engaged in the performance of duties as a teacher.[45] The Supreme Court of Oregon held that the religious dress statute did not violate, among other things, the First Amendment, stating: "If such a law is to be valid, it must be justified by

37 See Kathleen Sullivan, "The New Religion and the Constitution," 116 *Harv. L. Rev.* 1397 (2003), providing an in-depth discussion of interpretations of the Free Exercise and Establishment Clauses

38 Stefanie Walterick, "The Prohibition of Muslim Headscarves from French Public School and Controversies Surrounding the Hijab in the Western World," 20 *Temp. Int'l & Comp. L. J.* 264 (2006).

39 494 U.S. 872 (1990).

40 Ibid. at 878–82.

41 Amarsect S. Bhachu, "A Shield for Swords," 34 *Am. Crim. L. Rev.* 197, 204 (1996).

42 Thomas Berg, "The New Attacks on Religious Freedom Legislation, and Why they are Wrong," 21 *Caradozo L. Rev.* 415, 415 (1999).

43 723 P.2d 298 (Or. 1986), appeal dismissed, 480 U.S. 942 (1987).

44 Ibid. at 312.

45 Ibid. at 300.

a determination that religious dress necessarily contravenes the wearer's role or function at the time and place beyond any realistic means of accommodation."[46] The court maintained that by excluding teachers, whose dress is a constant visual reminder of their religious commitment, the law seeks to respect the right of free exercise of the *students*.[47] Although the court admitted that Cooper had not been trying to proselytize to her students, it felt that the repetitive and constant nature of her appearance could have more of a proselytizing effect than she imagined, and therefore her Sikh clothing should not be permitted in schools.[48] What is most ironic is that the Oregon statute limiting religious garb in public schools had originally been passed by supporters of the Ku Klux Klan in an effort to exclude Catholic nuns from teaching in public schools. The legislative intent of the law had been explicitly to religious freedoms, and, years later, a liberal Oregonian administration has been fighting to keep it on the books as a protection of neutrality in schools. In reality, the statute was enacted to protect a form of extremism in the public school system.

To those that doubt the weight of a State Supreme Court decision such as *Cooper*, it should be noted that the U.S. Court of Appeals for the Third Circuit relied on *Cooper* in 1990, following the Supreme Court's dismissal of the appeal, in reaching its analysis of a case brought by Muslim public school teacher under Title VII.[49] Accordingly, as one commentator noted, prevailing case law "suggest[s] that states can prohibit public school teachers from wearing religious garb in the interest of preserving religious neutrality without violating the free exercise rights of teachers as long as the prohibition applies equally to all religious dress and does not target or burden one religious group over others."[50] It may not be surprising, then, that some argue that a ban on conspicuous articles of faith in public schools is "not completely unthinkable in the United States," and that the religious rights of a turbaned Sikh public student after 9/11 are "tentative" at best.[51]

In 1993, however, Congress passed the Religious Freedom Restoration Act (RFRA), which was designed to reinstate the "compelling interest" *Sherbert*

46 Ibid. at 307.

47 Ibid. at 311.

48 Ibid. at 312–13. Interestingly, Cooper's decision to manifest her faith at school could have been recognized by the court as an educational benefit, namely of teaching her students about the diversity of the society they inhabited, and as such, teaching them to appreciate and respect those who may not appear to be the same as themselves. The court, however, assumed that visible religious minorities that are active in their communities are in essence imposing their faith on others by simply adopting the symbols of their own personal beliefs.

49 *U.S. v. Board of Education for School District of Philadelphia*, 911 F.2d 882, 884 (3rd Cir. 1990).

50 Walterick, "The Prohibition of Muslim Headscarves from French Public School" at 267.

51 Ibid., p. 269.

test for free exercise claims.[52] The RFRA states that the "Government shall not substantially burden a person's exercise of religion even if the burden results from a rule of general applicability,"[53] unless the government has demonstrated that the burden is "in furtherance of a compelling governmental interest" and "is the least restrictive means of furthering that compelling governmental interest."[54] In 1997, the U.S. Supreme Court, in *City of Boerne v. Flores*, declared that the RFRA was unconstitutional as applied to individual states.[55] However, it held that it is still applicable to First Amendment violations alleged against the federal government.[56]

In 2006, the Supreme Court may have marked an expansion of free exercise protection. In *Gonzales v. O Centro Espirita Beneficente Uniado Do Vegetal*,[57] a Church that uses hallucinogenic tea in religious ceremonies claimed the enforcement of the Controlled Substances Act infringed on the Church's free exercise rights. The court unanimously sided with the Church, noting that the government must "demonstrate a compelling interest in uniform application of a particular program by offering evidence that granting the requested religious accommodations would seriously compromise its ability to administer the program." The court rejected the government's "slippery-slope concerns that could be invoked in response to any RFRA claim for an exception to a generally applicable law," namely, "If I make an exception for you, I'll have to make one for everybody, so no exceptions."[58] The court indicated that a case-by-case approach to evaluating exemptions to generally applicable religious laws was appropriate,[59] as was the case in the 2005 decision of *Cutter v. Wilkinson*.[60] Acknowledging that "there may be instances in which a need for uniformity precludes the recognition of exceptions to generally applicable laws under RFRA," the court did not find that the Controlled Substances Act was immune from exemptions "given the longstanding exemption from the Controlled Substances Act for religious use of peyote, and the fact that the very reason Congress enacted the RFRA was to respond to a decision denying a claimed right to sacramental use of a controlled substance."[61]

To the extent that the government may pass a ban on conspicuous articles of faith to promote secularity or a national identity, such an interest would likely not

52 *City of Boerne v. Flores*, 521 U.S. 507, 515 (1999).

53 42 U.S.CA § 2000bb-1(a).

54 42 U.S.CA § 2000bb-1(b).

55 Flores, 521 U.S. at 536.

56 See *Kikimura v. Hurley*, 242 F.3d 950, 959 (10th Cir. 2001), noting that "the separation of powers concerns expressed in Flores do not render RFRA unconstitutional as applied to the federal government" and that "when a portion of a statute is declared unconstitutional the constitutional portions of the statute are presumed severable."

57 *Gonzales v. O Centro Espirita Beneficente Uniado Do Vegetal*, 546 U.S. 418 (2006).

58 Ibid. at 421.

59 Ibid. at 436.

60 *Cutter v. Wilkinson*, 544 U.S. 709, 724–26 (2005).

61 Gonzales, 546 U.S. at 436.

pass under *Pierce v. Society of the Sisters of the Holy Names of Jesus and Mary*,[62] which soundly rejected a state interest in ensuring homogeneity of American children and achieving assimilation in public schools. The court stated: "The fundamental theory of liberty upon which all governments in this Union repose excludes any general power of the state to standardize its children."[63] To the extent that a government interest may be based on fear of fundamental Islam, that interest may be construed as discriminatory animus or perpetuating stereotypes, which would not please the court either.[64]

Assuming that the federal government can proffer a compelling state interest, which is highly unlikely, Sikhs may be able to obtain an exemption from a ban on conspicuous articles of faith without having to run into the "slippery slope" concern of the government, in part because of the fact that Sikhs have been permitted to wear turbans in the United States since their arrival.

* * *

Sikh migration has carried members of the faith to major Western countries, and as such, turbaned Sikhs have been involved in the necessary process of finding out the extent to which they – and their turbans in particular – will be accepted by their host countries. Our survey has indicated that the results have been mixed. France and other European nations, for example, have taken a hard-line approach to turbaned Sikhs in the aftermath of the 9/11 attacks. Accordingly, Sikhs with turbans are less welcome in the public spaces of these nations, and have struggled to find appropriate schooling as a result. By contrast, Britain has recognized the valuable military contributions that Sikhs have historically made to Empire, and has therefore immunized Sikh military and police members from the overall questioning of conspicuous articles of faith that has taken place in virtually all other arenas of British life. The closest comparison to France may be Canada, whose multicultural policy has benefited Sikhs in both public service and in ordinary aspects of residence. With respect to the United States, generous First Amendment protections would likely guard against the blanket animus that took hold in France after 9/11. Ironically, though, turbaned Sikh Americans have been turned away from the opportunity to exhibit bravery in defense of the United States.

Laws like those in France overlook a fundamental tenet of the globalized democratic state that has now become a reality – that "The co-existence of different life forms as equals also requires the integration of citizens – and the mutual recognition of their sub-cultural memberships – within the framework of

62 *Pierce v. Society of the Sisters of the Holy Names of Jesus and Mary*, 268 U.S. 510 (1925).

63 Ibid. at 535.

64 See *Larson v. Valente*, 456 U.S. 228, 252–54 (1982).

a common political culture."[65] In order for a democratic Western State to integrate immigrants and minorities into its own culture and political heritage, it must work with these groups, instead of against the most visible amongst them. Imposing a piece of assimilationist legislation might force everyone in a particular area to look the same in terms of their outward appearance, but a "melting-pot" culture cannot be created so easily. Both sides – minority and majority – must be willing to concede some aspects of their traditions, especially those that trample on the rights of others. Secularity, or *laïcité*, as applied by the French is perhaps at the furthest end of our integration spectrum, and will be interpreted by many as a direct attempt to force them to choose between religion and political citizenship.

All told, there should be little doubt that turbaned Sikhs after 9/11 encountered a global attack on their identity that consisted both of tangible violence and discrimination, as outlined in Part II, and of an intangible attack on visible religious identity generally, as noted in Part III. The legal and political remedies available to Sikhs have provided inconsistent results in the United States and across other nations.

Given the immediacy, depth, and global scale of the backlash against Sikhs, the question invariably is: what can they do about it? Part IV explores the Sikh community's response to the backlash against it, and also details the American government's reaction to the threats to Sikh civil rights posed in the post-9/11 era.

---

65 Jürgen Habermas, "Intolerance and Discrimination," *International Journal of Constitutional Law* 9 (February 2003).

Part IV
The Response to the Post-9/11 Climate

Growing up in a small town in upstate New York, Navinderdeep Nijher knew what it was like to be marked as someone different. He had heard comments about his turban and had his *patka* pulled off in school. But what happened on September 11, 2001 changed everything. After that, navigating bias and discrimination became a much more complicated task, and Dr. Nijher had become one of the backlash's first victims.

That morning, Dr. Nijher, a surgery resident, was sitting in a dark conference room looking at X-rays with his colleagues at Maimonides Medical Center in Brooklyn. When they learned about the attacks, he volunteered to help rescue survivors at Ground Zero. Barely sleeping for two days, he and a group of colleagues waited and watched at the trauma centers, hoping for a patient to come in. Instead, they were dispatched to count bodies and pronounce victims dead. It was a painful and difficult experience, and when he arrived home on September 13, Dr. Nijher was exhausted.

It was only when he awoke that he first realized the terror his own community was facing. His roommate was protective, and wouldn't allow Dr. Nijher to leave the apartment alone. He watched the news coverage and shook his head in anger at the image of a Sikh man (Sher Singh described in Part II) being pulled off his train because fellow passengers were afraid. As he walked down the street, Dr. Nijher heard the comments, saw the stares. And when he dropped off a roll of film to be developed at a local store, he was told that "for you people" it would cost $500. Within hours, one of the heroes of 9/11 had been turned into the enemy.

Looking back, despite everything he saw that week, Dr. Nijher says: "Sikhs are continuously equated with the terrorist image. That stays with me more than the actual events of the day."

* * *

The Sikh turban was under attack as soon as the towers themselves were hit by commercial airplanes used as missiles. We noted in Part II that Amrik Singh Chawla, a turbaned Sikh, was chased and called a "terrorist" in Manhattan just moments after the impact. Four days later, Balbir Singh Sodhi, a Sikh, was shot to death in Mesa, Arizona. Reports continued to pour in about the numerous ways in which turbaned Sikhs were being mistreated.

The Sikhs, however, had no meaningful legal or political advocacy apparatus in place. While they had been part of the American community for many years and had entrenched themselves from east coast to west, the Sikhs had no established framework to fall back on to respond to the harassment or hate violence, there were no familiar buttons to push, there were no set media contacts to alert. The community had to be rallied. But how to do so was an altogether new question. At this moment of crisis, Sikhs had to start from scratch.

This part describes how Sikhs managed in the immediate aftermath of the 9/11 attacks, and how they ultimately built a mechanism to tackle ignorance, bias incidents, and unfavorable policies. The Sikh response assumed many forms. There was the necessary formal reaction, which was the forging of a Sikh civil rights community that would liaise with the government, law enforcement, and the media. Amandeep Sidhu, one of the first Sikhs to mobilize the community and form a makeshift response team for addressing Sikh civil rights issues, offers his thoughts on the first days of the fight against the backlash, and Harmeet Dhillon, who has contributed countless hours of pro bono legal services to Sikhs after 9/11, reflects on her experiences in becoming a leading Sikh civil rights activist.

But there were other, less institutional means by which Sikhs could eradicate ignorance and spread understanding of their faith. For example, Valarie Kaur created a documentary film on the backlash against Sikhs in an attempt to promote understanding of Sikhs' rightful place in America. Sonny Caberwal, a turbaned Sikh, modeled for a Kenneth Cole campaign that sought to generate awareness through fashion. Both speak about their experiences here.

This part also discusses how the federal government responded to the hate crimes and other noxious conduct affecting turbaned Sikhs. Eric Treene, the Department of Justice's special counsel on religious discrimination, furnished us with an extensive statement on the steps the federal government has taken to address discrimination against turbaned Sikhs in the aftermath of the attacks.

Still, before the organizations could be set up and the channels to be power brokered, the Sikh response was a basic, primal one – to seek safety and ensure one's wellbeing. We begin this discussion with a sober insight into the human response to the backlash. In the first chapter, Partap Singh Ajrawat, a graduate student in Sikh studies, shares his experiences growing up as a Sikh in America, and as a turbaned Sikh New Yorker in the aftermath of the terrorist attacks.

Chapter 20
The Human Costs

Partap Singh Ajrawat

Being born in Buffalo, New York and the son of Sikh immigrants from the state of Punjab in northwest India, I wear a patchwork cloak of multiple identities. Therefore, at any given time I can be an American, a Sikh, a Punjabi, an Indian, or any combination of these identities. But the ability to always choose which of these identities I wear is not up to me. Upon seeing me, others can wrap their own veils around me, against my will, covering who I am and subsuming the diversity of my experiences into a singular entity of their choosing. This became most clear to me as I experienced at first hand the unfolding of the events of September 11, 2001 and subsequent harassment, discrimination, and racial profiling, ranging from individual citizens to public authorities, whether in movie theaters or at Grand Central Station in midtown Manhattan. For immigrants, such as my parents, who have emigrated from all parts of the globe and settled in the United States of America, faith in the American dream has outweighed the hardships they have faced as newcomers to a society with different cultural norms. However, for first-generation American progeny of these immigrants, myself included, the realization of the American dream starts with our unwillingness as Americans to make the silencing and assimilation of our religious and cultural differences the price of admission for participation in the American way of life. As Americans, whether born or naturalized as such, we must remember that the First Amendment to the Constitution of the United States of America ensures that those who would otherwise be persecuted for their religious beliefs and convictions are welcomed with open arms to practice their faith freely and publicly, guaranteeing that these values will not be judged against those who seek a better life for themselves and their descendents within the United States of America. Therefore, in this chapter, I have the honor and privilege to write and share my experiences with you as both all of and none of my professed identities, because my task is not just to expose the true identity of hatred, persecution, harassment, and discrimination as veils for ignorance, a fear of the unknown, but for you, the reader, to get to know me, as an American citizen, a friend, a human being.

As a child growing up in an American suburb on the east coast outside Washington, DC, I did not perceive much difference between my family life and the lives of other families. Although my father wore a turban as a marker of his belonging to the Sikh faith, he was first and foremost my father, and I viewed him as such. However, there were a few instances where my family was marked as being different from other families. Although these instances occurred when I was of a young age and therefore could not fully understand their significance at the time, they remain seared in my memory and are my first recollections of being treated differently because of my family's ancestry.

The first instance happened when I was seven or eight. I was sitting in the back seat of our Grand Marquis that was parked in our driveway, and I remember curiously staring at a police officer as he drove by in his police cruiser. My mother told me to turn away and not look at the officer. I am not sure if my parents had ever had an uncomfortable encounter before with the police or if something had happened in the neighborhood or the Sikh, Punjabi, or Indian community, but her apprehension struck me as odd. As a child attending public elementary school, I had been taught that authority figures, including police officers, were to be trusted if I ever needed help, but here I saw that the presence of the police made my mother apprehensive. Although the officer passed by without incident, it was the first time I became aware of the differences in perception between the way others viewed my family and my family's view towards others.

The second encounter where I clearly remember someone drawing attention to a feature of difference of a family member happened when I was eight, while attending the local grocery store with my father. Usually my mother, older sister, younger brother, and I would go to the grocery store together, while my father rarely accompanied us. However, in this instance my father and I went to the grocery store together. We were in the fruit and vegetable section when a child, probably not more than four or five years old, after seeing my father's turban, turned to her mother and said: "Look Mom, a genie!" The mother, clearly embarrassed, quickly told her child that my father was not a genie, and after smiling and nodding to my father, moved on with her shopping. Although I realized the cause for the child's statement – my father's turban – and her associating it with depictions from children's stories, coloring books, cartoons, or movies featuring genies with turbans, I was made aware that people did not immediately perceive my father and I as a father and son shopping together, but firstly recognized my father's appearance of being from a different ethnic background that was not European. When I reflect on this memory, I also believe that the mother was incapable of telling her child who my father was, what his religion was, or where he came from, and on the part of my father, there was a feeling that this was a child's observation, and therefore excusable with no further clarification necessary of his ethnic background to this mother and daughter.

Another experience happened when I was a teenager spending the afternoon with my father in a rowboat on the C&O Canal. As we were paddling down the canal, we got to a point where the canal met the Potomac River, with boats of various sizes sailing around the area. A man on one of the larger boats saw my father, and with both hands pressed together, nodded towards my father, gestures of greetings and respect within South Asian cultures. My father smiled and did the same towards this individual, and then the boat passed by and we rowed back into the canal to our camp site Although I knew what all these gestures meant, it was funny to see it coming from an individual from a non-South Asian background. Clearly this person had come into contact with either Sikhs or people from South Asia before and wanted to communicate his familiarity with South Asian cultures. Even though in this instance I was impressed with this person's knowledge of my family's cultural and ethnic heritage, this person also chose to first acknowledge our ancestry, rather than recognizing us as Americans first and foremost with a hand wave.

If there were differences between my family and American society because of my father's wearing of the turban and our skin color, there were also internal differences that I perceived between myself, other family members, friends, and the larger Sikh community because of my not having unshorn hair, which for orthodox Sikhs is a primary marker of Sikh identity. One experience where this became strikingly clear took place during an informal forum at the gurdwara (Sikh temple) for the parents and children to discuss issues regarding the tensions between rearing children with Sikh religious norms and American cultural values. The issues raised quickly narrowed into a discussion regarding those children who had cut their hair and those who had not, with some community members arguing that those who had cut hair were somehow less fervent in their adherence to the tenets of the Sikh faith, while those that kept their hair unshorn were "true" Sikhs. Although both male and female Sikhs are to keep their hair unshorn, males are also required to wear a turban, making them easily distinguishable in their adherence to this precept. In this light, it was interesting that my sister raised her voice and questioned the congregation about how they could rightly say that someone is a better Sikh than the next just because the outward symbols of orthodoxy were displayed. In her view, one could have unshorn but still be a bad Sikh in daily life, and therefore being a Sikh could not be reduced to one's appearance over and against the substance of what it meant ethically to be a Sikh.

What these childhood experiences are meant to indicate is that from an early age I was aware that there were both internal and external differences between myself, my family, American society, and the Sikh community that were sometimes highlighted because of differences in appearance, and particularly surrounding the wearing of a turban. What was striking from these examples was how easy it became for others to form an opinion of my family based on our appearance rather than their comprehension of who we were as individuals, a family, and as belonging to heterogeneous communities. For the most part, people first and foremost formulated their perceptions of us based on our dissimilarities, rather than on shared characteristics such as seeing a family similar to their own or as Americans pursuing the American dream, or a Sikh family attending services. What became frustrating was that people were not able to comprehend that I could inhabit all and none of these identities at the same time. I would not have the power to fully understand and articulate this position until the events of 9/11.

During high school, I had contemplated growing my hair and wearing a turban, but had always decided against it because I was not fully prepared to answer questions from family, friends, and community members regarding my choice. However, a year and a half before 9/11, I decided to keep my hair uncut as a marker of my Sikh identity. At the time of this decision I had joined the Sikh association at my university, befriended other American Sikhs, and through many conversations and discussions with them about their experiences of being reared with different cultural values, I felt more comfortable and confident to explore my identity as a Sikh. At the end of my freshman year of college, I began to wear a turban while interning in Washington, DC for the summer. I don't recall the first time I wore a turban, but I do remember the sense of enjoyment and pride I took in tying the turban in my own distinct style every morning. My old fears of not being able to adequately answer questions about my choice had disappeared, replaced with the knowledge and confidence that I had gained from my friends to explain to those that were interested my personal understanding of the religious significance for Sikhs of tying a turban. My old fears were dispelled when, after a couple of months, I realized to my surprise that there were no incidents of negative or awkward encounters with anybody over my wearing a turban, but rather the opposite: sincere and genuine interest from people from all walks of life that were open to engaging in a dialogue with me and willing to become aware of the Sikh worldview. Moreover, this engagement allowed me to easily meet and befriend different people and learn about their value systems while deepening an understanding of my own. I returned to Manhattan to start my second year of college, appreciative that I no longer felt uncomfortable wearing my identities, but could now proudly display them and clearly articulate what it meant to be American, Indian, Punjabi, and Sikh. On September 11, 2001, my cloak unraveled as the events of that day unfolded.

That morning, I was startled out of my sleep by my roommate shouting something about smoke billowing from a building. I left my bed to look out of the common room window of our fourteenth-floor apartment, which had a clear view of downtown Manhattan, and saw a huge plume of smoke rising from the top floors of one of the World Trade Center buildings. The image was incomprehensible. Unable to process the moment, I went ahead with my morning routine and got ready for class. I was staring out the window, about to leave, next to my roommate when we both saw the second plane fly in at a steep angle, creating a huge fireball explosion and thick charcoal smoke pouring from the second building. The image of that moment became both surreal. I was unable to assess what I had just witnessed, and because we did not have a radio or news coverage on the TV, I continued my day as if it was like any other, and walked towards downtown Manhattan to my first class, watching the smoldering World Trade Center buildings.

I saw the first tower collapse while walking down a main avenue that had a clear view of both the World Trade Center towers. I had not heard or seen any coverage of these events, nor had anybody else on the street; the only information available was what I and others had witnessed. Shocked, I went to class, hoping that someone there might be able to share some news. However, as soon as I had sat down, my professor began to give a lecture. After some minutes, a student raised their hand and told the professor that the World Trade Center buildings were smoking and that one of them had collapsed. At this time a university personnel opened the doors to the classroom and told us that classes were cancelled for the day. I walked out of the building, looked down at the World Trade Center buildings, and saw the second tower fall. A person stood on a box in the middle of the street, offering people free hugs, displaying the profoundness of the moment. Still not knowing what was happening, I went to a copy shop to get a reader for one of my courses, where they had a TV with live coverage and analysis of what had taken place.

It was surreal watching live TV coverage of something that was taking place right outside of the door to the copy shop. I soon become familiar with the names and images of men sitting around together, having light brown skin, long graying or white beards with white turbans wrapped in a style distinct to a region in Afghanistan, from the style of the mainstream American Sikh community that I, along with other Sikhs, wore where the turban, with minor variations, peaked in the front. I decided that I should go back to the dorm room and use my phone there to call my parents. As I began to walk uptown to Union Square, looking back frequently, I saw bodies emerging from the backdrop of ash and smoke, walking towards uptown Manhattan. When I reached Union Square, masses of people had gathered in the park and on the sidewalks, with people both in shock and confusion, unable to get through to others on their cell phones because of the communication lines being overwhelmed with calls. At this moment I spotted a *sardar* (a respectful term for a Sikh who wears a turban) give a fire extinguisher to a cab driver who was taking emergency supplies to the World Trade Center. As the cab driver drove away, someone from the crowd began to harass the very same *sardar* for his wearing a turban, before other New Yorkers immediately came to his defense and quieted this person.

> Within a few minutes of this incident, I arrived back at my dorm room at around ten o'clock that morning. When I walked in, my roommate told me that my parents had called and wanted me to call them back immediately. So I called my house, and my father, mother, sister, and brother were all on the phone. After telling them where I had been and that I was OK, my older sister got on the phone and began to talk to me. Deeply concerned for my wellbeing, and aware of the media images that were being broadcast, my sister asked me if I was going to continue wearing my turban.

* * *

Part II of this book generally focused on discriminatory acts that may constitute harms that could be redressed in the courts or in another supervisory forum. An action, however, need not rise to the level of a legally cognizable impermissible activity for it to warrant attention. Partap Singh Ajrawat's account is emblematic of that principle.

For example, verbal harassment, though generally protected by First Amendment considerations, may become problematic depending on the context (for example, schools) and on whether the offensive conduct generates a negative cumulative impact for the targeted individual. An individual stare or remark may not seem to be significant, but taken together over one's day-to-day life, they may attain momentum, with significant consequences for the particular Sikh.

In another example, earlier we wrote of a Sikh student whose family decided to move to Britain to avoid the post-9/11 turban-based harassment the student he was receiving in the United States. Margaret A. Gibson in her study similarly addressed Sikh students not participating in school activities as a result of the overall treatment they received from other students.[1] The Sikh Coalition's report quoted one student as saying "I used to have a turban. I used to get into fights, and then I cut my hair."[2] These are just some of the intangible, human affects of the post-9/11 environment on Sikhs in America.

From Part I of our conversation, it should be evident that the Sikh turban carries deep significance for Sikhs. Regrettably, one human consequence of the post-9/11 climate has been for Sikhs to reconsider their wearing of the turban – if hate is directed towards them on the basis of their appearance, and specifically their turbans and unshorn hair, then to avoid such mistreatment, an expedient and sensible course of action is to take off the turban and cut their hair, even if this means violating a central aspect of proper Sikh conduct.

---

1 Margaret A. Gibson, *Accommodation without Assimilation* (Ithaca, NY: Cornell University Press, 1988), p. 162.

2 Sikh Coalition, *Hatred in the Hallways: A Preliminary Report on Bias Against Sikh Students in New York City's Public Schools* (June 2007), p. 5, available at <http://www.sikhcoalition.org/advisories/documents/HatredintheHallwaysFinal.pdf>.

The suggestions that non-legal harms may give rise to social concern and other action, and that the human consequences of such mistreatment also warrant consideration, have been made by Dawinder S. Sidhu. Indeed, he makes clear that there is historical precedent for both ideas, grounded firmly in the nation's civil rights-era struggle to address discrimination against African Americans in the early 1960s.[3]

* * *

> Over fifty years ago, the United States Supreme Court held that Title II of the Civil Rights Act of 1964, which prohibited racial discrimination in public accommodations,[4] was a proper exercise of Congress's authority under the Commerce Clause of the U.S. Constitution.[5] The court noted that discrimination against African Americans by hotels had "a *qualitative* as well as *quantitative* effect on interstate travel by Negroes."[6] The court said that the qualitative effect "was the obvious impairment of the Negro traveler's pleasure and convenience that resulted when he continually was uncertain of finding lodging."[7] As for the quantitative effect, the court observed that "there was evidence that this uncertainty stemming from racial discrimination had the effect of discouraging travel on the part of a substantial portion of the Negro community."[8]
>
> This seminal ruling placed legal importance on the qualitative and quantitative effects on minorities subject to discrimination in ostensibly everyday circumstances. The ruling also recognized the ability of the legislature to address the qualitative and quantitative effects of discrimination. Moreover, the court focused not only on the *act* of excluding African Americans from places of accommodation, but the *experiences* of African Americans in enduring such exclusion, for instance, "having to

3 The following passage is reprinted from, Dawinder S. Sidhu, "The Chilling Effect of Government Surveillance Programs on the Use of the Internet by Muslim Americans," 7 *Univ. of MD. J. of Race, Religion, Gender & Class* 375 (2007), available at <http://ssrn.com/abstract=1002145>.

4 See 42 U.S.C § 2000a (2000).

5 *Heart of Atlanta Motel, Inc. v. U.S.*, 379 U.S. 241 (1964); see also *Katzenbach v. McClung*, 379 U.S. 294, 298 (1964), characterizing the "basic holding" of Heart of Atlanta as finding Title II of the Civil Rights Act of 1964 to be "a valid exercise of the power to regulate interstate commerce insofar as it requires hotels and motels to serve transients without regard to their race or color."

6 Heart of Atlanta Motel, 379 U.S. at 253, emphasis added; see also Jil L. Martin, note, "*United States v. Morrison*: Federalism Against the Will of the States," 32 *Loy. U. Chi. L.J.* 243, 268–69 (2000): "These combined effects on interstate commerce were found to be sufficient to enable Congress to regulate the conduct of such purely local activities."

7 Heart of Atlanta Motel, 379 U.S. at 253.

8 Ibid.

travel great distances to secure" lodging, or having "to call upon friends to put them up overnight" when accommodations were unavailable to them.[9]

Since the terrorist attacks of 9/11, Muslim Americans, Arab Americans, Sikh Americans, and South Asian Americans have been the recipients of a severe and persistent backlash. In the first week following the attacks, 645 bias crimes were directed at those perceived to be Middle Eastern.[10] In the first eight weeks after 9/11, over a thousand bias incidents were reported, including up to nineteen murders, assaults, harassment, and acts of vandalism.[11] The violence is ongoing. In 2006, for example, a turbaned Sikh in California was stabbed in the neck with a steak knife because, in the words of the local prosecutor, the perpetrator "wanted to seek revenge for Sept. 11 and attack a member of the Taliban."[12]

Reports on the post-9/11 backlash against certain ethnic groups almost exclusively focus on hate crimes and other tangible acts of discrimination. It is understandable that the discussion to combat the post-9/11 backlash focuses on tangible actions – as they are more easily reported, verified, and conveyed. Moreover, authorities such as the Federal Bureau of Investigation are charged with the responsibility to address legally cognizable discrimination, such as an assault or act of vandalism. It is beyond question that tangible acts of violence and discrimination deserve the attention of policymakers, the law enforcement community, and the public.

However, a lesson of *Heart of Atlanta Motel* is applicable post-9/11: the experiences of the affected minority groups need not rise to the level of a hate crime or punishable act to warrant the public's consideration or a response from the legislature. That is, the human consequences of discrimination can have legal implications and merit governmental action. For example, the court in *Heart of Atlanta Motel* addressed the act of hotels refusing to lodge African Americans as well as the fact that African Americans were discouraged from traveling due to such experiences.[13] Similarly, in the aftermath of 9/11 it is vital to examine not only instances where a turbaned Sikh has been ejected from an airplane on account of his perceived race or religion, but also where Sikh Americans have "stopped

---

9 Ibid. at 252–53.

10 *South Asian American Leaders of Tomorrow, American Backlash: Terrorists Bring War Home in More Ways than One* (2001), p. 3, available at <http://old.911digitalarchive.org/documents/BiasReport.pdf>.

11 Muneer I. Ahmad, "A Rage Shared by Law: Post-September 11 Racial Violence as Crimes of Passion," 92 *Cal. L. Rev.* 1259, 1261–62 (2004).

12 John Coté, "Hate Crime Alleged in Stabbing of Sikh; Santa Clara Suspect Could Face Life Term if He is Convicted," *San Francisco Chronicle*, August 2, 2006, p. B10.

13 Heart of Atlanta Motel, 379 U.S. at 253.

flying altogether in the months and, in some cases, years after 9/11 to avoid potential problems."[14]

Accordingly, to the extent that the experiences of African Americans during the civil rights era provoked social concern, led to congressional remedy, and earned judicial notice, the experiences of Muslim Americans, Arab Americans, Sikh Americans, and South Asian Americans should similarly trouble those interested in ensuring that all Americans are treated with equality, dignity, and without regard to their race, religion, or national origin.[15] Indeed, the post-9/11 backlash against Muslims and those perceived to be Muslim has received some press coverage.[16] For example, in 2006 the *San Francisco Chronicle* reported that a Muslim woman, who "removes the *hijab*, as the head scarf is commonly referred to, when she goes to job interviews or has to fly[,] … was frustrated by repeated airport security interrogations."[17] In addition, in 2007 a Sikh advocacy organization studied the harassment of Sikh students in New York City public schools and found, among other things, that some Sikh students cut their hair – though Sikhs are required by their faith to keep their hair unshorn[18] – in response to physical harassment.[19] Again, the value of these accounts is that they illuminate the human consequences of discriminatory treatment.

* * *

Partap Singh Ajrawat's story and countless others like his compelled action on the part of the Sikh community. The next chapter describes the beginning, form, and current shape of the Sikh civil rights movement.

---

14 June Han, "We are Americans Too: A Comparative Study of the Effects of 9/11 on South Asian Communities," Discrimination and National Security Initiative (September 2006), p. 20, available at <http://www.geocities.com/dnsinitiative/911_Report.pdf>.

15 See Thomas Ross, "Whiteness after 9/11," 18 Wash. *U. J. L. & Policy* 223, 237 (2005), remarking that "flying while brown" has "displaced its predecessor, 'Driving While Black.'"

16 See Pew Research Center, "Muslim Americans: Middle Class and Mostly Mainstream" (May 22, 2007), pp. 35–39, available at <http://pewresearch.org/assets/pdf/Muslim Americans.pdf>, addressing the worries of Muslims in America, including concerns "about government surveillance, job discrimination, and being harassed in public."

17 Matthai Chakko Kuruvila, "9/11: Five Years Later: Typecasting Muslims as a Race," *San Francisco Chronicle*, September 3, 2006, p. A1.

18 See Khushwant Singh, *A History of the Sikhs* (Delhi: Oxford University Press, 1978), p. 84, listing the five Sikh articles of faith, which include unshorn hair; see also *Cheema v. Thompson*, 67 F.3d 883, 884 (9th Cir. 1995).

19 Sikh Coalition, *Hatred in the Hallways*, p. 5. According to the report, one Sikh student noted: "I used to have a turban. I used to get into fights, and then I cut my hair."

Chapter 21
The Emergence of Sikh Advocacy

In those first few months after 9/11, Sikh Americans felt that they were, for lack of a better term, alone. There was little sense that the government knew about, much less was working to mitigate, the discrimination against Sikhs. This sentiment is not an indictment of the government. For one, it is understandable, to some degree, to expect any discrimination to impact Muslims where the terrorists themselves were Muslim, from predominantly Muslim nations. Accordingly, to direct attention on another group, from another area of the world and a wholly different religious belief system, may not have been anticipated. The severity of the connection between turbans and the terrorists may not have been foreseeable.

Moreover, Sikhs bore their own responsibility to inform the government of what was occurring with respect to discrimination against them, to sufficiently explain to them and others who Sikhs were, and to broadly appeal for tolerance. The Sikhs, however, did not have an established apparatus to contend with the significant backlash against them. Their task was daunting, complex, and multifaceted – one they had to generate essentially from the ground up. To mount an effective response, Sikhs would need to work with the government agencies charged with enforcing civil rights laws, law enforcement authorities to investigate and apprehend those attacking Sikhs, members of Congress to issue proclamations condemning the media regarding images of Sikhs and misconceptions of turbaned individuals, and educate neighborhoods and schools about Sikhs in the area, among other things.

The task, though challenging, needed to be done. Sikhs were being harassed, assaulted, refused air travel, and killed. There was no choice but to respond – Sikhs had to "move," to borrow a term from the 1960s civil rights movement, on their own behalf. Concerned Sikhs, like Amandeep Sidhu, emerged from the community and took the mantle of responsibility for the entire Sikh community in the United States. He and a select group of others blazed the trails in the halls of Congress and in other areas in which the Sikh experience needed to be communicated and addressed. In this chapter, Amandeep Sidhu describes how he converted his concern into action, and more generally, how the efforts of some individual motivated Sikhs coalesced and developed into a Sikh civil rights organization that continues to tackle Sikh civil rights concerns to date.

* * *

Amandeep Sidhu

On the morning of September 11, 2001, I left my apartment in North Arlington for work, heading down George Washington Parkway past the Pentagon. As I listened to the radio, I heard the announcer say: "We are getting reports that a plane hit the World Trade Center in New York" – I thought it was a mistake, or a random accident. But by the time I arrived at my office in Old Town Alexandria and made it upstairs, my colleagues were gathered in a conference room, glued to the television, watching smoke billow out of the first tower on CNN. Within a few minutes of my arrival at the office, the second tower was hit. It was clear that this was no accident. Then, before we even saw the news reports on TV, we looked out of our windows to see smoke rising into the sky from the direction of the Pentagon. Time seemed at a standstill as we saw horrific images of the third attack just a few miles from where we sat. My heart sank. My country had been attacked.

As we continued watching the news, however, my sadness turned to fear. Images of Osama bin Laden starting popping up on the screen, followed by videotapes of al Qaeda training camps and disgruntled Taliban leaders. *All wore turbans. All had beards.* I remembered the taunting and racism that I grew up with, but I knew that this was different. I think that all Sikhs knew, as we watched our television screens, that the public reaction to the 9/11 terrorist attacks would be unprecedented – something we had never experienced before and were not prepared to respond to as quickly as was necessary.

Within minutes of the 9/11 attacks in New York and Washington, DC, Sikh email listservs became notice boards for bias crimes occurring around the country. An elderly Sikh man was beaten with a spiked baseball bat on his way home from a Queens gurdwara (Sikh place of worship) where he had gone to pray for the victims just hours after the attacks. A Sikh physician who was one of the first medical responders to the World Trade Center site – a man who had worked tirelessly saving the lives of his fellow citizens – was chased down the streets of Manhattan by an angry mob yelling "Taliban!" and "Osama!" as he returned to his apartment. And as I drove home from work late that evening, I was forced off of the road by another driver swerving erratically into my lane, waving his arms and presumably yelling racial epithets. Stories like these were repeated in every city across the United States on September 11, and in the days, weeks, and months that followed. This would be our community's reality going forward.

That evening, I sat on my sofa watching the news with tears in my eyes. For the first time in my life – notwithstanding the varied levels of discrimination I faced growing up – I feared for my safety. Never before had the Sikh community in America been such an overwhelming target of unwarranted anger and hostility. When I returned to work, I was greeted by an outpouring of support from my colleagues. They knew I was a Sikh, and immediately understood what our community was going through. But when I walked out for coffee or went to grab lunch, I was greeted with blank stares, dismissive head-nodding, or in the worst instances, hurtful comments under people's breath: "Go home, towelhead!" "Go back to where you came from!"

Did they mean Arlington, where I lived? Or did they mean Richmond, Virginia, where I grew up? Perhaps Norfolk, Virginia, where I was born? They couldn't possibly be telling me to go back "home" to India, from where my parents emigrated in the 1970s, could they? Everyone knew that the terrorists were not from India, right? No, they meant "back home" to the Middle East. They associated the turban not with the Sikh faith, but with Islam – a completely separate and distinct religion. And they associated Islam not with the peaceful and loving religion that is followed by the vast majority of Muslims around the world, but with the radical minority that is represented by Osama bin Laden, al Qaeda terrorists, and the Taliban faithful. In America at that moment, and in the years that followed, a turban equaled terrorism in the eyes of many of our fellow citizens. Then, on September 15, just four days after the 9/11 attacks, Balbir Singh Sodhi – a Sikh small business owner living outside Phoenix, Arizona – was brutally murdered by a self-proclaimed "patriot." We knew that our generation of Sikhs born or raised in the United States had to do something – we could not afford to sit on our hands and hope that the situation would get better on its own.

I remember meeting with two Sikh friends in my apartment on the weekend after the 9/11 attacks to discuss what we could do to make things better. How would we define who we were as Sikhs without simply deflecting hatred and bias onto members of the Muslim community? How would we prevent the "but we're not Muslim" reaction that many members of the Sikh American community wanted to implement? Needless to say, we had to strike a careful balance to ensure not only that we grew stronger as Sikhs, but that our bonds to our fellow advocates in the Muslim, Arab, Hindu, and broader South Asian community were strengthened, not weakened. We resolved that our response would be: "We are Sikh, this is what Sikhs believe in, the Sikh faith is an independent religion from northern India, separate and distinct from Islam – and by the way, it is *not OK* to direct anger and frustration at innocent Muslims, Arabs, and South Asians." With this nuanced response, we would simultaneously respond to our mistaken identity and educate others about who we were as a people.

By the next weekend, our group of three had grown to ten. We were college students, consultants, law students, and lawyers, and we applied our collective skill set to finding a workable solution. We made plans to speak to the community, meet with local and national elected officials, and contact the media. We knew that an informal group of similarly motivated

Sikhs in the New York metropolitan area had created an online database on September 12 to allow hate crime and discrimination reporting – a seed that would quickly grow into the Sikh Coalition. We met every weekend (and many weeknights) at area college campuses and in our company's conference rooms to strategize our activities for the upcoming week. On Sundays, we split into groups and visited the various gurdwaras in metropolitan Washington, DC to educate the *sangats* (congregations) on their civil rights and reassure them that now, more than ever, was a time to stand proud of our identity as Sikh Americans, a vibrant and proud segment of our diverse nation. We contacted media outlets, seeking positive media coverage of the Sikh community that explained our faith and highlighted the myriad stories of hate crimes, employment discrimination, and airport profiling experienced by Sikhs around the country. We knocked on the doors of our elected representatives in Washington, DC in hopes that someone, somewhere would listen.

Eventually, our voice was heard. Two of our colleagues – one of whom grew up in Chicago – visited Senator Dick Durbin's (D-IL) office. In the course of our conversation, Senator Durbin's legislative aid suggested that we draft a resolution that addressed the concerns of the Sikh community; he was confident that Senator Durbin would sponsor such a resolution. A group of attorneys working with the Sikh Coalition quickly put together a draft resolution that identified what it means to be a Sikh, described the experience of Sikhs in the United States post-9/11, and called upon law enforcement authorities to prosecute hate crimes against Sikhs to the fullest extent of the law. Perhaps most importantly, the resolution solidified a label that we had first begun to use in the days after the 9/11 attacks – *Sikh American*. It was at that point in our history that we were transformed as a community from Americans who happened to be Sikh into Sikh Americans – *a new identity for a newly invigorated community*.

Senator Durbin sponsored the resolution in the Senate, and an identical resolution was sponsored in the House by Representatives Mike Honda (D-CA) and Chris Shays (R-CT). Amid the excitement of our legislators actually listening to the needs of the Sikh American community, our group of Washington outsiders instantly became lobbyists. Working with the Sikh Coalition, we put together briefing packages that included information about the Sikh faith and the community's unfortunate post-9/11 experience. We walked the halls of Congress day in and day out to reach as many of the 538 members of the House and 100 senators, seeking co-sponsorship and support. In mid-October, a little over a month after the 9/11 attacks, the resolution passed in the Senate and House and was incorporated into the Patriot Act legislation. Through this Act of Congress, our new identity was defined for generations to come – we were Sikh Americans.

On September 11, Sikh Americans were attacked twice – once as Americans, who love this country dearly and know it as our only home, and next as Sikhs, a faith targeted simply because of our unique identity. We could have responded to this unprecedented reality by hiding our identity or by pointing fingers and redirecting discrimination onto other ethnic or religious groups. But such a reaction would be inconsistent with our ideals as Sikhs to promote justice and equality for all people even in the face of tremendous obstacles. Furthermore, such a response would be incongruous with what we love most about these great United States of America – the idea that all people, regardless of gender, race, or religion, deserve to live a life free from discrimination and oppression. The Sikh American community rose to meet the challenge of fighting for the civil rights and civil liberties of all Americans. For over seven years, the Sikh Coalition and other Sikh advocacy organizations have been working tirelessly to uphold these principles of equality and justice that we hold so dear to our heart – not only as Sikhs, but also as Americans.

* * *

The seed planted by the group of Sikh volunteers that month grew in part into the Sikh Coalition. Although the coalition's work began by firefighting in a crisis, it has slowly evolved to a more proactive approach. Years after 9/11, though the wave of hate crimes may have dissipated somewhat, bias and discrimination against Sikhs has become more institutionalized. What was an acute problem has now become a chronic condition.

Amandeep Sidhu commented on the development of the organizational structure of the Sikh civil rights movement. Harmeet Kaur Dhillon, a partner at Dhillon & Smith LLP in San Francisco, California is one of the most prominent footsoldiers in the Sikh effort to combat discrimination against Sikhs in the courtrooms and in other forums. In this chapter, she recounts her experiences in shaping her career as a Sikh civil rights activist.

* * *

Harmeet Kaur Dhillon

The neighbor's son who threatened to "call the [Ku Klux] Klan" on our family in rural North Carolina. Classmates in public school who made fun of my long braids and funny name. Friends and relatives who were denied jobs unless they shaved their beards, cut their hair and removed their turbans. Friends who wanted to join the military but were turned away due to the government's uniform policy. In the wake of 9/11, Sikhs who were arrested for wearing their kirpans, targeted by slurs of "Osama bin Laden," "raghead," "towelhead," "diaperhead," and worse, or even firebombed, shot and killed, solely because of their religious appearance. A major airline employee who was demoted to a back office job because he insisted on wearing his turban in a customer service role. A qualified applicant to an optical devices company who was denied the job because he refused to cut a hair sample for a drug test. A family man who was denied entry to a chain restaurant in California because he wears a kirpan. A family of eight observant Sikhs, including children, asked to disembark a plane in New York after 9/11. The German car dealership applicant with a turban who passed all the tests with flying colors until the one where he was asked to "shave off" to present the clean-cut appearance desired by the company. The California prison guard applicant denied a job he was otherwise qualified for because the state insisted he shave his beard for a gas mask fit test not shown to be necessary to his job. – These are but some of the pieces that have made up the mosaic of a career devoted in part to protecting the free exercise of religion in American civil society.

For nearly half of my life, I have volunteered a substantial amount of my personal and professional time to safeguarding and advancing the legal rights of Sikhs in the United States. My motivations for advocating Sikh civil rights are manifold – my family background, my strong identification with the Sikh faith and its principles in action, my passion for equal justice, and my belief that America is a stronger nation when it includes the khalsa on an equal level with all other diaspora communities.

I belong to a Gursikh family. My parents and I left India when I was very young, moving to the UK, where my brother was born, and eventually to the U.S. From my early youth, prayer and religion were a daily part of my home life, and every day my mother stressed to my brother and me the importance of spirituality not just on Sundays or during our morning and evening prayers, but also in every action and aspect of our lives. We were taught the importance of implementing the teachings of the Gurus into our values, our behavior towards others, our life goals, and our service to the greater community.

Among the principles of Sikhism that I learned at home at a young age was the concept of *seva* in the form of *tan*, *man*, and *dhan* – selfless service to others through physical labor, mental effort, and contributions of monetary wealth. Unlike the teachings of some other religions, Sikhism believes that every member of the *saadh sangat* (fellowship of the holy) must contribute in all these ways in order to fulfill their obligations to the welfare of the community. During visits to India and weekly trips to the local gurdwara, my brother and I were taught to contribute a small part of our allowance to the community, to help weed the gurdwara garden, serve *langar*, and clean the kitchen, and to research Sikh history and share what we learned with the *sangat* through speeches, youth seminars, and even through "show and tell" at our local public schools. My parents followed the same example – my father, as a physician, offering free medical advice and treatment to needy members of the community, my mother offering guidance and support to troubled women in the community, and both parents contributing their *tan*, *man*, and *dhan*, according to the fullest extent of their resources, to the Sikh community and also to the broader community where we lived in rural North Carolina. Thus, by the time I left home to attend college, the concept of community service according to my means was almost as natural as breathing. But I had to encounter other challenges, and learn more about my faith, beyond the concept of *seva*, in order to reach the place where legal *seva* is a daily part of my life.

Many lawyers grew up aspiring to a legal career, inspired by television shows featuring glamorous role models or gritty criminal law scenarios. A rare few Sikh Americans may even have had lawyers in their families who inspired them to seek a career steeped in words and laws rather than medicine, or mathematics, or engineering, or business – all more common vocations than the law for Sikh immigrants. I came to the law through a circuitous path. Coming from several generations of doctors, military service personnel, and farmers, the idea of being a lawyer never really entered my head until I went to college at Dartmouth. Although my mother successfully invoked the U.S. Constitution's First Amendment Establishment Clause to put an end to Christian prayers to start off the day at my Smithfield, North Carolina elementary school and I used legalistic arguments to extract myself from tricky situations in boarding school, I aspired to a medical career. But Dartmouth's strange confluence of erudition and rigid, orthodox political correctness collided directly with my political worldview and my notions of fair play and reason. When editors and a photographer on my college newspaper were suspended merely for exposing a tenured professor's intolerant rants, the *Dartmouth Review* sued Dartmouth to get the students reinstated – and we won. In other words, armed with the power of the Constitution, sophisticated lawyers from New York and the support of the American Civil Liberties Union and free speech activists nationwide, a small group of teenager dissident students was able to defeat Dartmouth in the courts and vindicate important principles of academic free speech and due process.

Once bitten by the public interest litigation bug, I never looked back. Following a one-year stint as a thinktank journalist in Washington's Heritage Foundation, I headed straight for law school. I was privileged to study law at Thomas Jefferson's University of Virginia Law School in Charlottesville, Virginia. Law schools in the U.S. are often idealistic institutions, and law school provided many opportunities to serve the local community through legal clinics. In addition, there were several community-based public interest groups that offered the opportunity to work directly with people in need. Charlottesville at the time did not have a substantial Sikh population, nor were there any Sikh legal services or public interest groups offering legal services active in the United States. I volunteered during law school at a domestic violence shelter, helping to take calls from and counsel women suffering physical, mental, and emotional abuse at the hands of their partners. That experience was my first opportunity to apply my legal training to a deserving cause. Even though I was not directly aiding members of my own community, by helping women in need I was furthering the Sikh principle of *sarbat da bhalla*, as Sikhs pray every day in the *ardaas* prayer – "May all prosper," or "May peace come to all."

An equally important pair of concepts in the Sikh faith which shaped my pro bono career are the concepts of *miri piri* and the principle of self-defense and defense of righteous principles as embodied in the *kirpan*. *Miri piri* is the principle that a religious movement must also have political and physical power in order to survive and thrive. The unique marriage of spirituality and temporal power is literally represented by the two connected *nishaan sahibs* on the premises of *Harmandir Sahib* in Amritsar – the seat of both spiritual and political power of the Sikh *panth*. In the days of the Gurus, political and physical power literally meant having an army to protect the principles of Sikhism and the people of the region. Many Sikhs continue to believe that tangible political power is essential to protect a minority faith from oppression and corruption from other elements. Today, living and practicing here in the American diaspora community, having an army at one's disposal is not quite practical. Having political power, however, is within our grasp. And under the U.S. Constitution, free access to the courts allows Sikhs and Sikh lawyers to seek justice under the law despite their minority status. A community skillfully represented by lawyers to fight on the battlefields of the courtroom has an important socio-political tool with which to protect its interests.

Just as the kirpan symbolizes a Sikh's duty to protect herself and others from attack, the Sikh lawyer's effective deployment of legal tools such as legal research, oral advocacy, negotiation skills, and if necessary, battle in the courts are all weapons and tools that it is the duty of a Sikh lawyer to unsheath when justice demands their use. Any Sikh armed with the legal tools to help another Sikh fight injustice, or obtain redress for a private or societal wrong, is duty bound to use those legal tools. A Sikh lawyer who says "I'm too busy" or "I'd rather be watching football" rather than coming to the aid of someone in need might as well be a Sikh man or woman with a kirpan who stands idly by while a mugging takes place in front of their eyes.

Upon leaving law school, I was determined to contribute to the welfare of the Sikh diaspora as well as the broader American community of deserving people with unmet legal needs when I graduated from law school. Following a one-year clerkship at the United States Court of Appeals for the Fourth Circuit, I began my private practice of law at Shearman & Sterling, an international law firm headquartered in New York City. In addition to my heavy caseload of mergers and acquisitions, securities, and insurance coverage litigation in various federal courts, Shearman gave me the opportunity to volunteer on cases involving important legal rights asserted by civil rights plaintiffs, criminal defendants, and human rights petitioners.

I let my partners know that I was particularly interested in helping clients from India, hoping that they might let me know of any cases involving Sikh civil rights or human rights.

The first pro bono case that came my way through my firm in 1994 *was* from India, but not what I had expected. A partner called me to let me know that the Lawyer's Committee for Human Rights (now known as Human Rights Watch) was seeking a pro bono lawyer with Hindi or Urdu language skills to represent an Immigration and Naturalization Service (INS) detainee seeking political asylum – from India. Intrigued, I asked for more information. I learned from the Lawyer's Committee that the detainee was from Kashmir, that he alleged that his brother had been murdered by the Indian government for speaking on the radio about the plight of Kashmiris under occupation by military forces, and that his parents had disappeared after a military bombing of their poor neighborhood in Srinagar. My client obtained business visa papers and fled India, turning himself in at John F. Kennedy Airport in New York and declaring himself a political refugee.

During the period in question – the early 1990s – as a Sikh activist I knew that the Indian government was causing the "disappearance" of thousands of young Sikh men in its efforts to suppress dissent in Punjab, and I had read about similar atrocities in Kashmir, so it was not difficult for me to believe my client's story. However, the U.S. government at that time, and to this day, took a very dim view of claims of political persecution from Indian refugees, largely due to propaganda from India, which put pressure on the U.S. and other Western nations not to give credence to claims by Indian asylum-seekers. The Lawyers Committee told me that only about 5 percent of Indian political refugees seeking asylum in the U.S. received it. Thus, I was faced with a daunting task; and while I had passed the New York bar, I was still awaiting admission, a formality involving background and reference checks that took several months. I was not even a Sikh lawyer yet!

Nonetheless, I took up the challenge of the Kashmiri refugee's case, meeting him over the course of several months in the notorious Wackenhut detention facility in Queens (each time having to meet him in a grim meeting room to which he was brought handcuffed and wearing an orange prison jumpsuit). He didn't speak much English, and I spoke no Urdu, but we were able to communicate somehow through my broken Punjabi and his limited English. I quickly put together the story of terror and persecution at the hands of a powerful government. With the help of information from the Red Cross's search for my client's parents, newspaper reports, reports from Amnesty International, and numerous other third-party sources, as well as affidavits from my client's surviving relatives, I compiled a phonebook-sized brief and submitted it to the INS, which summarily rejected his claims.

I proceeded to trial before an administrative law judge, where my Kashmiri client's tears, the story of India's occupation of Srinagar by military force, and the reports from human rights groups together convinced the judge to grant my client political asylum. I will never forget the tears of gratitude in his eyes when I went to the prison to pick him up and gave him a one-way plane ticket to Florida, where his mother's brother lived. Contrary to the cynical comments of my community which teased me for being so gullible as to lend money and time to a penniless and stateless client, he paid me back for the ticket, thanked me profusely with his words and deeds, and kept in touch with me for several years. The decision in his case is framed and holds the primary place of prominence on my office wall of degrees and honors.

Bitten by the pro bono bug, I continued to search for opportunities to represent Sikh clients. But the next cases that came my way again were from asylum-seekers from other parts of the world. I successfully represented victims of persecution from Eritrea and Tibet. I found a tremendous personal and professional satisfaction in overcoming the odds and freeing these men from sure death sentences had they been returned, protesting, to their repressive home countries. These experiences allowed me to feel that I was upholding the principle of *sarbat de bhalla* while at the same time developing better legal skills to help my own community when the time came.

According to the same principle of helping whoever in the community needed with what I could offer, during my early years as a lawyer I represented several victims of domestic violence through a New York domestic violence organization. I was particularly interested in helping South Asian victims. My most memorable case was a Bangladeshi woman in her twenties with three children living in New York whose husband repeatedly and brutally beat her, sometimes in front of her children. But he refused to grant her a divorce according to Muslim rites, and he refused to cooperate with her civil divorce filings. In New York during that time, filing for divorce and obtaining custody of their three children in the face of her husband's opposition, and without a lawyer – particularly a lawyer who understood her religious need to be divorced according to sha'ariah law – was virtually an insurmountable task for my client.

I was able to convince the trial judge of my client's position, and through some aggressive arm-twisting by the court my client was granted a divorce by her husband, granted custody of her three children, and granted freedom from a lifetime of abuse. Again, I will never forget her tears of joy and the tears of her three children when they heard the news. She went on to remarry another observant Muslim husband, and stayed in touch with me for many years. She was but one of the needy women, some of whom were from Punjab or other parts of India, who I have represented over the years.

I have become an outspoken advocate of the rights of South Asian victims of domestic violence as a result of these experiences and others.

Finally, in the late 1990s, through the organization of groups such as United Sikhs in Service of America (U.S.SA, now known simply as United Sikhs) and the Sikh American Legal Defense and Education Fund (SALDEF), as a lawyer I was given opportunities to serve the Sikh community. U.S.SA's founders approached me to incorporate and obtain tax-exempt status for the organization in the U.S., a daunting and complex corporate task for a litigation lawyer, but it was the first opportunity I got, and I took it. I also incorporated and obtained tax-exempt status for the Logharh Sikh Educational Foundation, a Sikh summer camp founded by my brother, Mandeep, with the help of several east coast Sikh families. These were satisfying experiences for me and again, helped me expand my skills into new realms.

My first opportunities to serve Sikh clients hands-on came through SALDEF, which was already organized and contacted me several times to render advice to Sikh students and job seekers or employees who were victims of employment discrimination. The second most populous category of Sikh civil rights plaintiffs is in the area of public accommodation – Sikhs denied the right to enter a restaurant, or nightclub, or courthouse, or public school, or other venue ostensibly open to the public. A third category is Sikhs who are victims of hate crimes or hate speech, including bullying in their schools or taunting at sporting events. This category of offenses is pervasive, but reached a peak in the months following the terrorist attacks on our country on September 11, 2001.

In over a decade of representing Sikh clients, usually at the counseling stage, but occasionally in courtroom battles, what I found time and time again was that many Sikh clients encountered unique challenges in finding lawyers to advance their claims. The typical pattern is of a jobseeker who passes his qualification testing, but then is told he must cut his hair or shave his beard in order to take the job; or she is told she cannot wear her small kirpan on the job; or they are told they cannot wear their *kara*, or their turban, or any other article of faith on the job. But these qualified, determined, and presentable Sikh clients almost always find other – sometimes better – jobs very soon, thus their damages are so limited from the traditional point of view of a plaintiff's lawyer that very few lawyers are willing to take on their cases on a paying or contingency basis. And sadly, there are still very few Sikh lawyers in private practice willing to set aside their caseloads to take up a non-paying case that vindicates the principle of free exercise of religion in the workplace as guaranteed by the United States Constitution, Title VII, and numerous other statutes at the federal, state, and local levels. Similarly, in public accommodation and hate crimes cases, damages are typically very limited and the public interest relatively narrow. In most cases, unless a Sikh lawyer steps forward to advance such a case pro bono publico, the complaint never ripens to a legal challenge.

Over the years, I have successfully represented Sikh employees or job applicants in numerous cases, ranging from a Sikh denied a customer service job with a major airline (he then obtained a better job, but won damages in a settlement brokered by the EEOC as we approached trial), a Sikh who wanted to work in a sales job on the floor of a major German automobile dealership (he won an apology and took a better job elsewhere), and several Sikhs who were denied the right to wear their kirpans on the job or to job-qualification tests (we reached settlements in all the cases, including company-wide changes to employment policies).

Most recently, a Sikh was denied the right to take the final test to be employed as a prison guard in California because he refused to shave his beard to take the gas mask fit test. After years of stubborn, incalcitrant rejection by the California prison authorities, and some of the most obnoxious litigation conduct I have seen in my entire career, with co-counsel from the Sikh Coalition I took the prison guard case to trial before the State Board of Personnel, and won a written opinion that the California Department of Corrections and Rehabilitation had failed to accommodate our client's religious observance, and ordering the department to process his application forthwith. To date, litigation in that matter is still pending, and may well proceed into federal court in the near future. Thus, that client's victory has been bittersweet – after years of litigation and patient following of the rules, he still has not been allowed to take the test or obtain the job he otherwise qualifies for at the Department of Corrections.

Public accommodation cases are another major category of civil rights abuses suffered by Sikhs. Some cases involve Sikhs being barred from restaurants or nightclubs, usually because they are wearing a turban, but occasionally because they are wearing a kirpan. In the turban discrimination cases, pre-litigation advocacy in the form of letters, calls, and if necessary local political pressure, usually result in a prompt settlement in the form of a changed admission policy, as the law is very clear and well settled on the side of the Sikh complainant. Kirpan cases in voluntary public accommodation present a particular challenge because criminal ordinances governing open display of weapons sometimes clash with the right to wear a religious article of faith. The law concerning these types of situation is in flux, and a pro bono practitioner on behalf of the Sikh community must be careful to aggressively push only those cases that are more likely than not to yield positive precedent, rather than select extreme cases whose pursuit will likely yield restrictive decisions negatively affecting future, and possibly less extreme, factual situations.

Public accommodation cases involving government settings, such as courthouses and schools, again pose particular challenges. Turban accommodation cases are, again, far easier to resolve in this context through letter writing, political pressure, and in some instances, the involvement of civil rights groups such as the American Civil Liberties Union. Surprisingly, even within the past five years courts, and occasionally public schools, have barred Sikhs wearing turbans from entry. A particularly memorable case in which I was involved concerned a Texas judge's refusal to permit a Sikh wearing a turban to enter the courtroom to protest his traffic ticket. It took increasingly vociferous threats of judicial disciplinary proceedings and federal civil rights litigation to resolve that matter. As one would expect, it is often very difficult to find a lawyer practicing in a particular jurisdiction to threaten disciplinary sanctions against a judge before whom he might appear, or to threaten civil rights litigation against a school district attended by his or her children or their neighbors' children. This is where a broad network of Sikh civil rights advocates around the country prepared to act in other jurisdictions would be particularly useful, yet here again where our legal community falls far short of serving our spiritual community's needs.

This need is even greater in what may be considered a category of "public accommodation" cases affecting our community – Sikhs unfortunately ensnared in the criminal justice system. In California alone during my last two years of practice, my assistance has been sought in the cases of several Sikh criminal defendants or adjudicated convicts who were denied the right to wear their turbans and/or unshorn hair, in clear violation of state and federal law. In these cases, even the Sikh community usually fails to seek assistance for these individuals, either because the crimes of which they have been accused (including murder or violent assault) are so horrific, or because the individuals have been convicted, either by a court or in the court of public opinion, and the community deems them unworthy of protection. In these cases, due to a paucity of Sikh lawyers in the criminal defense (or prosecution, for that matter) fields, court-appointed or retained defense counsels typically do not have enough knowledge about Sikhism to raise an adequate challenge to blatantly discriminatory and even unconstitutional practices, and they have little recourse to publicly available information or precedent sufficient to address the civil rights issues. In any event, in most cases criminal defense attorneys are solely focused on getting their clients acquitted, with civil rights concerns distant or non-existent. As a result, the burden often falls upon bar associations or national Sikh civil rights organizations to advance the causes of these inmates or detainees – if they are even made aware of the cases.

All Sikhs are painfully aware of the high incidence of anti-Sikh bias that arose in the wake of 9/11 – incidents of shouted epithets comparing Sikhs to terrorists, violent and even fatal attacks, and casual comments or social slights that affected every Sikh family, particularly those with family members who wore turbans and/or beards. Many of us wept to see our own family members subjected to attacks. Many of us cringed to see our community reflexively resorting to pasting American flag stickers in their back windows to avoid being targeted for abuse. Yet many of us are aware that such incidents of violence, hatred and abuse were not a novel but despicable side-effect of 9/11 – they are phenomena we have been living with for generations. Growing up in the deep South, in rural North Carolina, I remember my family being subjected to racial epithets and threats that the Ku Klux Klan would "get us." They didn't "get us," but perhaps that was in part because we proudly maintained our values while conspicuously taking weapons training courses and being actively involved in the community. I am convinced that my mother's dozen years of service as a Republican elections judge in rural Johnston County had something to do with the esteem in which my family was held, despite our "strange" appearance. Communities in which Sikhs have segregated themselves, and refused to participate in daily civic activities, tend to be those communities in which nameless, faceless cowards have felt free to attack our families.

In the wake of 9/11, when I felt fear for the safety of my own family, I was a founder of a Sikh civil rights group in Silicon Valley called the Sikh Communications Council, which included my brother Mandeep, a fellow Sikh lawyer, and several Sikh entrepreneurs, professionals and business executives. Our goal was simple: to educate the U.S. media and intelligentsia about Sikhs, our principles, and our social values. Perhaps nothing focused each of our self-knowledge about Sikhism and the limits of our beliefs as much as this coruscating experience – all around us, Sikh friends and brothers were cutting their hair and attempting to hide who they were. A Sikh family man in Arizona was murdered; a young Sikh man in Rhode Island was taken off an Amtrak train and arrested for wearing his kirpan. We were all afraid for our lives.

Then a senior associate at a Silicon Valley law firm, I appealed to my firm for the opportunity to use its resources to quickly research and compile a report on hate crimes, kirpan right-to-carry, and immigration issues pertaining to the Sikh community for use as an emergency resource in the pressing crisis. I am grateful that the firm responded positively, allowing me to deploy several associates across the U.S. to conduct research on various issues pertaining to Sikh civil rights issues specifically related to the 9/11 attacks. The hundreds of pages of reports we compiled were distributed to Sikh groups around the country, and are still a useful resource for me today.

A related incident that I will never forget, in that heated 9/11 atmosphere, was being asked to speak at a Silicon Valley Indian American business forum a few months after the attacks. I was a panelist in a session concerning the impact of 9/11 on Indian Americans. One of the leading Sikh American venture capitalists in Silicon Valley was a fellow panelist. The majority of the several hundred attendees were Indian Americans, with a sprinkling of mainstream media in the audience. I recounted several incidents of Sikh

Americans being stopped at security and missing their flights from Bay Area airports, or being asked to leave airplanes because fellow passengers were uncomfortable with their presence – a phenomenon that since has widely been described as "flying while brown." As murmurs of dismay traveled through the audience, the venture capitalist in the audience – a fellow Sikh – authoritatively interjected: "I don't know what you are talking about. I have flown around the country and around the world many times since 9/11, and no one has treated me any differently. I don't think there is any prejudice against Indians today."

One could have heard a pin drop in the audience at this obvious cognitive dissonance, as the audience waited to see if any panel member would challenge this canard. I did – and I pointed out to the venture capitalist that perhaps he had not encountered any problems because he had left his turban and beard behind many decades ago, and he no longer identified himself or was identified by the public with the Sikh faith. It was primarily identifiable Sikhs – and not just "Indians" – who were singled out for hatred and abuse. And who had to stand up and reaffirm what they believed, and why their values were consistent with our communities. And I could not help but remember that the Gurus asked Sikhs to adopt a distinctive identity for the very reason that in times of strife and challenge, they could not hide and they must – *must* – stand up for what they believed. The venture capitalist had no response, and never has since in the years that I have met him publicly on numerous occasions. For how can anyone credibly deny that Sikhs have borne the brunt of the fearful and ignorant backlash triggered by 9/11? Certainly no civil rights lawyer who hears such complaints on a weekly or monthly basis.

I believe I have striven throughout my career to serve the civil rights needs of the Sikh community, consistent with my personal values, my *dharma* or duty, and my understanding of the specific requirements of our faith which require us to serve our communities according to our abilities to defend and persuade. I continue, however, to be concerned and even haunted by the "ones who got away." I will recount perhaps the starkest example of this – a Sikh lawyer who would not help himself, and certainly would not help others.

As a young lawyer, I received a call from another young Sikh lawyer about a law student from his school – one of the top ten law schools in the country – who was facing an employment problem. The student had a blue-chip college background, and was a top student at the law school. I spoke to him and learned that during law firm recruiting season, he had been offered employment by a leading law firm in the South – a firm known for hiring only the cream of the crop. During the offer call, the hiring attorney informed the young Sikh law student that the summer internship was his, as long as he removed his turban and shaved his beard. The student was very shaken by this incident, which had taken place only days earlier. I reassured him that his credentials were strong, and that he would get other offers. His duty, *as a Sikh*, was to report this law firm to the law school recruiting department immediately. For an egregious violation of this nature, that law firm could have been barred from recruiting on campus by all law schools across the country.

The law student promised to think about what I had said. I stayed in touch with him, even offered to help him file the complaint and sue for discrimination, but beseeched him to at least file the complaint with his law school so that other law firms would think many times before making such blatantly discriminatory requests. The student, as predicted, went on to receive job offers from even better law firms, one of which he accepted. Yet he still refused to act to record this instance of blatant religious discrimination at his law school; refused, selfishly, to act to protect other Sikh law students from similar discrimination, and refused to punish the big Southern law firm for its outdated, offensive and illegal discrimination. Even with the safety of a job offer from a more prestigious New York law firm, where he interned and ultimately accepted the job offer, that young Sikh lawyer rejected his duty to himself and his community. The small act of reporting an incident of discrimination – which would have helped to protect many others less fortunately situated, with fewer job offers and lesser qualifications – was too much to ask. Today, that lawyer is successful. I am not one to judge, but I can venture to guess that he has not logged very many legal hours in the past decade on behalf of those less fortunate.

* * *

Unfortunately, the story of that young Sikh man is all too common. He turns into the privileged young Sikh lawyer who does not help his community even by the small act of standing up for himself. Or the young Sikh professional who simply denies that an act of discrimination has not just happened to her, but potentially hobbled the careers of others. Or the Sikh hourly worker who silently suffers abuse on the job or rejection from more desirable jobs, accepting this as his fate in a country whose laws decree that such treatment is no one's fate. It is up to the next generation of Sikh lawyers to help educate our communities that it is no American's fate to be discriminated against because of their faith, that it is no Sikh's fate to silently suffer minor and major slights relating to their religious observances, and that it is no Sikh American's fate to accept any unfair treatment in a civil society where all citizens and voters are empowered with the ability to change their circumstances through their own actions and the actions of their communities.

Chapter 22
Non-traditional Efforts

In our law review article, we noted that:

> the American legal system is unlikely to protect Sikhs from the most common form of discrimination – verbal insults such as "bin Laden," "raghead," and "terrorist" – though the nation's laws may protect Sikhs from a more drastic and wide-reaching policy of prohibiting Sikhs from wearing turbans in public schools. Sikhs, however, must continue to utilize non-legal methods to ensure that discriminatory activities do not occur in the first place, primarily by educating individuals who are unfamiliar with the Sikh turban or who are likely to associate it with terrorism.[1]

Such non-legal efforts formed part of the overall Sikh community's response to the backlash against turbaned Sikhs. In other words, Sikhs did not rely exclusively upon redressing their grievances in the courts or seeking favorable policy developments in Congress; instead, they had to draw upon every tool they had at their disposal to prevent further discrimination from occurring by educating others about Sikh identity.

Sikhs have taken the bait. For example, a group of consisting of mainly second-generation Sikhs formed a community service organization called Sikhcess, which has launched a number of "feed the homeless" campaigns in various corners of America. As of mid-2009, Sikhcess had provided free food to over 155,000 individuals. Sikhcess not only puts the Sikh ideal of selfless service into practice, but also demonstrates to non-Sikhs exactly what Sikhs stand for and believe in. In that respect, Sikhcess is a means by which Sikhs have informed others of their faith and identity and thereby helped to eradicate the ignorance which allows for hate violence to occur.

One Sikh, Navnit Singh, developed a turbaned cartoon character in the hopes that turbans would be seen as something "cool."[2] One can understand the reasoning for developing an alternative characterization of the turban when others may tend to associate it with bin Laden or view it as a marker for ideological extremism.

Sikh actor Waris Ahluwalia rose in popularity around the same time. He recognized the need to use his position to educate the public about Sikhs. During a

---

1 Neha Singh Gohil and Dawinder S. Sidhu, "The Sikh Turban: Post-9/11 Challenges to this Article of Faith," 9 *Rutgers J. L. & Religion* 10, 70 (2008).

2 See Rama Lakshmi, "A Ritual Slowly Unravels in India: Alarm Grows as More Sikh Youths Give Up Turbans," *Washington Post*, March 29, 2009.

brief scene in a Denzel Washington movie, Waris managed to work in a discussion about the suspicious eye that law enforcement and the public cast on his turban. Waris remembers that his discussion of the turban was not in the script. He made it up as he went along.

Another Sikh American, filmmaker Valarie Kaur, chose to chronicle Sikh stories. She made a documentary film, *Divided We Fall: Americans in the Aftermath*, on the backlash against Sikh Americans after 9/11. In 2005, Kaur reflected on her decision to create the film as she stood at the very location that precipitated the post-9/11 era – Ground Zero.

* * *

Valarie Kaur

> The film began as a student project in summer 2001. I was a 20-year-old Stanford student, majoring in religion and international relations, home for the summer before my junior year. But I was not planning to be at Stanford in the fall. I had gotten the school to pay for a trip to Punjab, India, where I would spend four months wandering through villages that bordered Pakistan, asking people my grandparents' age to tell me their memories of the 1947 Partition of India – that terrible violent event when Britain freed India but left it bleeding in two pieces. …
>
> And my cousin Sonny agreed to go with me. He was 18, just graduated from high school, and spoke Punjabi fluently. It was a perfect plan. We were planning to leave for India in late September. I was in my pajamas in front of the television set when it happened. And I could not move. After mugshots of a turbaned and bearded bin Laden, the president appeared on television and said that the country was unified in grief and resolve against the terrorists.
>
> But on email lists I began to hear stories of violence against brown-skinned Americans on our own streets. Four days later, on September 15, 2005, there was news that a turbaned Sikh man had been killed in a hate crime in Arizona. His name was Balbir Singh Sodhi. He was a friend of family friends in Phoenix. The one who killed him, yelled, "I am a patriot." His murder felt like the death of an uncle. …
>
> Then I began to remember. The violence of Partition was never really documented. Neither were the murders and disappearances of Sikhs in 1984. So too these full stories of hate crimes against Sikh, Muslim, and Arab Americans were not making headlines. I had a camera. I had time. I could document them. …
>
> Within days, I was on the road in my old silver Honda with my cousin as cameraman. He held the camera, I held the list of questions, and we entered the whirlwind. …

For the next four months I traveled across the country, up and down California, across to Arizona, over to Washington, DC and New York City. We spoke with dozens of Sikh American, Muslim American, and Arab-American families, and captured their stories in over 100 hours of footage. They were stories of fear and unspeakable loss, but also resilience and hope. The journey ended in Punjab, India, where I met and interviewed the widow of Balbir Singh Sodhi.

We spent four months on the road. Fourteen American cities. One hundred hours of footage. Two students. And the question: Why? The stories I heard moved me deeply. They deserved recognition. I wanted so badly to raise them up into the light and get them to the big screen ….

All this violence still defies my comprehension, but I believe that there is redemption in hearing and retelling these stories. These people have endured terrorism, discrimination, detention, displacement, torture, and war. Many of them live in ways invisible and unrecognizable to the public. Their suffering is not recognized, not dignified, not grievable.

But when they tell their stories – when the Afghan widow weeps beside me, when the turbaned Sikh boy wants his uncle back, when the black woman wonders why no one cares – they make me see them, recognize them and remember them.

Standing at Ground Zero, remembering each story, I began to see a common anguish. And I began to hear a common cry – *that it could be otherwise*. We have the resources to build a state and society that does *not* persecute minorities in times of war, that does *not* allow the poor to suffer, that does *not* engender more violence. It is possible to work towards this common vision.

On this four-year anniversary, we can retell and remember the stories of people who died on September 11, *and* the people whose lives have been broken in its ongoing aftermath, and *respond* in ways that stop cycles of violence, in big steps and small gestures, starting now.

My hope is that this film can be a small part of the solution.

For me, many things have changed in the last four years. I am stronger and steadier than when I first set out across the country to make this documentary. But in other ways, I feel the same as I did at 20. I am nervous and vulnerable. My fears are still with me.

And once again, I am thick in the confusion of events outside my control. It is just days after the terrible bombings in London. And there is news of backlash against Sikhs, Muslims, and Arabs in Europe. Mosques and Sikh gurdwaras and have been vandalized. The tension is high. Yet again, there is a need, a life-and-death need, for us to hear each other's stories.

My hope is that this film tells a rich and complex story about the impact of fear and division in America and abroad. The story is about the struggle for recognition. It is an American struggle, the struggle for human dignity.

In a nation and world where divisions abound, this message is important now more than ever.

* * *

A few years later, another Sikh, Sonny Caberwal, was selected to participate in a Kenneth Cole fashion campaign that intended to encourage social change through presenting the views and images of different people. The campaign, "Awearness," featured individuals who defied the traditional mold of a high-end model and came from different walks of life with unique backgrounds. Caberwal's images as a fashion icon offer an alternative depiction of Sikhs that differs markedly from the wholly negative imagery of bin Laden. Moreover, his affiliation with a high-end label in Kenneth Cole lends instant and well-recognized credibility to his images, and to the Sikh turban more generally. In his spreads, which have been seen from Manhattan to Germany, Caberwal described his experiences as a turbaned Sikh in the United States in the aftermath of the 9/11 terrorist attacks. A video clip entitled "We all Walk in Different Shoes" accompanied the campaign. In that, he explained why he participated in the program:

> My name is Sonny Caberwal and I am an entrepreneur. I am a member of the Sikh religion – Sikhism is a monotheistic religion started in the 1500s in India. As part of our religion, we believe that Sikh men maintain a very strong visual identity. We're often, in this day and age, mistaken for Muslims. I always drew strength from keeping this unique identity to remind me that I am different. For me, it's just a matter of reinforcement. For others, it's become a symbol of hate and a symbol of fundamentalism.
>
> When September 11th happened, I was in law school. I was watching TV. with all my peers, and I looked around and the Taliban came on TV. They looked just like Sikh people. As soon as I walk into a room, people have this certain association or what they think that someone who would wear a turban what they must behave like, what they must think like, whether it comes in the form of people talking slowly to you, people being disrespectful, or people flat-out naming-calling or even to the point of violence.
>
> You try to combat it and do the best you can because, at the end of the day, if I didn't have my identity I would have traded that away. That's why I think it's important for people to respect other people's differences, not because you agree with those differences, but because being able to put yourself in different people's shoes may impact how *you* think about how you behave, and it may help you grow and behave in ways that you never even thought were possible before.[3]

3 The clip is available at <http://www.youtube.com/watch?v=r60pjTdsmj0>.

As images can create and reinforce unintended stereotypes – for example, that anyone with a turban may be like bin Laden – the Sikh entry into media and the arts was of critical importance, and itself represented a major non-traditional means by which ignorance of Sikh identity could be ameliorated. For example, in 2004, Dawinder S. Sidhu contemplated whether the rise of certain elements of South Asian culture in the United States – including two movies and a song – could "represent an alternative, and perhaps more expedient, route to the advancement of South Asians," as "appealing for tolerance and restraint have only gone so far" and "South Asians have not yet entrenched themselves in legislatures or on Washington's K Street."[4] As Sikhs continue to work to counter the ignorance about Sikh turbans and the apparent link between turbans and terrorism, they will be prudent to explore and expand non-traditional avenues to inform others about their identity and religious teachings. Indeed, this book itself is a manifestation of the same interest to improve understanding about Sikhs through non-traditional means.

4 Dawinder S. Sidhu, "The Revolution Must Be Televised," *Pennsylvania Gazette*, March/April 2004.

Chapter 23
Government Appeals for Tolerance

On the morning of September 11, 2001, over 3,000 innocent men, women, and children were killed. Millions of people watched in horror and were fearful of falling victim to an another catastrophic attack that might take place in Los Angeles, Chicago, or Main Street, U.S.A, in a shopping mall, airport, or high-rise building. The nation was at war, to be sure, but it was also in a state of crippling terror.

The moment the nation realized it was under attack, the leaders of the government were compelled to react. They had two overlapping and critical goals – to track down those responsible and hold them to account, and to prevent them from exacting another act of terror on the United States. In his memoir, former Assistant Attorney General and current Harvard law professor Jack Goldsmith writes that the administration was "under pressure to stop a second attack by an enemy it couldn't see and didn't fully understand," that the president held the "ultimate obligation" to ensure another attack did not take place, and that government was "largely in the dark about where or how the next terrorist attack will occur."[1] As Vice President Dick Cheney's counsel told Goldsmith, if a second attack did occur, "the blood of hundred thousand people who die in the next attack will be on *your* hands."[2]

Understandably, the federal government concerned itself with the prosecution of a military campaign and the necessary investigative inquiries into the perpetrators of the worst terrorist attack on American soil since Pearl Harbor, the defining event of a generation. Operating in this environment, one may suspect that the government would have been uninterested in discrimination against Muslims or those perceived to be Muslim, particularly given the pressing demands of their new roles and the uncomfortable fact that the terrorists invoked Islam to justify the 9/11 attacks. Even if they thought about it, some of those government officials viewed engagement with the Muslim American community as serving just one purpose – counter-radicalization of the internal enemy.

Still, despite the pressure accompanying the attacks and the naysayers, high-level government officials nonetheless responded shortly after the backlash began, to condemn hate violence against Muslims or those perceived to be Muslim. They strove to indicate that the war was not against Islam or Muslims, to portray Islam as a religion of peace, and to convey the message that to harass or harm innocent

1 Jack Goldsmith, *The Terror Presidency* (New York: W.W. Norton, 2007), pp. 67–69, 75.

2 Ibid., p. 71; emphasis in original.

Americans did not represent the best of the country's ideals and character. For example, six days after the attacks, President George W. Bush visited a mosque and reminded the public:

> America counts millions of Muslims amongst our citizens, and Muslims make an incredibly valuable contribution to our country. Muslims are doctors, lawyers, law professors, members of the military, entrepreneurs, shopkeepers, moms and dads. And they need to be treated with respect. In our anger and emotion, our fellow Americans must treat each other with respect.
>
> Women who cover their heads in this country must feel comfortable going outside their homes. Moms who wear cover must be not intimidated in America. That's not the America I know. That's not the America I value.
>
> I've been told that some fear to leave; some don't want to go shopping for their families; some don't want to go about their ordinary daily routines because, by wearing cover, they're afraid they'll be intimidated.
>
> That should not and that will not stand in America.
>
> Those who feel like they can intimidate our fellow citizens to take out their anger don't represent the best of America, they represent the worst of humankind, and they should be ashamed of that kind of behavior.

At first, Sikhs were not explicitly included in these or similar remarks by federal government officials, even though Sikhs were encountering significant discrimination almost immediately after the towers fell. Almost two weeks after Balbir Singh Sodhi's death, President Bush addressed the targeting of turbaned Sikhs:

> An American Sikh has been killed, unjustly so. These citizens bring their hearts with them, and I can assure them that our government will do everything we can to not only bring those people to justice, but also to treat every human life as dear, and to respect the values that made our country so different and so unique. We're all Americans, bound together by common ideals and common values.

Chapter 24
Federal Enforcement and Outreach

The federal government did more than just discuss the backlash against Muslims, Arabs, South Asians, and Sikhs. Within months, a Special Counsel on Post-9/11 National Origin Discrimination was established at the Department of Justice. The agency also set up a working group on such discrimination. At present, the Department of Homeland Security's Office of Civil Rights and Civil Liberties assumes responsibility for working with community leaders and ensuring that government security policies take into account the civil rights concerns of the affected groups. The Justice and Homeland Security agencies continue to spearhead the government's relationship with Muslim, Arab, and South Asian Sikh advocacy organizations and efforts to temper security policies with respect and sensitivity towards members of the targeted groups. For example, regularly held inter-agency meetings serve as a platform for community leaders to directly address problems on the ground or potential issues with pending policy initiatives.

While these efforts have been helpful, bias about the Sikh turban remains rampant even in the halls of power. For example, in 2007, the Transportation Security Administration made an overnight decision to place turbans on a list of "suspicious headwear" that must be secondarily searched at U.S. airports. The decision was made with little prior research and without any consultation with community groups. TSA officials met with Sikh advocacy groups in the aftermath of the new policy's rollout. At that meeting, the Sikhs asked the policy-makers whether they had ever seen a turban from the inside, whether they knew how it was tied? The answer was "No." Instead, they had created a regulation that effectively singled out Sikhs without understanding who they were.

The Special Counsel on Religious Discrimination at the Department of Justice has worked tirelessly to address some of these internal attitudes and the resulting policy implications. To describe in greater detail his office's response to the post-9/11 backlash against turbaned Sikhs, Eric W. Treene, the Department of Justice's Special Counsel on Religious Discrimination, has provided the following account. Titled "The Sikh Turban After 9/11: Observations from Inside the Federal Government," it has not been issued or published elsewhere. Perhaps more than any other federal government official, Mr. Treene has been at the forefront of responding to the mistreatment against Sikhs after 9/11.

* * *

Eric W. Treene

The Sikh experience with post-9/11 backlash has been one of shock and frustration, but also of courage and steadfastness. I write as a non-Sikh who has witnessed the post-9/11 experience of the Sikh community from the vantage point of an attorney with the Civil Rights Division of the Department of Justice. In that role, I have overseen the federal government's efforts to protect religious liberty generally, and protecting against post-9/11 backlash in particular. I have also coordinated the DoJ's outreach efforts to affected communities. I note at the outset, however, that I am offering my personal observations, and write only in my personal capacity, and not as a representative of the government.

Before 9/11, most Americans did not know very much about Sikhs or Sikhism. Turbans were simply seen as exotic, perhaps associated with India, but more generally just vaguely representative of the East. Hollywood movies might put a character in a turban to suggest mysticism, mystery, and sometimes menace, but always to evoke a faraway place. Sometimes Sikhs were portrayed in more fully developed characters, as with the sergeant in *The English Patient*, but such portrayals were the exception.

I have been involved in the field of religious liberty law for more than fifteen years, and so before 9/11 I had more exposure than most Americans to minority religious practices, including those of Sikhs. As litigation director at a public interest law firm, the Becket Fund for Religious Liberty, from 1996 to 2002, I was involved in the representation of an elderly Sikh priest arrested for carrying his kirpan in Ohio. I also followed a handful of other kirpan cases around the country. But the turban was barely on my radar screen. This is not to say that there were no cases out there – there was one published case involving a Sikh turban during the 1990s,[1] and one unpublished case in 2002.[2] And Sikhs were involved in coalitions seeking to enact the Workplace Religious Freedom Act, a bill that has been introduced in Congress in various forms since 1994 which would strengthen the ability of workers to obtain accommodations of religious practices on the job,[3] so I heard concerns from Sikh groups about problems and conflicts regarding wearing turbans at work. But turban cases nonetheless seemed to

1 *Kalsi v. New York City Transit Authority*, 62 F.Supp.2d 745 (EDNY1998).

2 *Birdi v. UAL Corp.*, 2002 WL 471999 (ND Ill. 2002).

3 See Georgetown University Law Center Federal Legislation Clinic, *Title VII and Flexible Work Arrangements to Accommodate Religious Practice & Belief* (2005), available at <http://www.law.georgetown.edu/workplaceflexibility2010/definition/general/FWA_TitleVII.doc>; testimony of Richard T. Foltin, House Education and Labor Subcommittee on Health, Employment, Labor, and Pensions, February 12, 2008, available at <http://edlabor.house.gov/testimony/2008-02-12-RichardFoltin.pdf>.

be an interesting issue I might encounter some day, not a pressing present reality.

That all changed with 9/11. As recounted more fully elsewhere in this book, the fact that Osama bin Laden, other al Qaeda figures, and members of the Taliban in Afghanistan wore a type of turban created an association in many people's minds between turbans and terrorism. Since in the United States turbans are rare in any community but Sikhs, Sikhs bore the brunt of this association. An incident in which a turbaned Sikh man on an Amtrak train from Boston to New York on September 12 set off a wave of panic among other passengers who were convinced he must be a terrorist seems absurd, but unfortunately it was not an aberration. Sikhs after 9/11 faced a wave of backlash violence and discrimination.

Hate Crimes Against Turbaned Sikhs

As described earlier in this book, there was a dramatic surge in hate crimes against Muslims, Sikhs, Arabs, and South Asians after 9/11. The crimes included murder, assault, threats, arson, and vandalism. And it was a Sikh man, Balbir Singh Sodhi, who was the first victim of 9/11 backlash murder crime when he was shot during a drive-by shooting at a gas station in Mesa, Arizona. He was singled out as a victim because of his turban. In the three months after 9/11, the Department of Justice investigated more than 300 potential federal hate crimes against Muslims, Sikhs, Arabs, and South Asians. Nationwide in 2000, there were 28 hate crime incidents against Muslims reported to the FBI from all sources, including federal, state, and local law enforcement.[4] In 2001, that number jumped to 481.[5] There are no separate numbers for Sikhs in the FBI report. However, prosecutors who work on hate crime cases say that there was a significant jump in Sikh hate crimes, and I hear the same thing from the Sikh community. Preliminary results[6] from a study under way at the Civil Rights Division of post-9/11 backlash crimes shed additional light on the impact of 9/11 hate crimes involving Sikhs wearing turbans. Out of a sample in the study of 271 cases where the religion of the victim was identified as a factor in the crime, 49 of the victims were Sikh and 209 were Muslim. Of particular note is the fact that of the 62 cases in which the victim was wearing identifiable religious

---

4 Federal Bureau of Investigation, *2000 Hate Crime Statistics*, p. 7, Table 1.

5 Ibid., p. 9, Table 1.

6 These numbers are based on the 559 cases that the Civil Rights Division has analyzed to date, out of a total of more than 800 such cases for which the division has opened files. I have no reason to believe that these 559 are not representative of the patterns in the larger data set. However, the breakdowns by type of crime, victim, and presence of religious garb cited here should be viewed only as tentative indicators of the patterns in post-9/11 backlash crimes.

garb, 38 were Sikhs wearing turbans. Of the 258 cases identified in the study thus far involving assault, in-person threats, or murder, 34 involved Sikhs wearing turbans, or more than one in eight.

By any measure, the impact on Muslim, Sikh, Arab, and South Asian communities was dramatic. On September 13, 2001, a man set fire to cars in the parking lot of a Seattle mosque, then opened fire with a gun on worshipers as they came out to see what was happening. That same day a man in Utah attempted to burn down a Pakistani restaurant. There were numerous other violent crimes in these first days after 9/11.

These crimes were all based on the twisted logic that a terrible attack on innocents should be avenged by attacking other innocents who had no other connection to the terrorists than their religion or ethnicity, or the appearance of shared religion or ethnicity. Ordinary Muslims, Sikhs, Arabs, and South Asians in the United States were of course no more culpable than any other Americans for the 9/11 attacks. Indeed, many members of these groups died in the World Trade Center attacks, and people from these ethnic and faith groups were just as worried about the possibility of further terrorist attacks as everyone else. The President, the Attorney General, and other government officials spoke out swiftly against the backlash attacks on innocent Americans. On Thursday September 13, Attorney General Ashcroft said:

> Since Tuesday the Justice Department has received reports of violence and threats of violence against Arab Americans and other Americans of Middle Eastern and South Asian descent. We must not descend to the level of those who perpetrated Tuesday's violence by targeting individuals based on their race, their religion, or their national origin. Such reports of violence and threats are in direct opposition to the very principles and laws of the United States and will not be tolerated.[7]

On September 17, President Bush spoke specifically to the issue of those wearing religious head coverings being targeted:

> I've been told that some fear to leave; some don't want to go shopping for their families; some don't want to go about their ordinary daily routines because, by wearing cover, they're afraid they'll be intimidated. That should not and that will not stand in America.[8]

---

7 Remarks of Attorney General John Ashcroft, September 13, 2001, available at <http://www.usdoj.gov/crt/legalinfo/dojstatements.php>.

8 Speech at the Islamic Center of Washington, DC, September 17, 2001, available at <http://www.usdoj.gov/crt/legalinfo/bushremarks.php>.

And on September 26, at a meeting at the White House with Sikh leaders, the President said of the murder of Balbir Singh Sodhi:

> An American Sikh has been killed, unjustly so. These citizens bring their hearts with them, and I can assure them that our government will do everything we can to not only bring those people to justice, but also to treat every human life as dear, and to respect the values that made our country so different and so unique. We're all Americans, bound together by common ideals and common values.[9]

The Department of Justice aggressively pursued these cases. The DoJ to date has brought federal prosecutions against 46 defendants for backlash hate crimes, yielding 41 convictions thus far, with three cases pending. Sentences have been quite severe, such as more than four years in prison for a man who sent bomb threats to a Jordanian man and a 911 operator in Wisconsin in September 2001, more than 15 years in prison for a man who attempted to burn down a mosque in El Paso, Texas in 2004, and six years' imprisonment for a man in California who shot a turban-wearing Sikh postal carrier in the neck with an air rifle in July 2002. There also have been more than 150 prosecutions at the state and local level, in many cases with substantial assistance from the DoJ, such as the *Balbir Singh Sodhi* case, which resulted in a conviction and a death sentence, and the prosecution of a group of teenagers in upstate New York who burned a gurdwara to the ground on November 18, 2001.

During this period immediately after 9/11, the Sikh community, to its great credit, consistently stressed that all attacks on innocent people in backlash to terrorist attacks were wrong. It would have been very easy for Sikh leaders to point out that Sikhism was an entirely different religion from Islam, and that the Sikh turban was different from Arab, Muslim, and Afghani head coverings. The organized Sikh community, however, stressed the wrongfulness of such scapegoating broadly.

The number of these attacks dropped off precipitously after the initial spike in hate crimes. The DoJ opened 93, 109, and 71 investigations in September, October and November of 2001, respectively. By December, the number of investigations opened had dropped to 39. In 2002, January, February, and March saw 24, five, and 14 new investigations, respectively, after which the numbers fell consistently below 10 per month for the rest of that year. How much of the drop was due to the aggressive prosecutorial response and the efforts of government and diverse religious leaders to denounce the backlash crime, and how much is due to a natural drop-off due to the passage of time is hard to say. I believe, however, that the aggressive stance of the federal government played an important role.

9 Remarks to Sikh Community Leaders, September 26, 2001, available at <http://www.usdoj.gov/crt/legalinfo/bushremarks.php>.

Outreach to the Sikh Community

I was hired by the Civil Rights Division in June 2002 to fill a newly created position, Special Counsel for Religious Discrimination. Prior to the creation of the position, there had never been an attorney assigned to focusing on and coordinating religious discrimination and religion-based hate crimes, although the primary civil rights statutes enforced by the DoJ against discrimination in employment, education, housing, public accommodation, and public facilities all include religion as a protected classification along with race, sex, and national origin. Furthermore, religion-related claims appeared to be on the rise. For example, employment discrimination claims involving religion rose 69 percent from 1992 to 2005, whereas national origin discrimination rose a relatively moderate eight percent during that period, and racial discrimination dropping by 9.5 percent.[10] In addition, enforcement of the Religious Land Use and Institutionalized Persons Act (RLUIPA), enacted in 2000, was assigned to the Civil Rights Division, and the Special Counsel was tasked with developing enforcement mechanisms. And, of course, the backlash to the 9/11 attacks against Muslims and Sikhs, not only in hate crimes but in various forms of discrimination, created the need for a comprehensive approach.

In meetings with the Muslim, Sikh, Arab, and South Asian communities at the Civil Rights Division, it soon became apparent that while the mechanisms the division had in place were doing a good job of identifying and pursuing hate crimes and discrimination in the areas within the Civil Rights Division's enforcement jurisdiction, there were many broader civil rights issues involving the federal government that the communities were having trouble raising with the appropriate agency. When we would meet with groups, they would thank us for our enforcement work, but would ask about profiling of Muslims and Sikhs wearing religious head coverings on airplanes, problems with searches of religious head coverings at airports, and similar issues. The groups did not know what federal agency to address with which claims. For example, if a stewardess takes a certain action, do you complain to the Department of Transportation or the Department of Homeland Security? How does someone file a complaint about an inappropriate airport search? How many watch lists are there, who keeps them, and where does one go for redress? We realized that we did not know all of the answers either. The community groups also complained of general ignorance among law enforcement officials about articles of faith such as the turban, leading to misunderstandings and uncomfortable situations such as incidents of government officials touching the turban or asking for it to be removed.

10 *Report on Enforcement of Laws Protecting Religious Freedom: Fiscal Years 2001–2006* (Department of Justice, 2007), p. 4.

In response, the Civil Rights Division developed a regular series of meetings, held every six to eight weeks, that bring together community leaders from the Muslim, Sikh, Arab, and South Asian communities with representatives from a wide range of agencies, including various Department of Homeland Security (DHS) components, including the Transportation Security Administration (TSA), Customs and Border Patrol (CBP), Citizenship and Immigration Services (U.S.CIS), Immigration and Customs Enforcement (ICE), the Departments of State, Treasury, and Transportation, the FBI, and the Equal Employment Opportunity Commission. The idea of the meetings is to identify civil rights issues, and either produce a solution at the meeting or ensure that the proper agency is assigned the issue. These meetings have been instrumental in addressing issues involving Sikh turbans, such as airport screening policies, policies towards Sikh turbans in the Coast Guard and other federal agencies, and problems involving turban-wearing Sikhs who are immigration detainees, among many other issues.

Numerous proactive measures by the federal government have grown out of these meetings as well. One concern expressed by the community was a lack of cultural awareness by law enforcement and other government officials who interact with the public. The DHS responded by implementing various training measures, including a training video about Sikhs. The Civil Rights Division and the DHS's Office of Civil Rights and Civil Liberties collaborated on producing and widely distributing two posters, one showing common Muslim head coverings,[11] and the other showing common Sikh head coverings.[12] Thousands of copies were produced and distributed to federal, state, and local law enforcement throughout the country. The Sikh poster shows the *pagri* (turban), a boy with a *patka* (under-turban), and a woman in a *chunni* (headscarf), and gives very basic cultural awareness information: what Sikhism is, its origins, and why the turban is worn. The poster also gives basic information regarding searching turbans, such as explaining why a search needs to be conducted, offering private rooms if available, having someone of the same sex conduct any search, and showing respect. I knew these posters were having an impact when a wag at a South Asian-American blog produced a spoof entitled "Common Redneck Head Coverings."[13] Imitation may be the sincerest form of flattery, but satire gets the word out.

Another effective education measure was a law enforcement training video produced by the DoJ's Community Relations Service (CRS) on

11 U.S. Department of Justice, Civil Rights Division, *Common Muslim American Headcoverings*, available at <http://www.usdoj.gov/crt/legalinfo/muslim_poster.pdf>.

12 U.S. Department of Justice, Civil Rights Division, *Common Sikh American Headcoverings*, available at <http://www.usdoj.gov/crt/legalinfo/sikh_poster.pdf>.

13 See <http://www.sepiamutiny.com/sepia/archives/000799.html>.

Sikhs entitled *On Common Ground*, produced in consultation with Sikh organizations. The video explains Sikhism and the articles of faith, with guidance on how law enforcement should interact with Sikhs. Its length is designed to make the video conducive to being shown during roll-calls at the beginning of police shifts. Copies of the video have been distributed on DVD throughout the country, and it is available on the CRS website.[14]

Civil Enforcement Involving Turbans

The Civil Rights Division has seen issues involving turbans arise in a wide variety of the statutes it enforces, including public facilities, public accommodation, employment, and education.

Public accommodation and public facilities The Civil Rights Division has opened several investigations involving Sikhs wearing turbans turned away from nightclubs and other public accommodation. Title II of the Civil Rights Act of 1964[15] prohibits discrimination based on race, color, religion, or national origin in any place of public accommodation. Public accommodation under Title II basically encompasses hotels and motels, restaurants, and other places serving food or drink, and places of entertainment such as movie theaters.[16] The DoJ is authorized to bring an action where there has been an allegation of a pattern or practice of a violation of Title II.[17]

The most straightforward turban cases are ones in which there is evidence that the Sikh turban has been excluded where other head coverings are permitted. For example, the Civil Rights Division reached a settlement agreement in 2003 with F & K Management, Inc., d/b/a Hard Times Cafes and Santa Fe Cue Clubs in a case in which a Sikh man was excluded from a nightclub in Springfield, Virginia on September 23, 2001. The nightclub had a policy permitting cowboy hats and baseball caps, but excluding other headwear. There also was evidence that Sikhs had been able to wear turbans at the club prior to 9/11. Under the settlement, F & K rescinded its head covering policy and took remedial action.

The turban public accommodation cases are particularly interesting because the discrimination is typically overt. Title II was designed to address the problem, widespread in the 1960s, of segregated lunch counters, restaurants, and hotels that would not serve African Americans, and segregation at movie theaters. In recent years, the Civil Rights Division's Title II cases as a general matter have been more subtle, such as cases

14 See <http://www.usdoj.gov/crs>.
15 42 U.S.C § 2000a.
16 2000a(b).
17 42 U.S.C § 2000a-6(a).

in which African Americans are made to wait an excessively long period to be seated at a restaurant, or otherwise made to feel uncomfortable at public accommodations, rather than facing the overt "no Negroes allowed" policies of the Civil Rights era. These newer cases are more difficult to prove. But with the turbans, there is often the sort of overt discrimination found in the early years of Title II enforcement. This is beneficial from the standpoint of law enforcement, since when the Civil Rights Division opens investigations, the establishments typically settle.

A more difficult issue arises when there is a uniformly enforced, blanket policy on head coverings in a public accommodation such as a restaurant. This of course has a disproportionate impact on turbaned Sikhs, Jews wearing yarmulkes, and Muslim women wearing headscarves. There have been no published cases addressing this issue under Title II. One argument is that since Title II, like the original rule against employment discrimination based on religion in Title VII in the Civil Rights Act of 1964, does not address religious accommodations or disparate impact, Title II should be interpreted as courts did in the early 1970s with regard to Title VII. In such cases, the courts had ruled that since Title VII at the time only barred "discrimination," there was no duty on employers to accommodate to religion-neutral workplace rules.[18] Since Congress responded to these decisions by amending Title VII to add a religious accommodation requirement, but did not amend Title II or other sections of the Act, this argument goes, Title II should not be read to include a religious accommodation requirement. On the other hand, when Congress amended Title VII in 1972 to add a religious accommodation requirement, Senator Randolph, the amendment's sponsor, stressed that the purpose was to restore what was "originally intended by the Civil Rights Act."[19] By this reading of the original intent, Title II is designed to end all segregation based on race, national origin, and religion in public accommodation, and should protect Sikhs who must wear religious head coverings from being excluded from public accommodation, even when the management is applying a policy aimed at both secular and religious head coverings. How courts will address this issue under Title II remains to be seen.

The Civil Rights Division also has the authority to bring actions under Title III of the Civil Rights Act of 1964, 41 U.S.C § 2000b, which authorizes the Attorney General to bring suit in cases in which a person is denied equal protection of the laws, on account of race, color, religion, or national origin, by being denied equal utilization of a public facility "which is owned, operated, or managed by or on behalf of any State or

18 See *Dewey v. Reynolds Metals Co.*, 402 U.S. 689 (1971) (per curiam), aff'g by an equally divided court, 429 F.2d 324 (6th Cir. 1970); *Riley v. Bendix Corp.*, 330 F. Supp. 583 (MD Fla. 1971).

19 See 118 *Cong. Rec.* 705–6 (1972).

subdivision thereof." Title III requires that the Attorney General certify that the complainants are unable to bring a suit on their own, and that a suit by the DoJ would "materially further the orderly progress of desegregation in public facilities." The Civil Rights Division has looked into several cases involving persons with turbans having problems with access to public buildings, but has not brought any such actions under Title III. As with Title II, there are no published decisions involving discrimination against persons with religious garb.

Employment discrimination Title VII of the Civil Rights Act of 1964[20] prohibits discrimination in public and private employment on a number of bases, including religion. It also requires employers, under the 1972 amendments discussed above, to make reasonable accommodation of employees' religious observances and practices, unless doing so would cause the employer undue hardship. The DoJ has responsibility for bringing suits under Title VII against state and local governmental employers. Under § 706 of Title VII,[21] individual cases of discrimination against state and local governmental entities must be filed first with the Equal Employment Opportunity Commission (EEOC), which can refer cases to the Civil Rights Division. When a pattern or practice of discrimination by a governmental entity is alleged, the DoJ may file suit on its own volition under § 707 of Title VII.[22] Suits involving allegations of discrimination by private businesses and labor unions are handled by the EEOC.

The EEOC does not have pre-9/11 records on the number of complaints filed by Sikhs alleging religious discrimination. However, as noted above, religious discrimination cases in general have been on the rise since the early 1990s. For this book, however, the EEOC provided me with figures on the number of complaints filed by Sikhs alleging religious discrimination for the years 2002–2008. There were a total of 119 complaints filed, broken down by year as follows:

FY02 – 19
FY03 – 26
FY04 – 12
FY05 – 20
FY06 – 13
FY07 – 14
FY08 – 15

20 42 U.S.C § 2000e.
21 42 U.S.C § 2000e-5.
22 42 U.S.C § 2000e-6.

These statistics represent a significant number of cases involving Sikhs. The 45 complaints in fiscal years 2002 and 2003, for example, make up a little less than 1 percent of all religious complaints filed in those years (0.88 percent). However, given that there are an estimated 270,000 Sikhs in the United States,[23] making up less than 0.1 percent of the population, this is a significant number of cases. While these numbers are not broken down by type of complaint, given the patterns I have seen in the cases reviewed by the Department of Justice, and trends in published cases, a meaningful number of these 119 cases are likely turban cases.

The Civil Rights Division has filed two pattern-or-practice cases under Title VII involving religious head coverings since 2001. In *United States v. New York Department of Corrections*,[24] the United States reached a settlement requiring implementation of a procedure to assess claims by corrections officers requesting exceptions to uniform and grooming rules that conflict with their religious practices. A similar suit that remains ongoing is *United States v. New York Metropolitan Transit Authority*,[25] in which the United States is suing on behalf of Muslim and Sikh bus and subway operators who have been forbidden from wearing turbans and headscarves with their uniforms unless they agree to attach MTA logos, which the employees find religiously objectionable. The suit alleges both that the MTA has failed to make a reasonable accommodation of Muslim and Sikh employees, and also that it has not uniformly enforced its policy regarding the wearing of non-regulation head coverings with the uniform.

Under Title VII, an employer may decline to accommodate a sincere religious practice of an employee if the employer can demonstrate that the accommodation would cause an undue hardship on the employer's operations. In the *New York MTA* case, the MTA has argued that it has a "right as an employer to present *its* chosen image to the public,"[26] and that it therefore can require employees to wear turbans and headscarves with MTA logos on the front, or ban them completely. The employees, who have religious objections to placing logos on their religious head coverings, offered instead to wear turbans and headscarves in a uniform color, and wear additional insignia or MTA photo identification cards on their collars or other prominent places on their uniform. The MTA rejected this proposed accommodation. The United States' brief argued in response to the MTA's public image argument that the MTA "has provided no explanation as to

23 C. Alan Joyce (ed.), *World Almanac and Book of Facts* (New York: World Almanac Books, Simon & Schuster, 2009), p. 682.

24 No. 07 Civ. 2243 (DC) (SDNY, settlement entered January 18, 2008).

25 No. CV-04 4237 (EDNY, complaint filed September 30, 2004).

26 Defendants' Motion in Support of its Motion for Summary Judgment, *United States v. New York Transit Authority* (EDNY Civil Action No. 04-CV-4237 (SLT)(MDG)) at 24–25, 36.

how allowing Muslim and Sikh employees to wear turbans or *khimars* without TA logos would adversely affect its chosen public image or detract from the perceived professionalism of its work force."[27] The brief notes: "There is no evidence in the record that the TA's public image was harmed in any way during the more than ten years that these employees wore their turbans and *khimars* without TA logos."[28] The United States' arguments are similar to the conclusions of the court in *E.E.O.C. v. Alamo Rental Car. Inc.*,[29] which held that it was not an undue hardship on a rental car company to permit a Muslim employee to wear a headscarf while working in public contact positions behind the rental counter.

Employers cannot escape the duty to accommodate by claiming that while they do not want to discriminate against Sikhs, their customers do not want to be served by someone identifiable as a Sikh. The customer preference argument has been rejected in the context of sex and race discrimination, such as a case in which customer preference for female flight attendants was held to be an invalid basis for discriminating against men,[30] and a case in which customer preference for clean-shaven pizza delivery persons was held not to be a valid basis for a no-beards rule, which had disparate impact on black males suffering from skin conditions making shaving difficult or impossible.[31] This customer preference argument should be equally invalid in the religious context. The EEOC Compliance Manual, whose religious discrimination section was updated in July 2008, specifically states that customer preference is an invalid basis to engage in religious discrimination, and uses as its example a hypothetical scenario in which customers of a coffee shop are uncomfortable after 9/11 with a Sikh counter worker wearing a turban.[32]

Discrimination in schools The Civil Rights Division also enforces Title IV of the Civil Rights Act of 1964,[33] which prohibits discrimination based on religion in public primary and secondary schools, as well as public colleges and universities. In primary and secondary schools, Title IV is triggered when a student is "deprived by a school board of the equal protection of the laws." In the higher education context, Title IV only applies when a student is "denied admission or not permitted to continue" on the basis of protected

27 United States' Memorandum in Opposition to Defendants' Motion for Summary Judgment, *United States v. New York Transit Authority* (EDNY Civil Action No. 04-CV-4237 (SLT)(MDG)) at 41.

28 Ibid.

29 432 F. Supp. 2d 1006 (D. Ariz. 2006).

30 *Diaz v. Pan Am. World Airways*, 442 F.2d 385, 389 (5th Cir.), cert. denied, 404 U.S. 950 (1971).

31 *Bradley v. Pizzaco of Nebraska, Inc.*, 7 F.3d 795 (8th Cir. 1993).

32 *EEOC Compliance Manual*, Section 12II-B (July 22, 2008).

33 42 U.S.C § 2000c-6.

classifications, such as religion.

In contrast to Europe, where there are numerous unresolved controversies involving students wearing religious head coverings, this for the most part is simply not an issue in the United States. While the Civil Rights Division has been watching for such cases, very few have arisen, and most of those involved either misunderstandings or legitimate questions of whether a student in fact had a sincere religious belief. The exception was *Hearn and United States v. Muskogee Public School District*,[34] in which the Civil Rights Division filed suit to protect the rights of a sixth-grade Muslim girl who was suspended from school for refusing to remove her headscarf (*hijab*). School officials insisted that she remove the *hijab* in light of the school's "no-hats" policy in the school system's dress code. The dress code had not been applied consistently, however. Students with thinning hair due to medical reasons were permitted to wear scarves. The school had also allowed students to wear "Cat in the Hat" hats for Dr. Seuss's birthday, and to wear hats on other special days. Moreover, school officials reserved the right to make exceptions to the dress code on a case-by-case basis.

The girl, through her father, filed a private suit, and the Civil Rights Division intervened. The division reached a consent decree with the school that permitted the girl to wear her *hijab*, and which requires the school district to make similar religious accommodation for any other student in the school system who has a bona fide religious objection to the dress code.

The *Hearn* case was successful because the school had treated non-religious requests for exemptions better than religious ones, and because the fact that the school reserved the right to make exceptions to the dress code on a case-by-case basis. Title IV of the Civil Rights Act provides enforcement power to the DoJ, but the cause of action is based on the Equal Protection Clause of the Fourteenth Amendment. Thus the differential treatment of secular and religious reasons created a clear Equal Protection Clause cause of action. Such differential treatment, or a situation that gives a government actor the discretion to make individualized determinations of who will get an exemption and who will not, can also create a cause of action under the Free Exercise Clause.

While the Supreme Court held in *Employment Division v. Smith*[35] that neutral, generally applicable government policies that have the incidental effect of creating substantial burdens on religious observance do not give rise to any special scrutiny under the Free Exercise Clause, laws that are not in fact truly applicable to all are subject to heightened scrutiny. A policy is not "generally applicable" if it includes a system of "individualized exemptions" under which government officials permit exemptions to an

34 No. Civ. 03 598-S (ED Okla. 2003).

35 494 U.S. 872 (1990).

applicable policy based upon a case-by-case "assessment of the reasons for the relevant conduct" and the "particular circumstances" involved.[36] Based on this principle, the *Third Circuit in Fraternal Order of Police Newark Lodge No. 12 v. City of Newark*[37] held that the Free Exercise Clause rights of Muslim police officers who were barred from wearing beards for religious reasons had been violated, since the city had allowed beards for officers who had a skin condition making it painful or impossible to shave. Thus, even in the face of school uniform rules barring head coverings, there are avenues of recourse available for students who must wear turbans or headscarves for religious reasons. And as a practical matter, in my experience schools in the United States generally are accommodating to student religious needs to wear religious head coverings.

Conclusion

The Sikh turban has created many challenges for the Sikh community in the wake of 9/11: dealing with an increased threat of violence due to wearing this article of faith; facing discrimination in a variety of contexts, particularly employment and exclusion from public accommodations; and concerns about profiling by law enforcement and security personnel. The Sikh community has met these challenges in a commendable fashion, resisting the temptation to deflect attention to other religious groups. The community has instead worked to address these civil rights challenges head-on, and alongside other religious groups. The community also has been an active partner with the federal government on civil rights issues. As someone who has been involved from within the government, I have seen how this approach of the Sikh community has been invaluable.

Many challenges remain. While hate crimes against turbaned Sikhs have diminished, they continue to be a serious problem that requires continued vigilance. Conflicts involving the turban continue to arise in other contexts, particularly in employment and public accommodations. The federal civil rights laws provide powerful tools for addressing discrimination against Sikhs in these and other areas. As noted above, however, the application of these anti-discrimination protections to the various contexts in which conflicts can arise involving the turban are complicated and fact-intensive. Protecting the rights of Sikhs to wear this article of faith free of violence and discrimination will remain a challenge for the Sikh community, civil rights advocates, and the federal government as we continue to work toward a just, free and equal society in a post-9/11 world.

* * *

36 Ibid. at 884. See also *Church of the Lukumi Babalu Aye, Inc. v. City of Hialeah*, 508 U.S. 520, 531 (1993).

37 170 F.3d 359, 365 (3d Cir. 1999) (Alito, J).

As noted by Special Counsel Treene, outreach and awareness efforts are an important way to address the significant mistreatment of Sikhs, not only by members of the general public, but also by security personnel who are charged with safeguarding America's airports, courthouses, and other locations. These efforts have the ability to effect real change on the ground, where Sikhs interact with others, but also symbolize the ongoing working relationship between the Sikh community and the federal government. Such a relationship is necessary for Sikhs to address their grievances and for the government to be able to effectively respond to Sikh concerns. The Special Counsel's narrative also reflects the fact that the Sikhs are working not only with the government, but side by side with other groups affected by the post-9/11 backlash.

Conclusion

In the aftermath of the terrorist attacks on the United States of September 11, 2001, turbaned Sikhs have been conflated with Osama bin Laden and others responsible for those attacks. Accordingly, this book has attempted to answer two fundamental, overlapping questions: (1) how have turbaned Sikhs in America been targeted for discriminatory behavior, and (2) how have turbaned Sikhs globally been subject to marginalization on account of their conspicuous religious identity?

A necessary precondition for this discussion is examining who Sikhs are – what they believe in, how the faith has developed over time, and perhaps most importantly, why the Sikh turban is an essential part of the Sikh identity. In order to understand the problematic nature of noxious post-9/11 conduct that is premised on the Sikh turban, one must grasp why the turban itself is of significance to the Sikh people.

The post-9/11 experience of Sikhs is not only a story of discrimination in terms of hate violence or calls for physical assimilation, but is also one about how a modest minority rose up in the face of hate. A critical consequence of the post-9/11 climate has been the reactionary response to address the mistreatment and social isolation that attended the attacks. In addition to an immediate ad hoc response, Sikhs met these challenges head-on through the creation of a sustained, multifaceted Sikh civil rights movement. Today, that movement includes new organizations, relationships with the government, creative educational endeavors, and ongoing legal advocacy, among other things.

Accordingly, in Part I we explored the history of the Sikh faith and traced its founding in the Punjab region of South Asia. Specifically, we discussed its emergence in a time of religious strife with messages of humanity, equality, and civic engagement and its evolution into an army of saint-soldiers with an intent to achieve justice and with the turban as part of its mandatory uniform.

In Part II, we described how, in various contexts and settings, turbaned Sikh Americans have been subject to a post-9/11 backlash in which their distinct appearance has been used as a proxy for the identity of a terrorist or terrorist sympathizer. This backlash, the disproportionate brunt of which fell on the shoulders of Sikh Americans, spans practically every corner of the American landscape, and has seeped through every year since the 9/11 attacks.

In Part III, we noted how major nations in the West have tried to achieve integration by eliminating Sikh articles of faith from the public sphere. Sikh migration to Britain, Canada, the United States, and other places has come across increased hostility since the attacks, despite meaningful and long-lasting contributions that Sikhs have made to these very societies, including the Sikh sacrifices to their armed forces.

In Part IV, we noted the Sikh community's reaction to this animus, with the creation of Sikh civil rights groups, working closely with government agencies and authorities, and engaging in innovative ways to replace ignorance with a friendly familiarity or an appreciation for turbaned Sikhs. These traditional and non-traditional means are the backbone of the Sikh response to the post-9/11 difficulties. Those difficulties remain in the United States, and may expand in the event of another attack or national crisis. The welfare of the Sikhs in the West, and in the United States in particular, may very well depend on these tactics – especially the non-legal forms of Sikh advocacy.

Indeed, in the course of this discussion, we have observed that the American legal system is unlikely to protect Sikhs from the most common form of mistreatment – verbal insults such as "bin Laden," "raghead," and "terrorist" being lobbed at them on the streets, in their grocery stories and at their schools – though the nation's laws may protect Sikhs from a more drastic and wide-reaching policies like the French ban on Sikhs wearing turbans in public schools. As a result, Sikhs would be wise to continue to turn to non-legal methods to stem discrimination at its source. The goal of these educational efforts is not just to disassociate the turban from terrorists, but to a promote a positive connotation of the turban with the principles of equality, honesty, and service. Because redress through the courts takes significant amounts of time and is not certain to produce desired results, a preventative approach in which Sikhs educate others about their identity is likely to be the more effective means by which Sikhs are seen as a distinguishable, but still a welcome, part of the American experiment. Through non-legal avenues, such as awareness and outreach efforts, the discrimination experienced by this minority community will hopefully cease, and will not re-emerge with increased fervor if there is another act of terrorism on American soil. We are not there yet.

* * *

As noted in the preliminary pages of this book, the Sikh experience following the 9/11 terrorist attacks is not an examination of one subset of people – it is a reflection of America and its values. In a large sense, this book is not only about Sikhs, but is more appropriately about the United States itself. It examines another episode in our nation's history of balancing civil rights against national security interests and emotions.

In World War II, the United States was at war with the Japanese Empire. Following the bombing of Pearl Harbor, the west coast of the United States was considered to be in grave danger. Accordingly, with the national security of the nation in mind, President Franklin D. Roosevelt signed an executive order calling for the mandatory and forcible evacuation of individuals of Japanese descent from the western part of the nation. Over 120,000 Japanese individuals were placed in internment camps in one of the most disgraceful episodes in American history.

In the aftermath of the 9/11 attacks, some Asian Americans recognized that a similar situation was affecting Muslims and others – namely, that they were thought to be suspicious, disloyal, and/or dangerous because of appearance or ancestry alone. Commenting on history repeating itself after 9/11 is Saburo Masada, a survivor of the Internment.

* * *

Saburo Masada

My name is Saburo Masada, and I'm from Fresno, I'm 75 years old. My inmate number is 9534.

I am an American, a second-generation, born in Fresno of parents who emigrated from Japan in the early 1900s. My parents were so proud of America, even though discrimination laws in our country prevented them from becoming American citizens.

My parents brought me up to love my country and to be proud of being an American, and to be the best example of a citizen, especially because they were not allowed to become citizens. For me, Japan was like "the other side of the moon." In fact, I knew very little about my grandparents and about Japan. I knew nothing.

On December 7, 1941, Japan bombed Pearl Harbor, Hawaii.

I remember vividly, on Sunday, December 7, our family was working on our farm by the house, and as we worked our way back to the house, we would take a break and listen outside to the radio in the back of the house.

As we listened, our radio program was interrupted around 11 a.m. with the announcement that Pearl Harbor had been attacked by Japan warplanes. I remember we were shocked and couldn't believe it! I remember saying, "What a dumb thing Japan is doing to our country!"

To our dismay, a short time thereafter we were being associated with Japan's attack on Pearl Harbor. I remember our family gathering anything that associated us with anything Japanese, like photos, pictures, magazines, and phonograph records, and things like rifles and knives we buried, or burned, or destroyed, lest these things be used against us.

When we heard rumors that the Japanese in America would be rounded up and imprisoned by our government, none of us could believe that our beloved country would do such a thing. We had faith in our country and our Constitution, which we were studying in school.

But soon thereafter, we were being targeted as the enemies, even though we were Americans! That was the biggest shock to us. None of us thought that anyone would question our loyalty.

Within ten weeks of the Pearl Harbor attack by Japan, our President, Franklin Delano Roosevelt, signed Executive Order 9066. Five months after Pearl Harbor was bombed, I remember climbing into the back of an

> army truck with my family and being taken to the Fresno Fairgrounds, which was quickly set up to become our prison.
>
> I can still see the gates that closed behind us, and seeing a few non-Japanese people who were on the other side of the fence, talking to their friends on the inside. Once the gates were closed, our family identity became like that of a prisoner. After five months in the Fresno Fairgrounds camp, our family was sent by train to a barbed-wired camp in Jerome, Arkansas. The 120,000 Americans and legal alien residents were incarcerated for up to three-and-a-half years in these American "concentration camps."
>
> A frequent question that we are asked is: "Can it happen again?"
>
> I would like to think that in our modern times, it cannot happen again. Yet, there is still a widespread ignorance and prejudice towards other groups of people, who are looked upon as "them," and not a part of "us." How often do we hear people still say, "Go back to where you came from," as if people, even if they are true-blue Americans but who look different from us, must be from somewhere else.
>
> But, *look at the bigoted and racist attitudes toward people of Middle Eastern heritage or of Muslim tradition today, and the racial profiling towards them.*
>
> Can it happen again? It can to one group or another, *if* we are not vigilant and make our leaders accountable for their actions. George Santayana, American philosopher and poet, born in Madrid, Spain, wrote: "Those who do not remember the past are condemned to repeat it."

* * *

In the decades since World War II, the Japanese Internment has been rightfully recognized as a national embarrassment. It is a stain on the American principles of equality and due process, where blanket guilt based on ancestry was allowed to predominate, and where the judiciary abdicated its constitutional role by refusing to check overzealous executive claims of national security.

A primary lesson of the Japanese Internment should have been clear – shared appearances or national origin should not, on their own, be equated with suspicion or disloyalty to the United States. This book calls into question whether, over sixty years after the Internment, we have learned that lesson. This is more than an academic exercise; it is vitally important to determining the substantive content of our current and future behavior. The past will invariably repeat itself absent any meaningful understanding of what has already occurred. More than this, these past mistakes obtain harmful momentum: such mistakes will not only repeat themselves, but may become progressively worse as time progresses, as long as our society fails to appreciate its conduct. This same theory was eloquently advanced by Justice Robert H. Jackson, who in reviewing the constitutionality of the Internment warned that each qualification on equality during wartime would be enshrined, and that equality could be eroded further in subsequent military conflicts.

Accordingly, only through reflecting on our wrongful behavior will it be possible to move beyond such invidious treatment, to restore the basic principles of individualized suspicion and equality, and to validate the pluralistic ideal that was set forth by the Framers. If so, members of certain identifiable groups will not be subject to the stigmatization of being subversive or disloyal simply because their race, religion, or homeland is engaged in a military conflict with the United States. If not, the problems of hate crimes and racially motivated discrimination may continue with impunity in the event of another terrorist attack or military conflict involving the United States.

Put differently, the question remains whether, in a future time of crisis, the public and private agents of this nation will continue to resort to appearance or immutable characteristics in placating their security concerns. The stories contained in this book suggest that the nation is not yet prepared to relieve itself of this convenient proxy.

The discrimination encountered by Sikhs in the aftermath of the 9/11 attacks may not arouse the same disappointment when placed in comparison with the Internment of Japanese Americans. To be sure, features of 9/11 do not duplicate each aspect of the Internment. But the thought process underlying both phenomena is strikingly similar. While overt racial hostility towards and wholesale movement of Sikhs and others did not take place after 9/11, identity again has been used as a proxy for disloyalty in times of national emergency. Citizen minorities have once again become the scapegoats.

The Sikh experience in the post-9/11 era may not agitate the people's conscience for another reason – today, over eight years after the attacks, we are still under the clouds of a distant enemy and the specter of future terrorist activity. But once those dark parts of the national sky begin to dissipate, and the sanitizing light of calm reason reemerges and replaces the passions of insecurity, the post-9/11 backlash will be properly viewed as yet another failure in the American capacity to preserve its values when the nation is in crisis. This book has provided the factual predicate for that most unfortunate and imminent judgment.

Index

Where a Sikh has only two names, the name is listed without alteration (Prabhjot Singh is under 'P'). Where there are three names, the third name is used as a surname (Gurinder Singh Mann is under 'M').
An entry in **bold** type indicates a long quoted section from that person. Page numbers in *italics* refer to tables or figures. Where the page number is followed by *f* and a number, it refers to the footnotes on that page.